Know Your SHIPS

Guide to Boats & Boatwatching Great Lakes & St. Lawrence Seaway

© 2001 — Updated Annually

ISBN: 1-891849-04-2
ISSN: 0190-5562

Marine Publishing Co. Inc.

P.O. Box 68, Sault Ste. Marie, MI 49783
(734) 668-4734 — phone & fax

www.knowyourships.com

Editor & Publisher: Roger LeLievre
Listings Researchers:
Philip A. Clayton, John Vournakis
Contributing Researchers: Jody Aho, Rod Burdick,
Angela S. Clayton, Neil Schultheiss, George Wharton

Founder: Tom Manse, 1915-1994

Front cover: *Cuyahoga transits her namesake river.* (Dave Marcoux)
Back cover: *Burns Harbor leaves the Soo Locks.* (Roger LeLievre)

CONTENTS

Canada Steamship Lines'
Jean Parisien.

The information contained herein was obtained from the St. Lawrence Seaway Authority, the Lake Carriers' Association, the Institute for Great Lakes Research, Jane's Merchant Ships, Lloyd's Register of Shipping, the U.S. Army Corps of Engineers, www.boatnerd.com, 'Seaway Review,' 'Great Lakes Log' and publications of the Great Lakes Maritime Institute, the Toronto Marine Historical Society and the Marine Historical Society of Detroit.

***Courtney Burton* meets *Gordon C. Leitch* at dusk.** *(Roger LeLievre)*

WELCOME ABOARD

This year's edition of **"Know Your Ships"** begins with a twist on our recently established "Vessel of the Year" feature. For 2001, we have elected to nominate not a single ship, but a fleet: Canada's **Lower Lakes Towing Ltd**. Founded in 1995 with the christening of the **Cuyahoga**, the company is quickly becoming a major player in the lakes and Seaway cargo-hauling game, in the process giving new life to several older lakers. The story behind these boats is a fascinating one and we trust you will agree. We wish them continued smooth sailing.

Back this year is Jody Aho's historic feature, Marine Milestones, as well as the popular Vessel Spotlights, which take a closer look at familiar lake vessels. In addition, we have responded to the requests of many readers to list vessel horsepowers and other engine data, which you will find for the U.S. and Canadian fleets in an appendix beginning on Page 96. Once again, listings editor Philip A. Clayton has worked his usual magic compiling the statistical data that is at the heart of this book. You can rest assured – if it floats, it's here.

Then there are the pictures, which speak for themselves. Thanks to everyone from around the Great Lakes and St. Lawrence Seaway who sent in photos. As usual, there were far too many to include.

Why not climb aboard and take a look for yourself?

— *The 'Know Your Ships' staff*

Cuyahoga upbound in the Welland Canal. (Jim Hoffman)

LOWER LAKES TOWING

Fleet of the Year 2001

In 1995, Canada's Lower Lakes Towing Ltd., founded just a year earlier, startled the shipping industry by buying the obsolete, U.S.-flag, self-unloading steamer **J. Burton Ayers**, which had been awaiting sale for scrap at Toledo, refurbishing it and successfully putting it back to work. Now sailing as **Cuyahoga**, the vessel is one of the busiest on the lakes.

In 1999, Lower Lakes, based at Port Dover, ON, repeated its success story by purchasing the surplus American Steamship Co. steamer **John J. Boland**, which had spent that season laid up at Superior, WI. She emerged in time for a few trips late that year under her new name, **Saginaw**.

Keeping the momentum going in 2000, LLT's U.S. subsidiary, Lower Lakes Transportation Co., chartered the idle self-unloader **McKee Sons** from its owner, Lake Services Shipping Co.,and brought the saltwater tug **Invincible** to the lakes to push it.

Finding new life in old lakers seems to be Lower Lakes Towing's speciality.

LLT starts the 2001 shipping season with three more new vessels chartered by Lower Lakes Transportation Co., the veteran U.S. self-unloaders **Calcite II, Myron C. Taylor** and **George A. Sloan** (new names are still pending at press time). Built in 1929, the Calcite II and Taylor are two of the oldest operating vessels on the Great Lakes.

Seen in the context of history, these six boats are really something special. ▶

Veteran lakers are finding new careers under LLT's colors.

4

Saginaw enters port at Grand Haven, MI. *(Don Geske)*

Cuyahoga, built in 1943 at Lorain, OH, is the last "cruiser-stern" maritime class vessel built during World War II still sailing the lakes (the tenth of 16 such craft built from 1942-'43 to meet wartime iron-ore tonnage requirements) and the eldest Canadian vessel in Seaway service. Until she was repowered with a Caterpillar 3608 marine diesel engine during the winter of 1999-2000, she was also the last vessel on the lakes operating with a Lentz-Poppet four cylinder compound steam engine. Lower Lakes Towing bought the vessel from the Oglebay Norton Co. after 52 years in American registry, where she sailed as **J. Burton Ayers** under the flags of Great Lakes Transit Co., Wilson Marine Transit Co. and the Kinsman Marine Transit Co., as well as Oglebay Norton. When she was laid up in 1990, a victim of small capacity and high operating costs, waterfront watchers were certain she would never sail again.

Cuyahoga seen from atop a Welland Canal lift bridge. (Richard I. Weiss)

The story is almost the same for the John J. Boland.

After 46 years working for American Steamship Co., the **John J. Boland** was put out to pasture and offered for sale in 1999. LLT came to the rescue again. Purchase was completed and the Boland was towed down the lakes for refurbishing and renaming at Sarnia, ON, before the 1999 shipping season ended. At the time of her transfer to the Canadian flag, the Boland was the third vessel to bear the name of the pioneer Great Lakes vessel owner who co-founded American Steamship Co. with Adam E. Cornelius in 1907.

In 2000, LLT chartered another older self-unloader, **McKee Sons**, which had operated for American Steamship Co. since its conversion in 1945 from a World War II troop transport until its final days as a steamer in 1980. Upper Lakes Towing Co., Escanaba, MI, leased the vessel in 1990, converted her to a barge by removing her after cabin and engines and installing a notch in her stern for use by the pusher tug **Olive L. Moore**. The two operated as a pair from 1992-2000, when that lease arrangement ended.

After being refurbished and repainted at Sarnia during the summer of 2000, McKee Sons was paired with the ocean articulated notch tug **Invincible**, built at Jacksonville, FL, in 1979. Under the charter, McKee Sons hauls primarily stone,

McKee Sons waits to load at Toledo. *(Jim Hoffman)*

aggregates, coal and salt. Her name honors the 11 offspring of the three McKee brothers, principals of Lake Services Shipping Co. of Detroit, which still owns the boat. **Myron C. Taylor, Calcite II** and **George A. Sloan,** meanwhile, sailed for the once-huge U.S. Steel fleet of "Tinstackers" (now the USS Great Lakes fleet) their entire careers, an unusual accomplishment all on its own.

Whether painted with the grey hulls of the fleet's limestone division or, in later years, with traditional U.S. Steel iron ore-red hulls, the trio has always found steady work, mostly hauling bulk cargos on the lower lakes. All three started out their careers as standard bulk carriers, with self-unloader conversions in 1956 (Taylor), 1964 (Calcite) and 1965 (Sloan). Over the years, each had its original steam engine replaced with a more efficient diesel powerplant. Without such modernizations, it is certain none of the three would have ▶

Pusher tug Invincible entering the lakes via the Welland Canal. *(Roger LeLievre)*

7

Myron C. Taylor makes her last trip in USS colors under the Blue Water Bridge at Port Huron/Sarnia on 5 November 2000. (Roger LeLievre)

survived the purge of older bulk carriers from the U.S. Steel fleet during the 1980s. As they begin service this season, the trio of vessels will most likely be employed in the same trades they enjoyed for USS, perhaps with some of the same crew and for the same customers.

Part of LLT's success story must surely be its unusual owner-operator setup. Scott Bravener, the Cuyahoga's captain, is also Lower Lakes' president and CEO.

Flexibility is one of the main reasons for the fleet's success.

Jim Siddall, skipper of the Saginaw, is vice-president of operations. Frank Bravener, father of Scott, is the manager of purchasing and a shareholder. Several other key employees on the vessels are also shareholders from the beginning. Another experienced hand at LLT's helm is Robert S. Pierson, director of marketing, formerly of the Soo River Company which operated a number of vessels in lakes and Seaway service from 1975 to 1982.

In addition, job flexibility is a matter of course aboard the vessels in the fleet. Engineers might be found helping out on deck, and vice versa.

Then there's the handy ability of being able go where bigger boats can't, thanks to the smaller size of the Cuyahoga and her fleetmates.

"We can serve specialized markets particularly in ports that are only serviceable by smaller vessels due to draft of size restrictions – places like Cleveland and Saginaw," Scott Bravener told Seaway Review magazine recently. "And the fact that we are owner-operated means we can offer personal service and reliability of scheduling."

With those advantages in its favor, 2001 should be a busy year for the fleet. The company's success with its veteran vessels only goes to disprove the notion that new is always best and bigger is always better. Now if only they'd decide to pick up some laid up straight-deckers and go into the grain trade ...

– Roger LeLievre & George Wharton

George A. Sloan, downbound in the St. Clair River early in the 2000 season. (John Meyland)

Fleets & Vessels

Three veteran USS Great Lakes Fleet self-unloaders, **Calcite II**, **Myron C. Taylor** and **George A. Sloan**, sail this season for new operators (see page 4). The Calcite II and Taylor date from 1929 and are two of only a handful of vessels still at work on the lakes that predate 1930.

Observers are watching with interest bankruptcy proceedings surrounding LTV Corp., the nation's third-largest steel producer, which operates a mill in Cleveland served by Great Lakes vessels. Failure of the company could have consequences for several U.S. lake fleets. In addition, layoffs and cutbacks in the mining and steel industries have led to fears that a serious shipping slowdown may be ahead. Low water levels continue to plague ship owners, with a forecast for more of the same this season. The loss of one foot of water depth means about 3,240 tons less cargo carried per trip by a typical 1,000-footer.

Great Lakes Cruises Inc. is operating the Greek-flag, 1968-built passenger liner **Arcadia** on the Great Lakes and Seaway this season. A total of 24 cruises are planned on the vessel, which started out life as a passenger and auto ferry but was converted to a passenger ship in 1990.

Construction, Conversions & Casualties

Canada Steamship Lines' **Louis R. Desmarais** is the latest of the fleet's vessels to undergo rebuilding at Port Weller Drydocks over the winter. She sails this season with a new cargo section built to the maximum size allowed by the Seaway, plus a new name, **CSL Laurentien**. PWD

Tadoussac in the Detroit River. *(John C. Meyland)*

also rebuilt CSL's **Tadoussac** this past winter; she re-enters service this season wider and with a new self-unloading system. Meanwhile, reports indicate Canada Steamship Lines' **Manitoulin** may be at the end of a busy career.

Cason J. Callaway and **Philip R. Clarke** entered Fraser Shipyards in Superior early this year as part of a repowering project for the three AAA Class vessels of USS Great Lakes Fleet. After considering whether to convert the steamers to diesel power, turn them into tug-barge units or refurbish their turbines and boilers, the fleet has settled on the latter option. The five-year project began in 1999-2000 with renewal of one of the Callaway's two boilers. This year the project hit full ▶

Brand-new Great Lakes Trader carries its first cargo from Lake Superior 3 July 2000. (Roger LeLievre)

stride as the Callaway's turbine was refurbished and its boiler and engine controls were fully automated for pilothouse control. At the same time, both of Clarke's boilers were renewed. The Callaway's automation is expected to cut operating and maintenance costs. If it works as expected, the Clarke and **Arthur M. Anderson** will undergo similar work during the next three years.

The 740-foot, self-unloading barge **Great Lakes Trader** entered service 20 June 2000, pushed by the tug **Joyce L. Van Enkevort**. She loaded her first ore cargo at Escanaba, MI. and her second at Marquette, MI.

Casualties

On 28 April 2000, the **American Mariner**, downbound with ore from Marquette, experienced a steering failure that resulted in a collision with light number 7 in the Lake Huron Cut just north of Port Huron/Sarnia. A 30-foot by 10-foot tear in the forepeak and another six-inch-wide tear on the starboard bow stretching almost 25 feet led to serious flooding. With the help of the U.S. Coast Guard, which put additional pumps on board, the hull was temporarily patched and the vessel was allowed to proceed to Toledo for permanent repairs.

The Algoma Central self-unloader **Algowood**, loading at Bruce Mines, ON, settled to the bottom after a hull fracture amidships during the night of 2 June 2000. After almost a month of preparation, Algowood was refloated and towed to Port Weller Drydocks for repairs which included replacement of 30 feet of hull. She resumed service in late November.

A decades-old shipwreck is drawing a lot of interest in Lake Huron off the Canadian town of Grand Bend. Divers last year discovered the long-lost wreck of the **Wexford**, a 250-foot cargo vessel that sank with all hands during the Great Storm of 1913, one of eight that went down at that time on the lake. The wreck, which is sitting upright, is protected from looters by Canadian law.

The Wexford wreck was discovered by divers in Lake Huron during 2000.

Lay-up Log

Add **Seaway Queen**, **Canadian Trader** and **Algogulf** to the list of surplus lakeboat tonnage tied up indefinitely. The first two spent the 2000 season idle at Toronto, ON, the latter docked at nearby Hamilton. Meanwhile, **Edward L. Ryerson** continues inactive at Sturgeon Bay (she last sailed in 1998), **Kinsman Enterprise** is still in use as a grain storage hull at Buffalo, NY, (just up the road from the long-idle passenger liner **Aquarama**) and the **John Sherwin** continues her almost two-decade lay-up at Superior, WI. The cement carrier **S.T. Crapo** is still in use as a storage hull at Green Bay, WI, along with her former fleetmate **Lewis G. Harriman**. The 102-year-old **E.M. Ford** is still tied up as a cement storage hull at Saginaw, MI, while the retired cement carrier

John Sherwin (above). (Mike Sipper)

Quedoc's stack reveals the mark of past (Halco) and present (Paterson) owners at Thunder Bay (left).
(Colt Edin)

J.B. Ford, used for storage near Chicago the past several years, awaits an uncertain future, her usefulness in that role now at an end. The former Detroit River passenger steamers **Columbia** and **Ste. Claire** continue to deteriorate at a Detroit dock not far from where the **Edmund Fitzgerald** was launched in 1959. The former Inland Steel steamer **L.E. Block** is still sitting at Escanaba, MI, where she has been since 1981. The carferry **Viking** continues in idleness at Erie, PA along with the former Detroit River carferry and restaurant **Lansdowne**. The Paterson fleet's **Comeaudoc** remains in reserve at Montreal, as do **Vandoc** and **Quedoc** at Thunder Bay, ON. **Algontario** is

The former liner Aquarama, idle at Lackawanna, NY. (Roger LeLievre)

also at the Canadian lakehead, laid up there after a serious grounding in 1999. The **Willowglen** is still in use as a grain storage hull at Goderich, ON, a role she has filled since 1993.

MARINE MILESTONES

5 Years Ago 1996

The two billionth ton of cargo through the St. Lawrence Seaway passed through on board the **Algosoo** on 10 May. ... Despite the all-time record cold and snow during the winter of 1995-'96, many vessels operated late into the season. **Arthur M. Anderson** and **Cason J. Callaway** finally laid up 16 February 1996, each ending a season of more than 320 consecutive days in operation. The cold conditions caused problems to early season traffic in 1996, and Marquette still had ice in the harbor on 3 June. ... Continuing a trend in the 1990s, a new tug-barge unit, **Jacklyn M./Integrity**, enters service during the summer. This new construction joins several former lakers that were converted to barges earlier in the decade.

10 Years Ago 1991

The cement carrier **Alpena** enters service for Inland Lakes Management in June after undergoing conversion from the former straight-decker **Leon Fraser**. Later that summer, fleetmate **E. M. Ford** makes her last trip before entering long-term lay-up. ... 1991 was the first year in 100 that there was no active carferry service on Lake Michigan. The first carferry, **Ann Arbor No. 1**, sailed in November 1892, and the **Badger** laid up in November 1990 before resuming service under new ownership later in the decade.

20 Years Ago 1981

The **Columbia Star** is the last of the 1,000-footers to enter service, leaving Sturgeon Bay, WI, on her maiden voyage on 30 May. Except for tug-barge combinations, she is also the last new American-built Great Lakes vessel. The **Paul L. Tregurtha**, the longest carrier on the lakes, also enters service in 1981, sailing as **William J. DeLancey**. ... Many lakers sailed for the final time in 1981, ranging in age from the 76-year-old veteran **H.C. Heimbecker** to the 23-year-old youngster **John Sherwin**. The Heimbecker was scrapped not long afterward, and barring an unexpected return to service in 2001, the Sherwin will complete 20 years of lay-up at Superior, WI, in November 2001.

Veteran steamer H.C. Heimbecker sailed her last in 1981. *(Bob Campbell)*

Cement barge Integrity entered service five years ago. (Stephen Hause)

25 Years Ago
1976

The Superior Midwest Energy Terminal opened on 8 June with the loading of **John J. Boland**. The low-sulfur Western coal shipped through this facility has become an increasingly important commodity in the Great Lakes region. ... Many vessels sported Bicentennial markings this year. Perhaps most noteworthy included the vessels of U.S. Steel's Great Lakes Fleet, which were prominently decorated. ...The **James R. Barker** becomes the largest vessel on the Great Lakes when she enters service on 8 August.

50 Years Ago
1951

With Great Lakes shipyards busy, many fleets turn to saltwater as a source of new vessels. Construction begins in Sparrows Point, MD, on **Elton Hoyt 2nd**, **Johnstown** and **Sparrows Point**. **Cliffs Victory**, **Tom M. Girdler**, **Troy H. Browning** (later **Thomas F. Patton**) and **Charles M. White** are converted for Great Lakes service this year as former Victory-class and C-4 class ships, respectively.

Some vessels under construction in Great Lakes yards this year include the **Philip R. Clarke** and **Edward B. Greene**, the first of eight AAA-class vessels designed for Pittsburgh Steamship Co. and later adopted by other fleets. Canadian yards are especially busy building four large tankers that will primarily run between Superior, WI, and Sarnia, ON. The tankers enter service as the **Imperial Leduc**, **Imperial Redwater**, **Imperial Woodbend**, and **B.A. Peerless**. Within three years, all but one would be converted to dry bulk cargo vessels.

100 Years Ago
1901

The Pittsburgh Steamship Company is formed as a result of a merger of five other fleets. Throughout much of the next century, the fleet would remain among the largest on the Great Lakes, although the fleet is the smallest in its history as it enters its second century of operation.

— Jody Aho

GREAT LAKES GLOSSARY

AAA CLASS — Vessel design popular on the Great Lakes in the early 1950s. **Arthur M. Anderson** is one example.

AFT — Toward the back, or stern, of a ship.

AHEAD — Forward.

AMIDSHIPS — The middle point of a vessel, referring to either length or width.

ARTICULATED TUG-BARGE (ATB) — Tug-barge combination. The two vessels are mechanically linked in one axis, but with the tug free to move, or articulate, on another axis. **Jacklyn M / Integrity** is one example.

BACKHAUL — The practice of carrying a revenue-producing cargo (rather than ballast) on a return trip from hauling a primary cargo.

BARGE — Vessel with no engine, either pushed or pulled by a tug.

BEAM — The width of a vessel measured at the widest point.

BILGE — Lowest part of a hold or compartment, generally where the rounded side of a ship curves from the keel to the vertical sides.

BOOMER — Lakes slang for self-unloader.

BOW — Front of a vessel.

BOWTHRUSTER — Propeller mounted transversely in a vessel's bow under the waterline to assist in moving sideways. A sternthruster may also be installed.

BRIDGE — The platform above the main deck from which a ship is steered or navigated. Also: **PILOTHOUSE** or **WHEELHOUSE**.

BULKHEAD — Wall or partition that separates rooms, holds or tanks within a ship's hull.

BULWARK — The part of the ship that extends fore and aft above the main deck to form a rail.

DATUM — Level of water in a given area, determined by an average over time.

DEADWEIGHT TONNAGE — The actual carrying capacity of a vessel, equal to the difference between the light displacement tonnage and the heavy displacement tonnage, expressed in long tons (2,240 pounds or 1,016.1 kg).

DISPLACEMENT TONNAGE — The actual weight of the vessel and everything aboard her, measured in long tons. The displacement is equal to the weight of the water displaced by the vessel. Displacement tonnage may be qualified as light, indicating the weight of the vessel without cargo, fuels, stores; or heavy, indicating the weight of the vessel loaded with cargo, fuel and stores.

DRAFT — The depth of water a ship needs to float. Also the distance from keel to waterline.

FIT-OUT — The process of preparing a vessel for service after a period of inactivity.

FOOTER — Slang for 1,000-foot vessel.

FORECASTLE — (FOHK s'l) Area at the forward part of the ship and beneath the main cabins, often used for crew's quarters or storage.

FOREPEAK — The space below the forecastle.

FORWARD — Toward the front of an object on a ship.

FREEBOARD — The distance from the waterline to the main deck.

GROSS TONNAGE — The internal space of a vessel, measured in units of 100 cubic feet (2.83 cubic meters) = a gross ton.

HATCH — An opening in the deck through which cargo is lowered or raised. A hatch is closed by securing a hatch cover over it.

HULL — The body of a ship, not including its superstructure, masts or machinery.

INBOARD — Toward the center of the ship.

INTEGRATED TUG-BARGE (ITB) — Tug-barge combination in which the tug is rigidly mated to the barge. **Presque Isle** is one example.

JONES ACT — U.S. cabotage law that mandates cargos moved between American ports to be carried by U.S.-flagged, U.S.-built and U.S.-crewed vessels.

KEEL — A ship's steel backbone. It runs along the lowest part of the hull.

LAID UP — Out of service.

MARITIME CLASS — Style of lake vessel built during World War II as part of the nation's war effort. **Richard Reiss** is one example.

NET REGISTERED TONNAGE — The internal capacity of a vessel available for carrying cargo. It does not include the space occupied by boilers, engines, shaft alleys, chain lockers, officers' and crew's quarters. Net registered tonnage is usually referred to as registered tonnage or net tonnage and is used to figure taxes, tolls and port charges.

PELLETS — See **TACONITE**.

PORT — Left side of the ship facing the bow.

RIVER-CLASS SELF-UNLOADER — Group of vessels built in the 1970s to service smaller ports and negotiate narrow rivers such as Cleveland's Cuyahoga. **David Z. Norton** is one example.

SELF-UNLOADER — Vessel able to discharge its own cargo using a system of conveyor belts and a moveable boom.

SLAG — By-product of the steelmaking process which is later ground and used for paving roads.

STARBOARD — The right side of the ship facing forward.

STEM — The extreme forward end of the bow.

STERN — The back of the ship.

STRAIGHT-DECKER — A non-self-unloading vessel. **Edward L. Ryerson** is one example.

TACONITE — Processed, pelletized iron ore. Easy to load and unload, this is the primary method of shipping ore on the Great Lakes and St. Lawrence Seaway.

TRACTOR TUG — Highly maneuverable tug propelled by either a z-drive or cycloidal system rather than the traditional screw propeller.

Vessel Index

Cason J. Callaway, Algosound at the Soo Locks. *(Roger LeLievre)*

Vessel Name / Fleet Number	Vessel Name / Fleet Number	Vessel Name / Fleet Number
A	Alexandria Belle U-1	Anangel Fidelity.....................IA-10
A-390.......................................A-15	Alexis.......................................IT-11	Anangel Honesty IA-10
A-397.......................................A-15	Alexis-Simard A-6	Anangel Honour IA-10
A-410.......................................A-15	Algirdas......................................IL-6	Anangel Hope..........................IA-10
Abdul S.......................................IS-2	Algobay.............................A-7/S-7	Anangel Horizon......................IA-10
Abeer S.......................................IS-2	Algocape {2} A-7/S-7	Anangel Liberty IA-10
Abegweit {1}...........................C-26	Algocatalyst..............................A-7	Anangel Might IA-10
Abitibi Claiborne......................IR-5	Algocen {2} A-7/S-7	Anangel Prosperity IA-10
Abitibi Orinoco.........................IR-5	Algoeast A-7	Anangel Sky.............................IA-10
Abu Egila IT-7	Algofax A-7	Anangel Spirit IA-10
Acacia U-4	Algogulf {2} A-7/S-7	Anangel Triumph IA-10
ACBL 1613.................................D-15	Algoisle A-7/S-7	Anangel Victory IA-10
ACBL 1614.................................D-15	Algolake A-7/S-7	Anangel Wisdom IA-10
Achtergracht............................IS-28	Algomah A-18	Anax IP-16
Adanac P-14	Algomarine.........................A-7/S-7	Anchor Bay G-19
Adimon......................................IC-6	Algonorth A-7/S-7	Anderson, Arthur M. U-18
Adler..U-4	Algonova A-7	Andon IY-1
Admiral Ushakov...................IM-19	Algontario A-7/S-7	Andre H.......................................T-6
Admiralengracht IS-28	Algoport A-7/S-7	Andrea......................................IP-3
Advent......................................C-5	Algorail {2} A-7/S-7	Andrea Marie I D-3
Adventure IP-6	Algoriver.............................A-7/S-7	Andrew J.....................................E-5
Aegean I....................................IG-6	Algosar A-7	Andrie, Barbara A-15
Aegean Sea................................IE-4	Algoscotia A-7	Andrie, Candice.......................A-15
Agate Islands IN-5	Algosea {2}..............................C-36	Andrie, Clara A-15
Agawa Canyon A-7/S-7	Algosoo {2} A-7/S-7	Andrie, Karen {2}...................A-15
Aggie C...I-1	Algosound...........................A-7/S-7	Andrie, Mari Beth A-15
Aghia Marina IA-7	Algosteel {2} A-7/S-7	Anemone IP-16
Agiodektini IZ-1	Algoville A-7/S-7	Angelia P..................................IC-17
Agios Georgios IG-1	Algoway {2}.......................A-7/S-7	Angelicoussi, Maria IA-10
Agoming......................................T-7	Algowest A-7/S-7	Anglian Lady.............................P-14
Aiana...IN-5	Algowood...........................A-7/S-7	Angus, D. J. G-13
Aird, John B. A-7/S-7	Ali S...IS-2	Aniskin, Mekhanik IA-19
Aivik T-14	Alice A..M-19	Anita Dee T-2
Akebono Star IC-9	Alice E. E-7	Anita Dee II.................................T-2
Akrathos IA-7	Alka IS-29	Anita G. IP-3
Akti..IZ-1	Allegra IS-7	Anja IN-11
Aktis IL-5	Allied Chemical No. 12..............A-8	Anja C IC-4
Akvile IL-6	Allouez Marine............................A-9	Anjeliersgracht........................IS-28
Alabama {2} G-17	Alma IS-14	Ankergracht IS-28
Alam Jaya..................................IP-2	Almania IC-5	Ann Harvey C-5
Alam Karang..............................IP-2	Alouette Arrow IK-5	Antalina.....................................IT-5
Alam Kembong...........................IP-2	Alpena {2} I-4	Antares IA-9
Alam Kerisi IP-2	Alphonse des Jarnins...............S-17	Anthony IB-9
Alam Pari IP-2	Alsterstern IR-8	Antiquarian G-22
Alam Sejahtera........................IP-2	Alsyta...IP-3	Antwerpen C-36
Alam Sempurna........................IP-2	Altair...IN-7	Apache.......................................D-5
Alam Senang............................IP-2	Altis P IC-17	Apex Chicago A-16
Alam Tabah IP-2	Alycia IS-14	APJ Anand...............................IS-31
Alam Talang...............................IP-2	Amaryllis IP-16	APJ Angad.................................IS-31
Alam Tangkas IP-2	Amazonia IS-14	APJ Anjli IS-31
Alam Tegas IP-2	Amber Mae................................R-8	APJ Karan IS-31
Alam Teguh IP-2	AMC 100 ....A-13	APJ Sushma..............................IS-31
Alam Teladan.............................IP-2	AMC 200 ....A-13	Apollo C....................................IS-10
Alam Tenega IP-2	AMC 300 ....A-13	Apollogracht IS-28
Alam Tenggiri............................IP-2	American Freedom...................A-14	Appledore B-7
Alam Tenteram IP-2	American Girl G-9	Aptmariner................................IC-14
Alaska Rainbow IJ-2	American Mariner.....................A-14	Arabian Express.......................ID-1
Alba Sierra IA-11	American Republic A-14	Arcadia IG-6
Albert B.....................................M-19	Amherst Islander {2} O-4	Archangelgracht IS-28
Albert C...I-1	Amitie IG-8	Arctic..F-4
Alcona R-8	Amstelgracht IS-28	Arctic Kalvik...............................F-4
Alcor...T-13	An Guang Jiang IC-14	Arctic Viking C-1
Aldebaran IA-9	An Kang Jiang...........................IC-14	Arethusa IS-14
Aldo H.......................................M-19	An Qing Jiang IC-14	Argonaut...................................IS-26
Alexander K.............................IC-10	An Ze Jiang...............................IC-14	Argut..IF-4
Alexander, Sir William C-5	Ana Safi IK-1	Ariake Star IC-9
Alexandergracht IS-28	Anangel Ares...........................IA-10	Ariel...J-1
Alexandria...............IP-7, IT-7, IZ-1	Anangel Endeavor..................IA-10	Arion IW-2

19

U.S. Coast Guard cutters Katmai Bay (left) and Frank Drew. *(Roger LeLievre)*

Vessel Name / Fleet Number	Vessel Name / Fleet Number	Vessel Name / Fleet Number
Bremon IB-1	Canadian Progress U-16/S-7	Caribbean Express I ID-1
Brenda L. F-6	Canadian Prospector U-16/S-7	Caribou M-8
Bristol Bay U-4	Canadian Provider U-16/S-7	Caribou Isle C-5
Brochu F-4	Canadian Ranger U-16/S-7	Carl M. M-22
Brunto IW-3	Canadian Trader U-16/S-7	Carleton, George N. G-14
Buccaneer W-1	Canadian Transfer U-16/S-7	Caro IO-6
Buckeye {3} O-3	Canadian Transport {2} U-16/S-7	Carol Ann K-8
Buckley K-7	Canadian Venture U-16/S-7	Carola I. IH-3
Buckthorn U-4	Canadian Voyager U-16/S-7	Caroline K IF-1
Buffalo U-3	Canadiana MU-23	Caronia C-37
Buffalo {3} A-14	Canmar Conquest IC-1	Carrol C I M-19
Bunyan, Paul U-3	Canmar Courage IC-1	Carroll Jean A-9
Burns Harbor {2} B-11	Canmar Fortune IC-1	Cartier, Jacques C-33
Burro M-7	Canmar Glory IC-1	Cartierdoc {2} N-1
Burton, Courtney O-3	Canmar Honour IC-1	Cast Performance IC-1
Busch, Gregory J. B-23	Canmar Pride IC-1	Cast Privilege IC-1
Busse, Fred A. C-16	Canmar Spirit IC-1	Catherine-Legardeur S-17
	Canmar Triumph IC-1	Cavalier M-19
C	Canmar Valour IC-1	Cavalier des Mers C-31
c. Columbus IH-7	Canmar Venture IC-1	Cavalier Grand Fleuve C-31
C.T.C. No.1 .... H-4	Canmar Victory IC-1	Cavalier Maxim C-31
Cabot {2} C-20	Cantankerous E-12	Cavalier Royal C-31
Cabot Strait IC-5	Cap Streeter S-15	Cay IN-1
Cadillac {5} S-25	Cape Cod Light A-11	CEC Blue IE-3
Calabria IN-4	Cape Confidence IH-6	CEC Dawn IE-3
Calcite II L-14	Cape Hurd C-5	CEC Faith IE-3
California G-17	Cape May Light A-11	CEC Force IE-3
Callaway, Cason J. U-18	Cape Roger C-5	CEC Future IE-3
Calliroe Patronicola IO-4	Cape Syros IC-2	Celebrezze, Anthony J. C-21
Canadian Century U-16/S-7	Capetan Michalis IU-1	Celine M. IL-4
Canadian Challenger A-4	Capricorn IC-9	Celtic Sif IK-3
Canadian Empress S-22	Capt. Roy B-20	Cemba D-4
Canadian Enterprise U-16/S-7	Capt. Shepler S-13	CGB-12000 .... U-4
Canadian Leader U-16/S-7	Captain Barnaby K-4	CGB-12001 .... U-4
Canadian Mariner U-16/S-7	Captain Christos IG-1	Chada Naree IG-12
Canadian Miner U-16/S-7	Captain George F-8	Challenge G-21
Canadian Navigator U-16/S-7	Carey, Emmet J. O-7	Chalothorn Naree IG-12
Canadian Olympic U-16/S-7	Carib Alba C-25	Champion {1} C-12
Canadian Pioneer A-4	Carib Dawn C-25	Champion {3} D-15

20

Joseph H. Frantz upbound on Lake St. Clair. *(Gene W. Peterson)*

JOSEPH H. FRANTZ

Vessel Spotlight

JOSEPH H. FRANTZ	
Length	618'
Beam	62'
Depth	32'
Built	1925
Tonnage	13,600

Next time you spot the **Joseph H. Frantz** reliably going about her business on the Great Lakes, realize you are viewing history.

Built in 1925 at Great Lakes Engineering Works in River Rouge, MI, the Frantz is the second-oldest bulk carrier in service on the lakes. Built for the Columbia Steamship Co., she is operated today by Oglebay Norton Marine Services, a Columbia descendent. At the time of her launch, she was one of the largest carriers on the lakes; now she is among the smallest. She has carried the same name for all her 76 years and is very similar in design to Cleveland's museum ship, **William G. Mather**.

Although the Frantz is a veteran carrier, she has been extensively modernized. In 1955, her original triple expansion steam plant was replaced by a Skinner Uniflow steam engine. In 1965, that engine was replaced by a diesel, her triple-deck pilothouse was reduced to two levels and the Frantz was converted to a self-unloader. If the work had not be performed, the Frantz would have long ago gone the way of other vessels her age – to the scrapyard.

Luckily, the Frantz has found her niche serving smaller ports on the lower Great Lakes such as Saginaw, Muskegon and Marine City, MI, carrying mostly stone and coal, her smaller size an asset rather than a liability.

The Frantz early in her career. *(Tom Manse Collection)*

– *Roger LeLievre*

23

Montrealais under the unloading bridges at Indiana Harbor. (Gary L. Clark)

Vessel Name / Fleet Number		Vessel Name / Fleet Number		Vessel Name / Fleet Number	
Goki	P-14	Grayling	U-5	Halifax	C-3
Gold River	IC-8	Grazia	IS-7	Halton	M-22
Golden D	IG-7	Great Blue Heron	B-16	Hamilton Energy	U-16
Golden Laker	IJ-7	Great Laker	IB-14	Hammond Bay	L-12, U-3
Golden Shield	IT-10	Great Lakes {2}	K-6	Handymariner	IC-14
Golden Sky	IC-9	Great Lakes Trader	V-1	Hanlan, Ned	MU-15
Golden Sun	IC-9	Green, Maria	IH-3	Hanlan, Ned II	T-11
Gonio	IG-4	Green, Marion	IH-3	Hannah 1801	H-4
Goodtime I	G-11	Greenland Saga	IF-1	Hannah 1802	H-4
Goodtime III	G-12	Greenstone	U-7	Hannah 2801	H-4
Gorthon, Ada	IG-9	Grenfall, Sir Wilfred	C-5	Hannah 2901	H-4
Gorthon, Alida	IG-9	Greta V	M-19	Hannah 2902	H-4
Gorthon, Ingrid	IG-9	Grey Fox	U-8	Hannah 2903	H-4
Gorthon, Ivan	IG-9	Grey, Earl	C-5	Hannah 3601	H-4
Gorthon, Joh.	IG-9	Griffon	C-5	Hannah 5101	H-4
Gorthon, Lovisa	IG-9	Grue Des Iles	S-17	Hannah, Daryl C. {2}	H-4
Gorthon, Margit	IG-9	Guajira	IN-4	Hannah, Donald C.	H-4
Gorthon, Maria	IG-9	Gulf Star	S-26	Hannah, Hannah D.	H-4
Gorthon, Ragna	IG-9	Gulfbreeze	IC-12, IS-6	Hannah, James A.	H-4
Gorthon, Viola	IG-9	Gulfstream	IC-12, IS-6	Hannah, Kristin Lee	H-4
Gotia	IO-6	Gull Isle	C-5	Hannah, Mark	H-4
Gott, Edwin H.	U-18	Gunay A	ID-3	Hannah, Mary E.	H-4
Gouin, Lomer	S-17	Gur Maiden	IJ-8	Hannah, Mary Page {1}	S-8
Goviken	IT-3	Gur Master	IJ-8	Hannah, Mary Page {2}	H-4
Grace Pioneer	IM-2	Gutshof	IM-11	Hannah, Peggy D.	H-4
Grampa Woo III	L-5			Hannah, Susan W.	H-4
Grand Island {2}	P-6	**H**		Hanne Cartharine	IH-1
Grande Baie	A-6	H-9901	L-11	Hanseatic	IH-7
Grande Caribe	A-10	Habib	IC-20	Happy Day	IM-1
Grande Mariner	A-10	Haci Hilmi Bey	IB-7	Happy Ranger	IM-3
Grande Prince	A-10	Hai Ji Shun	IC-14	Happy River	IM-3
Grant Carrier	IJ-10	Haida	MU-10	Happy Rover	IM-3
Grant, R. F.	T-6			Harbor Builder	E-5

Joseph L. Block heads for a Lake Superior port with a cargo of limestone. (Roger LeLievre)

Vessel Name / Fleet Number	Vessel Name / Fleet Number	Vessel Name / Fleet Number
Livanov, Boris..........................IN-13	Maid of the Mist VII...................M-4	Massachusetts..........................G-17
Lois T.......................................N-2	Maine {1}..............................G-17	Matador VI................................K-2
Lok Maheshwari.......................IT-8	Maisonneuve S-18	Mather, William G. {2}..........MU-8
Lok Pragati...............................IT-8	Majestic Star {2}...................P-12	Matthew....................................C-5
Lok Prakash.............................IT-8	Makatsarija................................IG-4	MBT 10 ....M-27
Lok Pratap IT-8	Makeevka................................IA-16	MBT 20 ....M-27
Lok Pratima IT-8	Malden.....................................P-14	MBT 33 ....M-27
Lok Prem IT-8	Malene Sif IK-3	McAllister 132............................A-2
Lok Rajeshwari IT-8	Mallard....................................IN-3	McAllister No. 3.........................L-11
Looiersgracht.........................IS-28	Malte B IW-1	McAllister, Cathy L-11
Lootsgracht.............................IS-28	Malyovitza IN-6	McAllister, Daniel.....................MU-1
Lotus Islands............................IN-5	Mana IG-8	McAsphalt 401 ....M-17
Louie S.....................................R-6	Manco......................................M-19	McBride, Sam T-12
Louisbourg C-5	Manitou {1}.............................T-15	McCarthy, Walter J. Jr. A-14
Louise M-1	Manitou {2} M-5	McCauley.................................U-3
Louisiana.................................G-17	Manitou Isle M-6	McGrath, James E. U-16
Louis-Jolliet C-31	Manitoulin {5} C-3	McGuirl, May.............................R-2
Lovcen IJ-10	Manitowoc M-15, U-3	McKee Sons L-14
LST-325................................MU-30	Mantadoc {2}.............................N-1	McKeil, Doug {2}....................M-19
Lucien L...................................S-17	Maple....................MU-4, U-4	McKeil, Evans M-19
Lucien-Paquin T-14	Maple......................................ID-6	McKeil, Florence M-19
Luckyman IT-13	Maple City T-11	McKeil, Jarrett.........................M-19
Luedtke, Alan K. L-15	Maple Grove O-1	McKeil, Wyatt...........................M-19
Luedtke, Chris E. L-15	Mapleglen {2}..........................P-1	McKeller P-14
Luedtke, Erich R. L-15	Marcey.....................................M-7	McLane MU-30
Luedtke, Karl E. L-15	Marcosul Uruguay IF-5	Meagan Beth............................D-15
Luedtke, Kurt L-15	Marcoux, Camille.......................S-17	Mecta Sea IE-4
Luedtke, Paul L.........................L-15	Margaret Ann............................H-10	Med Glory...............................IM-10
Luna Verde.............................IP-14	Margaret M. A-1	Med Hope IM-10
Lunni IN-8	Marie-Clarisse F-2	Med Pride IM-10
Lynx IV-1	Marilis T....................................IT-5	Med Transporter IS-25
Lyra IN-1	Marine Star E-8	Medill, Joseph {2}....................S-8
M	Marine Supplier A-3	Medininkai................................IL-6
M. Melody IJ-8	Marine Trader............................A-3	Melkki.....................................IN-8
M/V Montreal.............................C-31	Marinette.................................IG-13	Menasha {2}...........................M-23
M-1..D-15	Marinor IB-12	Menier Consol............................T-9
Macado.....................................IB-1	Marinus C-5	Menominee..............................IG-13
Macassa Bay.............................E-4	Mariposa Belle M-14	Merkine IL-6
Mackenzie, Wm. Lyon T-10	Maritime Trader........................M-19	Mervine II................................C-19
Mackinac Express A-18	Marjan I..................................IS-29	Merweborg...............................IW-2
Mackinaw U-4	Marjolaine II.............................C-34	Mesabi Miner..............................I-6
Mackinaw City..........................M-1	Mark C.....................................IC-4	Meta.......................................IO-6
Madeline M-3	Marka L....................................IC-7	Metauro...................................IM-9
Madison M-1	Markborg.................................IW-2	Meteor...................................MU-24
Maersk Brooklyn IG-11	Market, Wm. M-26	Metis......................................U-16
Maersk Charleston IG-11	Marlyn.....................................S-15	Mette Clipper...........................IJ-15
Maersk Manila IP-9	Marquette {5}..........................S-25	Metz Beirut...............................IL-4
Maersk Savannah IG-11	Marquette {6}..........................C-17	Metz Italia IL-4
Maersk Takoradi IG-11	Martha A...................................H-9	Metz, Carl................................IL-4
Magnetic F-5	Martin, Argue M-19	Metz, Pablo...............................IL-4
Magpie....................................P-14	Martin, Rt. Hon. Paul J...............C-3	Metz, Pauline............................IL-4
Maid of the Mist M-4	Martinique................................IC-13	Michigan...................................U-3
Maid of the Mist III M-4	Mary C.......................................I-1	Michigan {10}...........................K-6
Maid of the Mist IV....................M-4	Mary C......................................IC-4	Michiganborg............................IW-2
Maid of the Mist V.....................M-4	Maryland {2}...........................G-17	Middle Channel........................C-12
Maid of the Mist VI....................M-4	Marysville G-1	Middletown................................O-3
		Midstate I..................................S-6
		Midstate II.................................S-6
		Milin Kamak..............................IN-6
		Millenium Amethyst..................IM-16
		Millenium Condor.....................IM-16
		Millenium Eagle IM-16
		Millenium Falcon......................IM-16
		Millenium Golden Hind IM-16
		Millenium Harmony IM-16
		Millenium Hawk.......................IM-16
		Millenium Leader IM-16
		Millenium Majestic IM-16

American Steamship Co.'s Sam Laud loading at Stoneport, MI. *(Jon LaFontaine)*

Vessel Name / Fleet Number		
Millenium Osprey IM-16	MOBRO 2005...........................D-15	Nanook....................................L-11
Millenium Raptor....................IM-16	Moby Dick.................................S-8	Nanticoke C-3
Millenium Yama IM-16	Moezelborg.............................IW-2	Nantucket Clipper.....................N-6
Milroy, Phil F-6	Mohawk L-3	Narragansett...........................IB-2
Milwaukee................................G-17	Montana G-17	Nathan S................................M-10
Milwaukee Clipper...................MU-5	Monterey IC-2	Nautica Queen J-3
Mimer.......................................IG-5	Montrealais U-16/S-7	Navcomar #1...........................L-11
Mina Cebi IP-5	Moor Laker IV-2	Navigo.....................................IR-2
Mindaugas IL-6	Moore, Olive M.........................U-15	Nea Doxa.................................IF-2
Miners Castle P-6	Morgan K-7	Nea Elpis IF-2
Minka C IC-4	Morgenstond IA-9	Nea Tyhi IF-2
Minnesota {1}.........................G-17	Morias IM-12	Neah Bay U-4
Minthi IO-3	Morillo IG-3	Nebraska.................................G-17
Miseford N-2	Morraborg................................IW-2	Necat A....................................ID-3
Mishe-Mokwa...........................M-6	Morris, George R-2	Nedlloyd Africa IP-1
Miss Brockville U-14	Morton Salt 74 ....M-29	Nedlloyd America IP-1
Miss Brockville IV U-14	Moslavina...............................IJ-10	Nedlloyd Asia...........................IP-1
Miss Brockville V......................U-14	Mott, Charlie.............................U-7	Nedlloyd Clarence....................IP-1
Miss Brockville VI.....................U-14	Mountain Blossom L-8	Nedlloyd Clement IP-1
Miss Brockville VII....................U-14	Mr. Micky..................................H-1	Nedlloyd Colombo....................IP-1
Miss Brockville VIII...................U-14	Mrs. C.....................................C-30	Nedlloyd Europa.......................IP-1
Miss Buffalo.............................B-21	MSC Baltic..............................IW-2	Nedlloyd Hongkong..................IP-1
Miss Buffalo II..........................B-21	MSC Boston.............................IG-2	Nedlloyd Honshu......................IP-1
Miss Edna..................................K-8	MSC Houston...........................IG-2	Nedlloyd Hoorn........................IP-1
Miss Ivy Lea II...........................I-11	MSC New York.........................IG-3	Nedlloyd Marne IP-1
Miss Ivy Lea III.........................I-11	Munksund IG-13	Nedlloyd Musi..........................IP-1
Miss Midland P-4	Munson, John G. {2}..............U-18	Nedlloyd Oceania.....................IP-1
Miss Munising..........................S-14	Murray R....................................F-6	Neebish Islander C-22
Miss Olympia...........................C-31	Musa IL-6	Neebish Islander II E-2
Miss Shawn Simpson M-19	Musinskiy, Vasiliy IN-12	Needler, Alfred..........................C-5
Miss Superior P-6	Muskegon {2}...........................K-8	Neeltje, Laurina IA-9
Mississippi................................G-17	Musky II.....................................U-5	Neeskay U-12
Missouri {2}............................G-17	Musselborg..............................IW-2	Nelvana C-36
Mistral IG-5		Nelvana {1} N-4
Misty..IN-4		Nememcha IS-23
Mljet...IA-14	**N**	Nenufar Atlantico.....................IH-9
Mobile Bay U-4	Nadia J....................................IN-10	Neptune...................................H-14
MOBRO 2000..........................D-15	Nadro Clipper............................N-2	Neptune III...............................D-6
MOBRO 2001..........................D-15	Nancy Ann M-12	Nereis P IC-17
	Nancy Anne.............................D-15	

Algogulf loads at Thunder Bay, ON. (Gene Onchulenko)

Yankcanuck is upbound in the Welland Canal 28 October 2000.

(Roger LeLievre)

YANKCANUCK

Vessel Spotlight

YANKCANUCK

Length	324' 03"
Beam	49'
Depth	26'
Built	1963
Tonnage	4,760

Built by Collingwood Shipyards, Collingwood, ON, this versatile vessel was launched 8 January 1963 as **Yankcanuck** for the Yankcanuck Steamship Co., Sault Ste. Marie, ON. She was the second lake vessel to bear that name, derived from the fact that her owner, Captain Frank Manzzutti, was Canadian and his wife, Eleanor Cox, an American (earlier vessels in the fleet bore the names **Mancox** and **Manzzutti**). Classified as a crane ship, the Yankcanuck was built to haul finished steel products from the Algoma Steel mill at the Canadian Soo to markets in Windsor and Detroit.

In 1970, the Yankcanuck was sold to Algoma Steel Corp. Ltd. of Sault Ste. Marie, ON, but her runs remained virtually unchanged. Capable of coastal trading and equipped with a hull strengthened for service in ice, the Yankcanuck has also used her crane to load steel into ocean-going ships. Other duties have included lightering grounded vessels and hauling salt, ore and coal. In 1981 she picked up a load of coal at Thunder Bay, ON, in just 37 minutes.

Algoma Steel sold the Yankcanuck in 1991 to Purvis Marine Ltd., Sault Ste. Marie, ON. Due to labor disagreements, she was operated a barge in 1991, then again as a powered vessel in 1993 after the dispute was settled. For Purvis, the Yankcanuck continues to actively sail as a crane ship, sometimes serving as a barge (Purvis' activities are focused around tug/barge operations).

The Yankcanuck is powered by a Cooper-Bessemer 1860 horsepower diesel engine and is equipped with a tracked extendable boom crane. A bowthruster was installed during the winter of 1999-'00. Three hatches feed into three holds where she can carry 4,760 tons at her maximum mid-summer draft of 21 feet, 6 inches.

"Skipper" Manzzutti, Yankcanuck's original owner, and his wife, Eleanor, both passed away in 2000.

— George Wharton

Vessel Name / Fleet Number	Vessel Name / Fleet Number	Vessel Name / Fleet Number
San Marino IR-3	Shamook C-5	Spirit of Rochester G-7
Sand Pebble..............................D-5	Shannon G-1, IC-2	Split IS-29
Sandpiper H-5	Shannon 66-5 ....T-5	Spray C-5
Sandra Mary M-22	Shark C-5	Spring Grace............................IM-2
Sandviken IT-3	Shark VII I-8	Spring Laker IS-17
Santiago IA-1	Sharon Jon S-16	Spring Ocean IS-17
Sapanca IS-25	Sheila P. P-14	Spring Trader IS-17
Saturn {4} A-7	Shelia Ann C-36	Spuds R-6
Sault au Couchon M-19	Shelter Bay..............................U-3	Spume C-5
Sauniere A-7	Sherwin, John {2} I-6	St. Clair {2} M-19
Savard, Joseph S-17	Shipka IN-6	St. Clair {3}............................A-14
Scan Arctic IS-5	Shirley Irene K-3	St. George IS-30
Scan Atlantic............................IS-5	Shirley Joy L-3	St. John, J. S. E-13
Scan Bothnia IS-5	Shoreline II S-15	St. Martin IS-30
Scan Finlandia.........................IS-5	Showboat Mardi Gras H-7	St. Mary's Cement...................B-14
Scan Germania IS-5	Showboat Royal Grace...........M-14	St. Mary's Cement II................B-15
Scan Hansa IS-5	Siauliai IL-6	St. Mary's Cement III...............B-15
Scan Oceanic...........................IS-5	Sideracrux IS-18	St. Thomas IS-30
Scan Pacific IH-9	Sidercastor IS-18	Stadt Essen.............................IH-9
Scan Partner IH-9	Siderpollux..............................IS-18	Stahl, Roger G-1
Scan Polaris IS-5	Sillery G-20	Stahl, Weser............................C-36
Scandrett, Fred T-11	Silver River IM-4	Stamon IS-1
Scarab......................................ID-8	Silversides MU-30	Star B IB-5
Schlaegar, Victor L. C-15	Simcoe C-5	Star Eagle IA-1
Schwartz, H. J. U-3	Simonsen U-3	Star of Chicago {2}..................S-15
Sea Castle M-11	Sioux {1} L-3	Star Savannah............................F-1
Sea Chief D-5	Sirri IN-8	State of Haryana.......................IT-8
Sea Colt S-5	Siscowet U-5	STC 2004 ....B-23
Sea Eagle IB-14	Sjard IB-13	Ste. Claire MU-27
Sea Eagle II B-15	Skagen IP-7	Steel Shuttle............................IH-3
Sea Falcon...............................S-5	Skradin IS-21	Steel Sprinter IH-3
Sea Flower IF-1	Sky Bird...................................IJ-4	Stefania I IF-8
Sea Fox II.................................S-4	Skyline Princess M-24	Stefanos IS-36
Sea Hound N-2	Skyline Queen M-24	Stella Borealis C-24
Sea Lion IF-1	Slano IA-14	Stellamare IJ-12
Sea Maid IF-1	Sloan, George A. L-14	Stellanova IJ-12
Sea Ox S-5	Smallwood, Joseph & Clara M-8	Stellaprima IJ-12
Sea Pilot S-5	Smaragda IJ-3	Stevns Bulk IN-10
Sea Queen II A-17	Smith, F. C. G...........................C-5	Stevns Pearl IN-10
Sea Rose IF-1	Smith, H. A. H-8	Stevns Sea IN-10
Sea Sparrow.............................S-5	Smith, L. L. Jr. U-13	Stevns Trader IN-10
Sea Wolf............................C-2, S-5	Solin IS-29	Stevnsland..................IN-10, IS-34
Seaflight I C-24	Solta IS-29	Still Watch T-4
Seaflight II C-24	Solymar IH-9	Stinson, George A. A-14
Seaglory ID-11	Soo River Belle........................N-11	St-Laurent, Louis S. C-5
Seaharmony II IT-9	Sooneck II-1	Stolt Alliance S-28
Seal VII I-8	Sora C-5	Stolt Aspiration S-28
Sealink IT-9	Sotka IN-8	Stolt Kent S-28
Sealion VII I-8	South Bass M-26	Storm IE-1
Searanger II IT-9	South Carolina G-17	Stormont M-19
Seaway Queen U-16/S-7	South Channel C-12	Storon IB-1
Seba M.....................................IR-1	South Islands IN-5	Straits Express A-18
Segwun....................................M-30	South Shore B-9	Straits of Mackinac II...............A-18
Selvick, Bonnie G. M-1	Southdown Challenger..............H-4	Strange Attractor......................IO-2
Selvick, Carla Anne S-8	Southdown Conquest................H-4	Strekalovskiy, Mikhail..............IM-19
Selvick, John M. S-8	Spanky Paine F-7	Strelkov, Petr..........................IN-12
Selvick, Sharon M. S-8	Spar...U-4	Suat Ulusoy IP-9
Selvick, William C......................S-8	Spar Garnet.............................IS-27	Sugar Islander II.......................E-2
Semena IJ-3	Spar Jade IS-27	Sumy IA-16
Seneca B-13	Spar Opal IS-27	Sun Bird IH-12
Sentinelle II C-31	Spar Ruby IS-27	Sun Glory.................................IT-1
Sentinelle III C-31	Spartan [42] {2}.........................L-2	Sundew U-4
Sentinelle IV C-31	Speer, Edgar B........................U-18	Sunniva IS-22
Sentinelle V C-31	Spence, John..........................M-19	Sunny Blossom........................L-8
Sequoia U-4	Spencer, Sarah G-23	Sunrise IS-31
Serenade IM-18	Spiridon, A. M. IS-15	Sunrise V S-9
Serendipity Princess..................P-4	Spiridon, S. M. IS-15	Sunrise VI................................S-9
Sevilla Wave IT-5	Spirit of Resolution IH-9	Superior {3}.............................G-17

ALL HANDS ON DECK ...

Looking for a future that's different than most? Your perfect career opportunity may be waiting aboard a Great Lakes vessel. There are shortages of qualified Merchant Marine officers to sail the lakes, reports the **Great Lakes Maritime Academy** at Northwestern Michigan College in Traverse City.

GLMA is a nonmilitary academy dedicated to educating and training officers for the commercial shipping industry on the Great Lakes. Cadets may choose the "deck" or "engine" program, and upon graduation, write the U.S. Coast Guard examinations for licensing as Third Mate Near Coastal of Any Tonnage and Great Lakes Mate and First Class Pilot (deck program) or Third Assistant Engineer, Steam or Motor Vessel of Any Horsepower (engine program). In addition, all graduates of the four-year program receive an associate's degree in Marine Technology and a Bachelor's

Cadets aboard the GLMA training vessel Anchor Bay.

Degree in Business Administration. Courses include seamanship, navigation and piloting, steam and diesel engineering and 270 days afloat training aboard Great Lakes freighters. Cadets attend classes in Traverse City and there are no age or marital restrictions. Graduates serve with every company operating on the Great Lakes and as pilots for ocean-going ships sailing the lakes, many as masters or chief engineers. Employment opportunities are excellent, with exceptional entry-level potential. Flexible work schedules and great benefits are part of the industry.

Interested? Call GLMA at (800) 748-0566, ext. 1200, for more information or to schedule a visit. On the web at www.nmc.edu/~maritime

Fleet & Vessel Listings

Algomarine waits her turn below the MacArthur Lock at the Soo. (Roger LeLievre)

U.S. & CANADIAN FLEETS

Listed after each vessel in order are; Type of Vessel, Year Built, Type of Engine, Cargo Capacity (at mid-summer draft in long tons) or Gross Tonnage* (tanker capacities are listed in barrels), Overall Length, Breadth and Depth (from the top of the keel to the top of the upper deck beam) or Draft*. The figures given are as accurate as possible and are given for informational purposes only. Vessels and owners are listed alphabetically as per American Bureau of Shipping and Lloyd's Register of Shipping format. Former names of vessels and years of operation under former names appear beneath the vessel's name. A number in brackets following a vessel's name indicates how many other vessels, including the one listed, have carried that name. For convenience, the following abbreviations have been used.

TYPE OF VESSEL

2B	Brigantine	ES	Excursion Ship	PF	Passenger Ferry
2S	2 Masted Schooner	EV	Env. Response Ship	PK	Package Freighter
3S	3 Masted Schooner	FB	Fire Boat	PT	Patrol Torpedo Boat
AC	Auto Carrier	FD	Floating Dry Dock	RR	Roll On/Roll Off
AV	Air Cushion Vessel	FF	Frigate	RT	Refueling Tanker
BB	Bum Boat	GA	Gambling Casino	RV	Research Vessel
BC	Bulk Carrier	GC	General Cargo	SB	Supply Boat
BK	Bulk Carrier/Tanker	GL	Gate Lifter	SC	Sand Carrier
BT	Buoy Tender	GU	Grain Self Unloader	SR	Search & Rescue
CC	Cement Carrier	HL	Heavy Lift Vessel	SS	Submarine
CF	Car Ferry	HY	Hydrofoil	SU	Self Unloader
CLG	Guided Missile Cruiser	IB	Ice Breaker	SV	Survey Vessel
CO	Container Vessel	KO	Corvette	TB	Tug Boat
CS	Crane Ship	LS	Lightship	TBA	Articulated Tug Boat
DB	Deck Barge	LST	Landing Ship Tank	TF	Train Ferry
DD	Destroyer	LT	Lighthouse Tender	TK	Tanker
DH	Hopper Barge	MB	Mail Boat	TT	Tractor Tug Boat
DR	Dredge	MS	Mine Sweeper	TV	Training Vessel
DS	Spud Barge	PA	Passenger Vessel	TW	Tanker - Wine
DV	Drilling Vessel	PB	Pilot Boat	WM	Medium Endurance Cutter
DW	Scow	PC	Passenger Catamaran		

PROPULSION

B ....Barge	**Q** ....Steam - Quad Exp. Compound Engine
D ....Diesel	**R** ....Steam - Triple Exp. Compound Engine
V........Batteries	**S**........Steam - Skinner "Unaflow" Engine
W........Sailing Vessel	**T**........Steam - Turbine
	U ....Steam - Uniflow Engine - "Skinner" Design

E-mail any updates, corrections or additions to **KnowYourShipsFix@Gateway.net.**

Fleet #.	Fleet Name Vessel Name	Type of Vessel	Year Built	Type of Engine	Cargo Cap. or Gross*	Overall Length	Breadth	Depth or Draft*
A-1	**A & L MARINE, INC., ST. JOSEPH, MI**							
	Margaret M.	TB	1956	D	167*	89' 06"	24' 00"	10' 00"
	(Shuttler '56 - '60, Margaret M. Hannah '60 - '84)							
A-2	**A .B. M. MARINE, THUNDER BAY, ON**							
	McAllister 132	DB	1954	B	7,000	343' 00"	63' 00"	19' 00"
	(Powell No. 1 '54 - '61, Alberni Carrier '61 - '77, Genmar 132 '77 - '79)							
	Radium 604	DB		B		150' 00"		
	Radium 611	DB		B		150' 00"		
	Radium 623	DB		B		150' 00"		
	Radium Yellowknife	TB	1948	D	235*	120' 00"	28' 00"	
	W. N. Twolan	TB	1962	D	299*	106' 00"	29' 05"	15' 00"
A-3	**ACME MARINE SERVICE, KNIFE RIVER, MN**							
	Dona	SB	1929	D	10*	35' 00"	9' 00"	4' 06"
	Marine Supplier	BB	1950	D	38*	57' 08"	15' 00"	7' 01"
	(Ted '50 - '50, Kaner 1 '50 - '98)							
	Marine Trader	BB	1939	D	60*	65' 00"	15' 00"	7' 06"

Fleet #.	Fleet Name Vessel Name	Type of Vessel	Year Built	Type of Engine	Cargo Cap. or Gross*	Overall Length	Breadth	Depth or Draft*
A-4	**ADECON SHIPPING, INC., MISSISSAUGA, ON**							
	Canadian Challenger	GC	1976	D	15,061	462' 07"	67' 02"	38' 06"
	Canadian Pioneer	GC	1976	D	15,251	462' 07"	67' 02"	38' 06"
A-5	**ALBERT JOHNSON, SCARBOROUGH, ON**							
	Deer Lake	ES	1925	D	104*	75' 00"		
A-6	**ALCAN ALUMINUM LTD., PORT ALFRED, QC**							
	Alexis-Simard	TT	1980	D	286*	92' 00"	34' 00"	13' 07"
	Grande Baie	TT	1972	D	194*	86' 06"	30' 00"	12' 00"
A-7	**ALGOMA CENTRAL CORP., SAULT STE. MARIE, ON**							

ALGOMA CENTRAL MARINE GROUP - A DIVISION OF ALGOMA CENTRAL CORP.

	Agawa Canyon	SU	1970	D	23,400	647' 00"	72' 00"	40' 00"
	Algobay	SU	1978	D	34,900	730' 00"	75' 10"	46' 06"
	(Algobay '78 - '94, Atlantic Trader '94 - '97)							
	Algocape {2}	BC	1967	D	29,950	729' 09"	75' 04"	39' 08"
	(Richelieu {3} '67 - '94)							
	Algocen {2}	BC	1968	D	28,400	730' 00"	75' 03"	39' 08"
	Algogulf {2}	BC	1961	T	26,950	730' 00"	75' 06"	39' 00"
	(J. N. McWatters {2} '61 - '91, Scott Misener {4} '91 - '94)							
	Algoisle	BC	1963	D	26,700	730' 00"	75' 05"	39' 03"
	(Silver Isle '63 - '94)							
	Algolake	SU	1977	D	32,150	730' 00"	75' 06"	46' 06"
	Algomarine	SU	1968	D	27,000	729' 10"	75' 04"	39' 08"
	(Lake Manitoba '68 - '87)							
	Algonorth	BC	1971	D	28,000	729' 11"	75' 02"	42' 11"
	(Temple Bar '71 - '76, Lake Nipigon '76 - '84, Laketon {2} '84 - '86, Lake Nipigon '86 - '87)							
	Algontario	BC	1960	D	29,100	730' 00"	75' 09"	40' 02"
	([Fore Section] Cartiercliffe Hall '76 - '88, Winnipeg {2} '88 - '94) ([Stern Section] Ruhr Ore '60 - '76)							
	Algoport	SU	1979	D	32,000	658' 00"	75' 10"	46' 06"
	Algorail {2}	SU	1968	D	23,750	640' 05"	72' 03"	40' 00"
	Algoriver	BC	1960	T	26,800	722' 06"	75' 00"	39' 00"
	(John A. France {2} '60 - '94)							
	Algosoo {2}	SU	1974	D	31,300	730' 00"	75' 05"	44' 06"
	(The Algosoo {2} was the last Great Lakes cargo vessel built with the traditional fore and aft cabins first used by the R. J. Hackett in 1869.)							
	Algosound	BC	1965	T	27,700	730' 00"	75' 06"	39' 00"
	(Don-De-Dieu '65 - '67, V. W. Scully '67 - '87)							
	Algosteel {2}	SU	1966	D	27,000	729' 11"	75' 04"	39' 08"
	(A. S. Glossbrenner '66 - '87, Algogulf {1} '87 - '90)							
	Algoville	SU	1967	D	31,250	730' 00"	77' 11"	39' 08"
	(Senneville '67 - '94)							
	(The Algoville's #1 hold can carry non-gaseous liquid cargoes such as vegetable oil.)							
	Algoway {2}	SU	1972	D	24,000	650' 00"	72' 00"	40' 00"
	Algowest	SU	1982	D	31,700	730' 00"	76' 01"	42' 00"
	Algowood	SU	1981	D	31,750	740' 00"	76' 01"	46' 06"
	Capt. Henry Jackman	SU	1981	D	30,550	730' 00"	76' 01"	42' 00"
	(Lake Wabush '81 - '87)							
	John B. Aird	SU	1983	D	31,300	730' 00"	76' 01"	46' 06"

SOCIETE QUEBECOISE D' EXPLORATION MINIERE - CHARTERER

	Sauniere	SU	1970	D	23,900	642' 10"	74' 10"	42' 00"
	(Bulknes '70 - '70, Brooknes '70 - '76, Algosea {1} '76 - '82)							

ALGOMA TANKERS LTD. - A DIVISION OF ALGOMA CENTRAL CORP.

	Algocatalyst	TK	1972	D	65,325	430' 05"	62' 04"	34' 05"
	(Jon Ramsoy '72 - '74, Doan Transport '74 - '86, EnerChem Catalyst '86 - '99)							
	Algoeast	TK	1977	D	64,956	431' 05"	65' 07"	35' 05"
	(Texaco Brave {2} '77 - '86, Le Brave '86 - '97, Imperial St. Lawrence {2} '97 - '97)							
	Algofax	TK	1969	D	119,277	485' 05"	70' 02"	33' 03"
	(Imperial Bedford '69 - '97)							
	Algonova	TK	1969	D	54,241	400' 06"	54' 02"	26' 05"
	(Texaco Chief {2} '69 - '87, A. G. Farquharson '87 - '98)							
	Algosar	TK	1974	D	104,333	435' 00"	74' 00"	32' 00"
	(Imperial St. Clair '74 - '97)							
	Algoscotia	TK	1966	D	81,764	440' 00"	60' 00"	31' 00"
	(Imperial Acadia '66 - '97)							

CLEVELAND TANKERS (1991), INC. - VESSELS CHARTERED BY ALGOMA TANKERS LTD.

	Gemini	TK	1978	D	75,298	432' 06"	65' 00"	29' 04"
	Saturn {4}	TK	1974	D	47,030	384' 01"	54' 06"	25' 00"

WINTER QUARTERS – A dock worker applies a new coat of paint to the Armco's hull during spring fit-out at Toledo **(above).** (Roger LeLievre)

Roger Blough looks as if she has come to a sudden stop in a field of tall grass (right). Don't worry – she's just in winter lay-up at Duluth. (Mike Sipper)

Fleet #.	Fleet Name / Vessel Name	Type of Vessel	Year Built	Type of Engine	Cargo Cap. or Gross*	Overall Length	Breadth	Depth or Draft*
A-8	**ALLIED SIGNAL, INC., DETROIT, MI**							
	Allied Chemical No. 12	TK	1969	B	1,545	200' 01"	35' 01"	8' 06"*
A-9	**ALLOUEZ MARINE SUPPLY, SUPERIOR, WI**							
	Allouez Marine	BB	1948	D	9*	35' 02"	11' 02"	3' 06"
	Barbara Ann {1}	BB	1948	D	5*	38' 00"	10' 00"	3' 00"
	Carroll Jean	BB		D	5*	38' 00"	10' 00"	3' 00"
A-10	**AMERICAN CANADIAN CARIBBEAN LINE, INC., WARREN, RI**							
	Grande Caribe	PA	1998	D	99*	182' 00"	39' 00"	9' 08"
	Grande Mariner	PA	1998	D	99*	182' 00"	39' 00"	9' 08"
	Grande Prince	PA	1997	D	99*	182' 00"	39' 00"	9' 08"
	Niagara Prince	PA	1994	D	687*	174' 00"	40' 00"	14' 00"
A-11	**AMERICAN CLASSIC VOYAGES CO., CHICAGO, IL**							
	DELTA QUEEN COASTAL VOYAGES - A DIVISION OF AMERICAN CLASSIC VOYAGES CO.							
	Cape Cod Light	PA	2001	D				
	Cape May Light	PA	2000	D				
A-12	**AMERICAN DIVING & SALVAGE CO., CHICAGO, IL**							
	Eric Z.	TB		D		42' 00"	12' 07"	5' 06"
	Lauren Z.	TB		D		50' 00"	13' 07"	5' 00"
A-13	**AMERICAN MARINE CONSTRUCTION, BENTON HARBOR, MI**							
	AMC 100	DB	1979	B	2,273	200' 00"	52' 00"	14' 00"
	AMC 200	DB	1979	B	2,273	200' 00"	36' 00"	11' 08"
	AMC 300	DB	1977	B	1,048	180' 00"	54' 00"	12' 00"
	Defiance	TB	1966	D	26*	44' 08"	18' 00"	6' 00"
A-14	**AMERICAN STEAMSHIP CO. - A DIVISION OF GATX CORP., WILLIAMSVILLE, NY**							
	Adam E. Cornelius {4}	SU	1973	D	28,200	680' 00"	78' 00"	42' 00"
	(Roger M. Kyes '73 - '89)							
	American Freedom	BC	1981	B	33,700	550' 00"	78' 00"	50' 00"
	American Mariner	SU	1980	D	37,200	730' 00"	78' 00"	45' 00"
	(Laid down as Chicago {3})							
	American Republic	SU	1981	D	24,800	634' 10"	68' 00"	40' 00"
	(American Gulf V '81 - '98)							
	Buffalo {3}	SU	1978	D	23,800	634' 10"	68' 00"	40' 00"
	H. Lee White {2}	SU	1974	D	35,200	704' 00"	78' 00"	45' 00"
	Indiana Harbor	SU	1979	D	78,850	1,000' 00"	105' 00"	56' 00"
	John J. Boland {4}	SU	1973	D	33,800	680' 00"	78' 00"	45' 00"
	(Charles E. Wilson '73 - 2000)							
	Ocean Venture	TBA	1975	D	173*	149' 00"	40' 00"	22' 00"
	(Eliska Theriot '75 - '84, Eliska '84 - '88, Exxon Golden State '88 - '93, S/R Golden State '93 - '99)							
	Sam Laud	SU	1975	D	23,800	634' 10"	68' 00"	40' 00"
	St. Clair {3}	SU	1976	D	44,000	770' 00"	92' 00"	52' 00"
	Walter J. McCarthy Jr.	SU	1977	D	78,850	1,000' 00"	105' 00"	56' 00"
	(Belle River '77 - '90)							
	STINSON, INC. - VESSEL MANAGED BY AMERICAN STEAMSHIP CO.							
	George A. Stinson	SU	1978	D	59,700	1,004' 00"	105' 00"	50' 00"
A-15	**ANDRIE, INC., MUSKEGON, MI**							
	A-390	TK	1982	B	39,000	310' 00"	60' 00"	19' 03"
	(Canonie 40 '82 - '92)							
	A-397	TK	1962	B	39,700	270' 00"	60' 00"	25' 00"
	(Auntie Mame '62 - '91, Iron Mike '91 - '93)							
	A-410	TK	1955	B	41,000	335' 00"	54' 00"	26' 06"
	(Methane '55 - '63, B-6400 '63 - '71, Kelly '71 - '86, Canonie 50 '86 - '93)							
	B-7	DB	1976	B	1,350	165' 00"	42' 06"	12' 00"
	B-16	DB	1976	B	1,350	165' 00"	42' 06"	12' 00"
	Barbara Andrie	TB	1940	D	298*	121' 10"	29' 06"	16' 00"
	(Edmond J. Moran '40 - '76)							
	Candice Andrie	CS	1958	B	1,000	150' 00"	52' 00"	10' 00"
	(Minnesota {2} '58 - ?)							
	Clara Andrie	DR	1930	B	1,000	110' 00"	30' 00"	6' 10"
	John Joseph	TB	1993	D	15*	40' 00"	14' 00"	5' 00"
	John Purves	TB	1919	D	436*	150' 00"	27' 07"	16' 00"
	(Butterfield '19 - '42, U. S. Army Butterfield [LT-145] '42 - '45, Butterfield '45 - '57)							
	Karen Andrie {2}	TB	1965	D	433*	120' 00"	31' 06"	16' 00"
	(Sarah Hays '65 - '93)							
	Mari Beth Andrie	TB	1961	D	147*	87' 00"	24' 00"	11' 06"
	(Gladys Bea '61 - '73, American Viking '73 - '83)							
	Rebecca Lynn	TB	1964	D	433*	120' 00"	31' 08"	18' 09"
	(Kathrine Clewis '64 - '96)							
	Robert Purcell	TB	1952	D	28*	45' 00"	12' 06"	7' 09"

Fleet #.	Fleet Name / Vessel Name	Type of Vessel	Year Built	Type of Engine	Cargo Cap. or Gross*	Overall Length	Breadth	Depth or Draft*
	LAFARGE CORP. - VESSELS MANAGED BY ANDRIE, INC.							
	Integrity	CC	1996	B	14,000	460' 00"	70' 00"	37' 00"
	Jacklyn M.	TBA	1976	D	198*	140' 02"	40' 01"	22' 03"
	(Andrew Martin '76 - '90, Robert L. Torres '90 - '94)							
	[Integrity / Jacklyn M. overall dimensions together]					543' 00"	70' 00"	37' 00"
A-16	**APEX OIL CO., GRANITE CITY, IL**							
	Apex Chicago	TK	1981	B	35,000	288' 00"	60' 00"	19' 00"
A-17	**APOSTLE ISLANDS CRUISE SERVICE, BAYFIELD, WI**							
	Eagle Island	ES	1976	D	12*	42' 00"	14' 00"	3' 06"
	(Grampa Woo '93 - '96)							
	Island Princess {2}	ES		D				
	Sea Queen II	ES	1971	D	12*	42' 00"	14' 00"	2' 07"
	Zeeto	3S		W		54' 00"	16' 00"	
A-18	**ARNOLD TRANSIT CO., MACKINAC ISLAND, MI**							
	Algomah	PK	1961	D	125	93' 00"	31' 00"	8' 00"
	Beaver	CF	1952	D	87*	61' 02"	30' 02"	8' 00"
	Chippewa {6}	PK	1962	D	125	93' 00"	31' 00"	8' 00"
	Corsair	CF	1955	D	98*	94' 06"	33' 00"	8' 06"
	Drummond Islander	CF	1947	D	99*	84' 00"	30' 00"	8' 03"
	Huron {5}	PK	1955	D	80	91' 06"	25' 00"	10' 01"
	Island Express	PC	1988	D	90*	82' 07"	28' 06"	8' 05"
	Mackinac Express	PC	1987	D	90*	82' 07"	28' 06"	8' 05"
	Ottawa {2}	PK	1959	D	125	93' 00"	31' 00"	8' 00"
	Straits Express	PC	1995	D	99*	101' 00"	29' 11"	6' 08"
	Straits of Mackinac II	PF	1969	D	89*	89' 11"	27' 00"	8' 08"
B-1	**BARGE TRANSPORTATION, INC., DETROIT, MI**							
	Cherokee {2}	DB	1943	B	1,200	155' 00"	50' 00"	13' 06"
B-2	**BASIC TOWING, INC., ESCANABA, MI**							
	Danicia	TB	1944	D	382*	110' 02"	27' 03"	15' 07"
	(USCGC Chinook [WYT / WYTM-96] '44 - '86, Tracie B '86 - '98)							
	Erika Kobasic	TB	1939	D	226*	110' 00"	26' 05"	15' 01"
	(USCGC Arundel [WYT / WYTM-90] '39 - '84, Karen Andrie {1} '84 - '90)							
	Escort II	TB	1969	D	26*	50' 00"	13' 00"	7' 00"
	L. E. Block	BC	1927	T	15,900	621' 00"	64' 00"	33' 00"
	(Last operated 31 October, 1981 — Currently laid up in Escanaba, MI.)							
B-3	**BAY CHALEUR MARINE LTD., BATHURST, NB**							
	Eddie Mac I	TT	1992	D	120*	84' 08"	23' 07"	7' 07"
B-4	**BAY CITY BOAT LINE, LLC, BAY CITY, MI**							
	Islander {1}	ES	1946	D	39*	53' 04"	21' 00"	5' 05"
	Princess Wenonah	ES	1954	D	96*	64' 09"	32' 09"	9' 09"
	(William M. Miller '54 - '98)							
B-5	**BAY OCEAN MANAGEMENT, INC., ENGLEWOOD CLIFFS, NJ**							
	Lake Carling	BC	1992	D	26,264	591' 01"	75' 09"	45' 07"
	(Ziemia Cieszynska '92 - '93)							
	Lake Champlain	BC	1992	D	26,264	591' 01"	75' 09"	45' 07"
	(Ziemia Lodzka '92 - '92)							
	Lake Charles	BC	1990	D	26,209	591' 01"	75' 09"	45' 07"
	(Ziemia Gornoslaska '90 - '91)							
B-6	**BAY SHIPBUILDING CO., STURGEON BAY, WI**							
	Bayship	TB	1943	D	19*	45' 00"	12' 06"	6' 00"
B-7	**BAYSAIL, BAY CITY, MI**							
	Appledore	2S	1989	W		85' 00"	19' 00"	9' 00"*
B-8	**BEAUSOLEIL FIRST NATION, CHRISTIAN ISLAND, ON**							
	Upper Canada	CF	1949	D	165*	143' 00"	36' 00"	11' 00"
	(Romeo and Annette '49 - '66)							
B-9	**BEAVER ISLAND BOAT CO., CHARLEVOIX, MI**							
	Beaver Islander	CF	1963	D	95*	96' 03"	27' 05"	9' 09"
	Emerald Isle {2}	CF	1997	D	95*	130' 00"	38' 08"	12' 00"
	South Shore	CF	1945	D	67*	64' 10"	24' 00"	9' 06"
B-10	**BEST OF ALL TOURS, ERIE, PA**							
	Lady Kate {2}	ES	1952	D		65' 00"	16' 06"	4' 00"
B-11	**BETHLEHEM STEEL CORP. - BURNS HARBOR DIVISION, CHESTERTON, IN**							
	Burns Harbor {2}	SU	1980	D	78,850	1,000' 00"	105' 00"	56' 00"
	Stewart J. Cort	SU	1972	D	58,000	1,000' 00"	105' 00"	49' 00"
	(The Stewart J. Cort was the first 1,000' long cargo vessel to operate on the Great Lakes.)							

Edgar B. Speer in the St. Clair River 22 July 2000. (Roger LeLievre)

Fleet #.	Fleet Name / Vessel Name	Type of Vessel	Year Built	Type of Engine	Cargo Cap. or Gross*	Overall Length	Breadth	Depth or Draft*
B-12	**BIGANE VESSEL FUELING CO. OF CHICAGO, CHICAGO, IL**							
	Jos. F. Bigane	RT	1973	D	7,500	140' 00"	40' 00"	14' 00"
B-13	**BILLINGTON CONTRACTING, INC., DULUTH, MN**							
	Coleman	CS	1923	B	502*	153' 06"	40' 06"	10' 06"
	Duluth	DR	1962	B	401*	106' 00"	36' 00"	8' 04"
	Faith	CS	1906	B	705*	120' 00"	38' 00"	10' 02"
	Houghton	TB	1944	D	21*	45' 00"	13' 00"	6' 00"
	Seneca	TB	1939	D	152*	90' 02"	22' 00"	9' 00"
	(General {1} '39 - '39, Raymond Card '39 - '40, USS Keshena [YTM-731] '40 - '47, Mary L. McAllister '47 - '81)							
	(The USS Keshena served as a net tender at Guantanamo Bay, Cuba during World War II.)							
B-14	**BLUE CIRCLE CEMENT CO., DETROIT, MI**							
	Lewis G. Harriman	CC	1923	R	5,500	350' 00"	55' 00"	28' 00"
	(John W. Boardman '23 - '65)							
	(Last operated 20 April 1980 — 5 year survey expired September, 1997.)							
	(Currently in use as a non-powered cement storage vessel in Green Bay, WI.)							
	St. Mary's Cement	CC	1986	B	9,400	360' 00"	60' 00"	23' 03"
B-15	**BLUE CIRCLE CEMENT CO., TORONTO, ON**							
	Sea Eagle II	TBA	1979	D	560*	132' 00"	35' 00"	19' 00"
	(Sea Eagle '79 - '81, Canmar Sea Eagle '81 - '91)							
	St. Mary's Cement II	CC	1978	B	19,513	496' 06"	76' 00"	35' 00"
	(Velasco '78 - '81, Canmar Shuttle '81 - '90)							
	St. Mary's Cement III	CC	1980	D	4,800	335' 00"	76' 08"	17' 09"
	(Bigorange XVI '80 - '84, Says '84 - '85, Al-Sayb-7 '85 - '86, Clarkson Carrier '86 - '94)							
	(Last operated 20 April 1980 — 5 year survey expires March, 2004.)							
	(Currently in use as a cement storage barge in Green Bay, WI.)							
	GREAT LAKES INT. TOWING & SALVAGE CO., INC. - CHARTERED BY BLUE CIRCLE CEMENT CO.							
	Petite Forte	TB	1969	D	368*	127' 00"	32' 00"	14' 06"
	(E. Bronson Ingram '69 - '72, Jarmac 42 '72 - '73, Scotsman '73 - '81, Al Battal '81 - '86)							
B-16	**BLUE HERON CO., TOBERMORY, ON**							
	Blue Heron V	ES		D		54' 06"		
	Great Blue Heron	ES		D		79' 00"		
B-17	**BLUE WATER EXCURSIONS, INC., FORT GRATIOT, MI**							
	Huron Lady II	ES		D				
B-18	**BLUE WATER FERRY LTD., SOMBRA, ON**							
	Daldean	CF	1951	D	145*	75' 00"	35' 00"	7' 00"
	Ontamich	CF	1939	D	55*	65' 00"	28' 10"	8' 06"
	(Harsens Island '39 - '73)							
B-19	**BOB-LO ISLAND, AMHERSTBURG, ON**							
	Courtney-O	CF	1998	D				
	Crystal-O	CF	1946	D	65*	65' 00"	28' 10"	8' 06"
	(St. Clair Flats '46 - '97)							
B-20	**BRIAN UTILITIES SERVICES, INC., MUSKEGON, MI**							
	Capt. Roy	TB	1987	D	27*	42' 06"	12' 08"	6' 06"
B-21	**BUFFALO CHARTERS, INC. / NIAGARA CLIPPER, INC., BUFFALO, NY**							
	Miss Buffalo	ES	1964	D	88*	64' 10"	23' 05"	7' 04"
	(Miss Muskoka {1} '64 - '69, Miss Niagara '69 - '72)							
	Miss Buffalo II	ES	1972	D	88*	86' 00"	24' 00"	6' 00"
	Niagara Clipper	ES	1983	D	65*	112' 00"	29' 00"	6' 06"*
B-22	**BUFFALO PUBLIC WORKS DEPT., BUFFALO, NY**							
	Edwin M. Cotter	FB	1900	D	208*	118' 00"	24' 00"	11' 06"
	(W. S. Grattan 1900 - '53, Firefighter '53 - '54)							
B-23	**BUSCH MARINE, INC., CARROLLTON, MI**							
	Gregory J. Busch	TB	1919	D	299*	151' 00"	28' 00"	16' 09"
	(Humaconna '19 - '77)							
	STC 2004	DB	1986	B	2,364	240' 00"	50' 00"	9' 05"
C-1	**C. A. CROSBIE SHIPPING LTD., MONTREAL, QC**							
	Arctic Viking	GC	1967	D	1,265	244' 06"	41' 03"	21' 11"
	(Baltic Viking '67 - '81)							
	Lady Franklin	GC	1970	D	3,627	339' 04"	51' 10"	27' 11"
	(Baltic Valiant '70 - '81)							
C-2	**CALUMET RIVER FLEETING, INC., WHITING, IN**							
	Des Plaines	TB	1956	D	175*	98' 00"	28' 00"	8' 04"*
	Sea Wolf	TB	1954	D	95*	72' 00"	22' 00"	7' 00"*
	Tommy B.	TB	1962	D	43*	45' 00"	11' 10"	4' 11"*
	Trinity	TB	1939	D	51*	45' 00"	12' 10"	5' 07"*

Fleet #.	Fleet Name Vessel Name	Type of Vessel	Year Built	Type of Engine	Cargo Cap. or Gross*	Overall Length	Breadth	Depth or Draft*
C-3	**CANADA STEAMSHIP LINES, INC., MONTREAL, QC**							
	ACOMARIT CANADA, INC. - MANAGERS							
	Atlantic Erie	SU	1985	D	38,200	736' 07"	75' 10"	50' 00"
	(Hon. Paul Martin '85 - '88)							
	Atlantic Huron {2}	SU	1984	D	34,600	736' 07"	75' 10"	46' 06"
	(Prairie Harvest '84 - '89, Atlantic Huron {2} '89 - '94, Melvin H. Baker II {2} '94 - '97)							
	CSL Laurentien	SU	1977	D	34,938	739' 10"	78' 01"	48' 05"
	(Louis R. Desmarais '77 - '00)							
	CSL Niagara	SU	1972	D	34,938	739' 10"	78' 01"	48' 05"
	(J. W. McGiffin '72 - '99)							
	CSL Tadoussac	SU	1969	D	29,700	730' 00"	78' 00"	42' 00"
	Ferbec	BC	1966	D	56,887	732' 06"	104' 02"	57' 09"
	(Fugaku Maru '65 - '77)							
	Frontenac {5}	SU	1968	D	27,500	729' 07"	75' 03"	39' 08"
	Halifax	SU	1963	T	30,100	730' 02"	75' 00"	39' 03"
	(Frankcliffe Hall {2} '63 - '88)							
	Jean Parisien	SU	1977	D	33,000	730' 00"	75' 00"	46' 06"
	Manitoulin {5}	SU	1966	D	28,100	729' 09"	75' 00"	41' 00"
	Nanticoke	SU	1980	D	35,100	729' 10"	75' 08"	46' 06"
	Rt. Hon. Paul J. Martin	SU	1973	D	34,938	739' 10"	78' 01"	48' 05"
	(H. M. Griffith '73 - 2000)							
	LAFARGE CANADA, INC. - VESSEL MANAGED BY CANADA STEAMSHIP LINES, INC.							
	English River	CC	1961	D	7,450	404' 03"	60' 00"	36' 06"
C-4	**CANADA WEST INDIES MOLASSES CO. LTD., MISSISSAUGA, ON**							
	San Juan	TK	1962	B	913*	195' 00"	35' 00"	12' 06"
	(5 year survey expired April, 1998 — Currently laid up in Hamilton, ON.)							
C-5	**CANADIAN COAST GUARD, OTTAWA, ON**							
	CENTRAL AND ARCTIC REGION, SARNIA, ON							
	Advent	RV	1972	D	72*	77' 01"	18' 05"	5' 03"*
	Bittern	SR	1982	D	21*	40' 08"	13' 06"	4' 04"
	Cape Hurd	SR	1982	D	55*	70' 10"	18' 00"	8' 09"
	Caribou Isle	BT	1985	D	92*	75' 06"	19' 08"	7' 04"
	Cove Isle	BT	1980	D	92*	65' 07"	19' 08"	7' 04"
	Griffon	IB	1970	D	2,212*	234' 00"	49' 00"	21' 06"
	Gull Isle	BT	1980	D	80*	65' 07"	19' 08"	7' 04"
	Limnos	RV	1968	D	460*	147' 00"	32' 00"	12' 00"
	Louis M. Lauzier	RV	1976	D	322*	125' 00"	27' 01"	11' 06"
	(Cape Harrison '76 - '83)							
	Samuel Risley	IB	1985	D	1,988*	228' 09"	47' 01"	21' 09"
	Shark	RV	1971	D	30*	52' 06"	14' 09"	7' 03"
	Simcoe	BT	1962	D	961*	179' 01"	38' 00"	15' 06"
	Sora	SR	1982	D	21*	41' 00"	14' 01"	4' 04"
	Spray	SR	1994	D	42*	51' 09"	17' 00"	8' 02"
	Spume	SR	1994	D	42*	51' 09"	17' 00"	8' 02"
	Tobermory	SR	1973	D	17*	44' 01"	12' 06"	6' 07"
	Westfort	SR	1973	D	22*	44' 01"	12' 08"	5' 11"
	MAJOR VESSELS – LAURENTIAN REGION, QUEBEC, QC							
	Des Groseilliers	IB	1983	D	5,910*	322' 07"	64' 00"	35' 06"
	E. P. Le Quebecois	RV	1968	D	186*	93' 00"	23' 10"	12' 03"
	F. C. G. Smith	SV	1985	D	439*	114' 02"	45' 11"	11' 02"
	George R. Pearkes	IB	1986	D	3,809	272' 04"	53' 02"	25' 02"
	Ile Des Barques	BT	1985	D	92*	75' 06"	19' 08"	7' 04"
	Ile Saint-Ours	BT	1986	D	92*	75' 06"	19' 08"	7' 04"
	Louisbourg	RV	1977	D	295*	124' 00"	26' 11"	11' 06"
	Martha L. Black	IB	1986	D	3,818*	272' 04"	53' 02"	25' 02"
	Pierre Radisson	IB	1978	D	5,910*	322' 00"	62' 10"	35' 06"
	Tracy	BT	1968	D	963*	181' 01"	38' 00"	16' 00"
	MAJOR VESSELS – MARITIMES REGION, DARTMOUTH, NS							
	Alfred Needler	RV	1982	D	959*	165' 09"	36' 09"	22' 01"
	Chebucto	RV	1966	D	751*	179' 02"	30' 10"	27' 02"
	Cygnus	RV	1982	D	1,211*	205' 01"	40' 00"	15' 05"
	Earl Grey	IB	1986	D	1,971*	230' 00"	46' 02"	22' 01"
	Edward Cornwallis	IB	1986	D	3,727*	272' 04"	53' 02"	24' 06"
	Hudson	RV	1963	D	3,740*	296' 07"	50' 06"	32' 10"
	Louis S. St-Laurent	IB	1969	D	10,908*	392' 06"	80' 00"	53' 06"
	Matthew	RV	1990	D	857*	165' 00"	34' 05"	16' 05"
	Parizeau	RV	1967	D	1,328*	211' 07"	40' 00"	21' 00"
	Provo Wallis	BT	1969	D	1,313*	209' 03"	42' 08"	16' 07"

Fleet #.	Fleet Name / Vessel Name	Type of Vessel	Year Built	Type of Engine	Cargo Cap. or Gross*	Overall Length	Breadth	Depth or Draft*
	Simon Fraser	BT	1960	D	1,353*	204' 06"	42' 00"	18' 03"
	Sir William Alexander	IB	1986	D	3,550*	272' 06"	45' 00"	17' 06"
	Terry Fox	IB	1983	D	4,234*	288' 09"	58' 06"	29' 08"
	Tupper	BT	1959	D	1,353*	204' 06"	42' 00"	18' 03"
	MAJOR VESSELS – NEWFOUNDLAND REGION, ST. JOHN'S, NF							
	Ann Harvey	IB	1987	D	3,854*	272' 04"	53' 02"	25' 10"
	Cape Roger	RV	1977	D	1,255*	205' 01"	35' 05"	22' 00"
	Henry Larsen	IB	1988	D	6,172*	327' 05"	64' 08"	35' 09"
	J. E. Bernier	IB	1967	D	2,457*	231' 04"	49' 00"	16' 00"
	Leonard J. Cowley	RV	1984	D	2,243*	236' 03"	46' 07"	24' 03"
	Sir Humphrey Gilbert	IB	1959	D	2,152*	237' 10"	48' 02"	21' 01"
	Sir Wilfred Grenfall	SR	1987	D	2,404*	224' 08"	49' 03"	22' 06"
	Teleost	RV	1988	D	2,337*	206' 08"	46' 07"	29' 02"
	Wilfred Templeman	RV	1981	D	925*	166' 00"	36' 09"	22' 01"
C-6	**CANADIAN FOREST NAVIGATION CO. LTD., MONTREAL, QC**							
	Pintail	BC	1983	D	28,035	647' 08"	75' 10"	46' 11"
	(Puncia '83 - '95)							
C-7	**CAPT. JOE BOAT SERVICE, CHICAGO, IL**							
	Eleanor R.	ES	1988	D	75*	90' 00"	22' 00"	4' 06"*
C-8	**CAPTAIN NORMAC'S RIVERBOAT INN LTD., TORONTO, ON**							
	Jadran	GC	1957	D	2,520*	295' 06"	42' 08"	24' 08"
	(Former Jadranska Plovidba vessel which last operated in 1975.)							
	(Currently in use as a floating restaurant in Toronto, ON.)							
C-9	**CAROL N. BAKER, PENETANGUISHENE, ON**							
	Dawnlight		1891	D	64*	75' 00"	24' 00"	12' 00"
	(Le Roy Brooks 1891 - '25, Henry Stokes '25 - '54, Aburg '54 - '81)							
C-10	**CELEST BAY TIMBER & MARINE, DULUTH, MN**							
	Essayons	TB	1908	R	117*	85' 06"	21' 02"	11' 09"
C-11	**CENTRAL MARINE LOGISTICS, INC., HIGHLAND, IN**							
	INDIANA HARBOR STEAMSHIP CO. - OWNER							
	Edward L. Ryerson	BC	1960	T	27,500	730' 00"	75' 00"	39' 00"
	(Last operated 12 December, 1998 — 5 year survey expires December 2001.)							
	(Currently laid up in Sturgeon Bay, WI.)							
	Joseph L. Block	SU	1976	D	37,200	728' 00"	78' 00"	45' 00"
	Wilfred Sykes	SU	1949	T	21,500	678' 00"	70' 00"	37' 00"
	(The Wilfred Sykes was the first U. S. Great Lakes cargo vessel to be constructed with a 70' beam.)							
C-12	**CHAMPION'S AUTO FERRY, INC., ALGONAC, MI**							
	Champion {1}	CF	1941	D	65*	65' 00"	29' 00"	8' 06"
	Middle Channel	CF	1997	D	97*	79' 00"	31' 00"	8' 03"
	North Channel	CF	1967	D	67*	75' 00"	30' 00"	8' 00"
	South Channel	CF	1973	D	94*	79' 00"	31' 00"	8' 03"
C-13	**CHARLEVOIX COUNTY ROAD COMMISSION, BOYNE CITY, MI**							
	Charlevoix {1}	CF	1926	D	43*	50' 00"	32' 00"	3' 09"
C-14	**CHICAGO CRUISES, INC., CHICAGO, IL**							
	Chicago II	ES	1983	D	42*	123' 03"	28' 06"	7' 00"
	(Star of Sandford '83 - '86, Star of Charlevoix {1} '86 - '87, Star of Toronto '87 - '87, Star of Chicago II '87 - '94)							
C-15	**CHICAGO FIRE DEPT., CHICAGO, IL**							
	Victor L. Schlaegar	FB	1949	D	350*	92' 06"	24' 00"	11' 00"
C-16	**CHICAGO FIREBOAT CRUISE CO., CHICAGO, IL**							
	Fred A. Busse	FB	1937	D	209*	92' 00"	23' 00"	8' 00"
C-17	**CHICAGO FROM THE LAKE LTD., CHICAGO, IL**							
	Fort Dearborn	ES	1985	D	72*	64' 10"	22' 00"	7' 04"
	Innisfree	ES	1953	D	34*	61' 08"	16' 00"	4' 06"
	Marquette {6}	ES	1957	D	29*	50' 07"	15' 00"	4' 00"
C-18	**CHICAGO WATER PUMPING STATION, CHICAGO, IL**							
	James J. Versluis	TB	1957	D	126*	83' 00"	22' 00"	11' 02"
C-19	**CHRISTOPHER LADD, PUT-IN-BAY, OH**							
	Ladler	DB	1950	B	100	100' 00"	26' 00"	5' 06"*
	Mervine II	TB	1942	D	22*	46' 08"	14' 00"	5' 01"*
C-20	**CLARKE TRANSPORT CANADA, MONTREAL, QC**							
	Cabot {2}	RR	1979	D	7,132	564' 09"	73' 11"	45' 09"
	(Cavallo '79 - '88)							
	Cicero	RR	1978	D	6,985	482' 10"	73' 11"	45' 09"
	Trans-St-Laurent	RR	1963	D	645	261' 11"	62' 04"	18' 00"

Fleet #.	Fleet Name / Vessel Name	Type of Vessel	Year Built	Type of Engine	Cargo Cap. or Gross*	Overall Length	Breadth	Depth or Draft*
C-21	**CLEVELAND FIRE DEPT., CLEVELAND, OH**							
	Anthony J. Celebrezze	FB	1961	D	74*	66' 00"	17' 00"	5' 00"
C-22	**CLIFFORD TYNER, BARBEAU, MI**							
	Neebish Islander	CF	1950	D	49*	55' 00"	20' 07"	6' 00"
	(Lillifred '50 - '56) **(Last operated in 1995 — Currently laid up at Neebish Island, MI.)**							
C-23	**CLINTON RIVER CRUISE CO., CLINTON TOWNSHIP, MI**							
	Clinton	ES	1949	D	12*	44' 00"	11' 01"	4' 00"*
	Gibraltar	ES	1984	D	47*	64' 11"	22' 00"	3' 00"*
C-24	**CLUB CANAMAC CRUISES, TORONTO, ON**							
	Aurora Borealis	ES	1983	D	277*	101' 00"	24' 00"	6' 00"*
	Jaguar II	ES	1968	D	142*	95' 03"	20' 00"	9' 00"
	(Jaguar '68 - '86)							
	Stella Borealis	ES	1989	D	356*	118 '00"	26' 00"	7' 00"
	SEAFLIGHT 2000 - VESSELS MANAGED BY CLUB CANAMAC CRUISES							
	Katran-2	HY	1995	D	135*	113' 02"	33' 10"	5' 11"
	(Seawing I '95 - '95)							
	Katran-3	HY	1996	D	135*	113' 02"	33' 10"	5' 11"
	Seaflight I	HY	1994	D	135*	113' 02"	33' 10"	5' 11"
	(Katran-1 '94 - '98)							
	Seaflight II	HY	1996	D	135*	113' 02"	33' 10"	5' 11"
	(Katran-4 '96 - '98)							
C-25	**COLONIAL MARINE INDUSTRIES, INC., SAVANNAH, GA**							
	Carib Alba	GC	1976	D/W	3,100	258' 06"	43' 07"	19' 08"
	Carib Dawn	GC	1975	D	2,997	258' 05"	43' 07"	19' 09"
C-26	**COLUMBIA YACHT CLUB, CHICAGO, IL**							
	Abegweit {1}	CF	1947	D	6,694*	372' 06"	61' 00"	24' 09"
	(Abegweit {1} '47 - '81, Abby '81 - '97)							
	(Former CN Marine, Inc. vessel which last operated in 1981.)							
	(Currently in use as a floating club house in Chicago, IL.)							
C-27	**CONSTANTINOS MAKAYDAKIS, ATHENS, GREECE**							
	The Straits of Mackinac	CF	1928	R	736*	202' 11"	48' 00"	16' 07"
	(Last operated in 1968 — 5 year survey expired Sept. 1971 — Currently laid up in Kewaunee, WI.)							
C-28	**CONTESSA CRUISE LINES, L.L.C., LAFAYETTE, LA**							
	Arthur K. Atkinson	PA	1917	D	3,241*	384' 00"	56' 00"	20' 06"
	(Ann Arbor No. 6 '17 - '59)							
	(Last operated in 1984 — 5 year survey expired August, 1985 — Currently laid up in Ludington, MI.)							
	Viking I	PA	1925	D	2,713*	360' 00"	56' 03"	21' 06"
	(Ann Arbor No. 7 '25 - '64, Viking {2} '64 - '96)							
	(Last operated 11 April, 1982 — 5 year survey expires May, 2001 — Currently laid up in Erie, PA.)							
C-29	**CONTINENTAL MARINE, INC., LEMONT, IL**							
	Brandon E.	TB	1945	D	19*	42' 01"	12' 10"	5' 02"*
C-30	**CORP. OF PROFESSIONAL GREAT LAKES PILOTS, ST. CATHARINES, ON**							
	J. W. Cooper	PB		D				
	Juleen I	PB		D				
	Mrs. C.	PB		D				
C-31	**CROISIERES AML, INC., QUEBEC, QC**							
	Cavalier des Mers	ES	1974	D	128*	105' 00"	21' 00"	4' 08"
	Cavalier Grand Fleuve	ES	1987	D	499*	145' 00"	30' 00"	5' 06"
	Cavalier Maxim	ES	1962	D	752*	191' 02"	42' 00"	11' 07"
	(Osborne Castle '62 - '78, Le Gobelet D' Argent '78 - '88, Gobelet D' Argent '88 - '89, Le Maxim '89 - '93)							
	Cavalier Royal	ES	1971	D	283*	125' 00"	24' 00"	5' 00"
	Louis-Jolliet	ES	1938	R	2,436*	170' 01"	70' 00"	17' 00"
	M/V Montreal	ES	1975	D	281*	106' 00"	24' 00"	
	(Island Queen {3} '75 - '79, Miss Kingston II '79 - '84)							
	Miss Olympia	ES	1972	D	29*	62' 08"	14' 00"	4' 08"
	Nouvelle-Orleans	ES	1989	D	234*	90' 00"	25' 00"	5' 03"
	Sentinelle II	ES	1993	D	9*	29' 09"	8' 00"	2' 00"
	Sentinelle III	ES	1993	D	9*	29' 09"	8' 00"	2' 00"
	Sentinelle IV	ES	1993	D	9*	29' 09"	8' 00"	2' 00"
	Sentinelle V	ES	1993	D	9*	29' 09"	8' 00"	2' 00"
	Tandem	ES	1991	D	102*	66' 00"	22' 00"	2' 02"
	Transit	ES	1992	D	102*	66' 00"	22' 00"	2' 08"
	Ville Marie II	ES	1947	R	887*	176' 00"	66' 00"	13' 06"
	(Laviolette '47 - '76, Bluewater Belle '76 - '79, Cadedonia '79 - '82)							
C-32	**CROISIERES DES ILES DE SOREL, INC., SAINTE-ANNE-DE-SOREL, QC**							
	Le Survenant III	ES	1974	D	105*	65' 00"	13' 00"	5' 00"

James Norris arrives at Marquette 26 July 2000. (Rod Burdick)

JAMES NORRIS

Vessel Spotlight

JAMES NORRIS	
Length	663' 06"
Beam	67'
Depth	35'
Built	1952
Tonnage	18,600

The steamer **James Norris**, serving the Seaway Marine Transport pool of Algoma Central Corp. and Upper Lakes Group self-unloaders, is a veteran member of the Canadian Great Lakes and Seaway fleet.

Norris entered service in 1952 for Upper Lakes Shipping after construction at the now-defunct Midland Shipbuilding Co. in Midland, ON. With her sistership, **Gordon C. Leitch** {1}, she sailed as a bulk carrier in grain, ore and coal trades until 1980, when she was converted to a self-unloader at Port Weller Drydocks to carry stone between the Lake Ontario ports of Colborne and Clarkson (the Leitch was scrapped in 1985). To aid in unloading, Norris' holds were lined with Teflon in 1987.

Misfortune struck in November, 1995, when a violent storm caught the Norris at the loading dock in Colborne, ON. Unable to depart, the vessel was slammed against the dock, holed and partially sunk. Some feared her career was over, but Upper Lakes Group put many millions of dollars into repairs and navigational equipment improvements at Port Weller Drydocks. Norris still steams with her original Skinner Uniflow engine and occasionally visits the Upper Lakes when her stone commitments on Lake Ontario are met.

– Rod Burdick

Fleet #.	Fleet Name Vessel Name	Type of Vessel	Year Built	Type of Engine	Cargo Cap. or Gross*	Overall Length	Breadth	Depth or Draft*
C-33	**CROISIERES M/S JACQUES-CARTIER, TROIS-RIVIERES, QC**							
	Jacques Cartier	ES	1924	D	441*	135' 00"	35' 00"	10' 00"
	Le Draveur	ES	1992	D	79*			
C-34	**CROISIERES MARJOLAINE, INC., CHICOUTIMI, QC**							
	Marjolaine II	ES	1904			92' 00"	27' 00"	9' 00"
C-35	**CROISIERES RICHELIEU, INC., SAINT-JEAN-SUR-RICHELIEU, QC**							
	Fort Saint-Jean II	ES	1967	D	109*	62' 09"	19' 10"	
	(Miss Gananoque '67 - '77)							
	Suroit IV	ES	1973	D	64*	58' 00"	16' 00"	10' 04"
	(Miss Montreal '73 - '99)							
C-36	**CSL INTERNATIONAL, INC., BEVERLY, MA**							
	CSL Asia	BC	1999	D	45,729	609' 05"	99' 09"	54' 02"
	CSL Atlas	SU	1990	D	67,308	746' 01"	105' 02"	63' 00"
	CSL Cabo	SU	1971	D	31,364	596' 02"	84' 04"	49' 10"
	(Bockenheim '71 - '80, Cabo San Lucas '80 - '95)							
	CSL Spirit	SU	2000	D	70,037	737' 10"	105' 07"	64' 00"
	CSL Trailblazer	SU	1978	D	26,608	583' 11"	85' 02"	46' 03"
	([Main Cargo Section] Colon Brown '74 - '75, Gold Bond Conveyor '75 - '78)							
	([Completed Vessel] Gold Bond Trailblazer '78 - '98)							
	M. H. Baker III	SU	1982	D	38,900	730' 00"	75' 10"	50' 00"
	(Atlantic Superior '82 - '97)							
	Shelia Ann	SU	1999	D	70,037	737' 10"	105' 07"	64' 00"
	MARBULK SHIPPING, INC. - MANAGED BY CSL INTERNATIONAL, INC.							
	PARTNERSHIP BETWEEN CSL INTERNATIONAL, INC. AND ALGOMA CENTRAL CORP.							
	Algosea {2}	SU	1983	D	37,263	730' 00"	75' 10"	50' 00"
	(Canadian Ambassador '83 - '85, Ambassador '85 - 2000)							
	Antwerpen	BC	1979	D	41,100	652' 11"	96' 04"	50' 05"
	(Antwerpen '79 - '96, Sea L '96 - '98, Sea Lion '98 - '98)							
	Bahama Spirit	BC	1995	D	46,606	615' 02"	105' 09"	52' 10"
	(San Pietro '95 - '99, Freeport Miner '99 - 2000)							
	Eastern Power	SU	1989	D	69,808	738' 02"	105' 09"	60' 01"
	(Milamores '89 - '96, Cereza '96 - '97)							
	Nelvana	SU	1983	D	74,973	797' 05"	105' 11"	66' 04"
	Pioneer	SU	1981	D	37,448	730' 00"	75' 10"	50' 00"
	(Canadian Pioneer '81 - '86)							
	Thornhill	SU	1981	D	35,463	635' 11"	90' 08"	48' 07"
	(Frotabrasil '81 - '87, Athos '87 - '89, Chennai Perumai '89 - '93)							
	Weser Stahl	SU	1999	D	47,257	630' 07"	105' 10"	51' 06"
	EGON OLDENDORFF LTD. - PARTNERSHIP WITH CSL INTERNATIONAL, INC.							
	Bernhard Oldendorff	SU	1991	D	77,548	803' 10"	105' 08"	60' 00"
	Christopher Oldendorff	SU	1982	D	62,732	747' 02"	106' 00"	63' 00"
	(Pacific Peace '82 - '86, Atlantic Huron {1} '86 - '88, CSL Innovator '88 - '93)							
	Sophie Oldendorff	SU	2000	D	70,037	737' 10"	105' 07"	64' 00"
D-1	**DALE T. DEAN — WALPOLE - ALGONAC FERRY LINE, PORT LAMBTON, ON**							
	City of Algonac	CF	1990	D	92*	80' 04"	26' 01"	6' 09"
	Walpole Islander	CF	1986	D	71*	74' 00"	33' 00"	7' 00"
D-2	**DALMIG MARINE, INC., QUEBEC, QC**							
	Dalmig	CF	1957	D	538*	175' 10"	40' 01"	11' 10"
D-3	**DAN MINOR & SONS, INC., PORT COLBORNE, ON**							
	Andrea Marie I	TB	1963	D	87*	75' 02"	24' 07"	7' 03"
	Susan Michelle	TB	1995	D	89*	79' 10"	20' 11"	6' 02"
	Welland	TB	1954	D	94*	86' 00"	20' 00"	8' 00"
D-4	**DAVID MALLOCH, SCUDDER, ON**							
	Cemba	TK	1960	D	151	50' 00"	15' 06"	7' 06"
D-5	**DAWES MARINE TUG & BARGE, INC., NORTH TONAWANDA, NY**							
	Apache	TB	1954	D	119*	71' 00"	19' 06"	9' 06"
	(Lewis Castle '54 - '97)							
	Fourth Coast	TB	1957	D	17*	40' 00"	12' 06"	4' 00"
	Sand Pebble	TB	1969	D	30*	48' 00"	15' 00"	8' 00"
	Sea Chief	TB	1952	D	390*	107' 00"	26' 06"	14' 10"
	(U. S. Army LT-1944 '52 - '62, USCOE Washington '62 - 2000)							
	Tommy Ray	TB	1954	D	19*	45' 00"	12' 05"	6' 00"
D-6	**DEAN CONSTRUCTION CO. LTD., BELLE RIVER, ON**							
	Americo Dean	TB	1956	D	15*	45' 00"	15' 00"	5' 00"
	Annie M. Dean	TB	1981	D	58*	50' 00"	19' 00"	5' 00"
	Neptune III	TB	1939	D	23*	53' 10"	15' 06"	5' 00"
	Wayne Dean	TB	1946	D	10*	45' 00"	13' 00"	5' 00"

Fleet #.	Fleet Name Vessel Name	Type of Vessel	Year Built	Type of Engine	Cargo Cap. or Gross*	Overall Length	Breadth	Depth or Draft*
D-7	**DENNIS DOUGHERTY, SAULT STE. MARIE, MI**							
	Gerald D. Neville	TB	1924	D	29*	50' 00"	13' 00"	4' 06"
	(Tobermory '24 - '41, Champion {2} '41 - '81)							
D-8	**DETOUR MARINE, INC., DETOUR, MI**							
	Resolute	TB	1935	D	17*	36' 10"	12' 05"	4' 00"*
D-9	**DETROIT CITY FIRE DEPT., DETROIT, MI**							
	Curtis Randolph	FB	1979	D	85*	77' 10"	21' 06"	9' 03"
D-10	**DIAMOND JACK'S RIVER TOURS, GROSSE ILE, MI**							
	Diamond Belle	ES	1958	D	93*	93' 06"	25' 10"	10' 01"
	(Mackinac Islander {2} '58 - '90, Sir Richard '90 - '91)							
	Diamond Jack	ES	1955	D	82*	72' 00"	25' 00"	8' 00"
	(Emerald Isle {1} '55 - '91)							
	Diamond Queen	ES	1956	D	94*	92' 00"	25' 00"	10' 00"
	(Mohawk '56 - '96)							
D-11	**DIRK SPLILLMAKER, EAST LANSING, MI**							
	Verendrye	RV	1958	D	297*	167' 06"	34' 00"	16' 07"
	(CCGS Verendrye '58 - '86, 500 '86 - '92) **(Currently laid up in Toronto, ON.)**							
D-12	**DISSEN & JUHN CORP., MACEDON, NY**							
	Constructor	TB	1950	D	14*	39' 00"	11' 00"	5' 00"
	James W. Rickey	TB	1935	D	24*	46' 00"	14' 00"	7' 00"
	Portside Belle	TB	1953	D	13*	35' 00"	10' 06"	6' 00"
D-13	**DOW CHEMICAL CO., LUDINGTON, MI**							
	DC 710	TK	1969	B	25,500	260' 00"	50' 00"	9' 00"
	E-63	TK	1980	B	60,000	407' 00"	60' 00"	20' 00"
D-14	**DUC d' ORLEANS CRUISE BOAT, CORUNNA, ON**							
	Duc d' Orleans	ES	1943	D	112*	112' 00"	17' 10"	6' 03"
	(HMCS ML-105 '43 - ?, HMCS Duc d' Orleans [ML-105] ? - '48)							
D-15	**DUROCHER DOCK & DREDGE, INC., CHEBOYGAN, MI**							
	ACBL 1613	DB	1966	B	1,200	195' 02"	35' 02"	10' 04"
	ACBL 1614	DB	1966	B	1,200	195' 02"	35' 02"	10' 04"
	Betty D.	TB	1953	D	14*	40' 00"	13' 00"	6' 00"
	Champion {3}	TB	1974	D	125*	75' 00"	24' 00"	9' 06"
	General {2}	TB	1954	D	119*	71' 00"	19' 06"	9' 06"
	(U. S. Army ST-1999 '54 - '61, USCOE Au Sable '61 - '84, Challenger {3} '84 - '87)							
	Joe Van	TB	1955	D	32*	57' 09"	16' 06"	9' 00"
	M-1	CS	1924	B	750	100' 00"	24' 11"	4' 11"
	Meagan Beth	TB	1982	D	94*	60' 00"	22' 00"	9' 00"
	MOBRO 2000	DB	1980	B	2,400	180' 00"	52' 00"	11' 04"
	MOBRO 2001	DB	1980	B	2,400	180' 00"	52' 00"	11' 04"
	MOBRO 2005	DB	1980	B	2,400	180' 00"	52' 00"	11' 04"
	Nancy Anne	TB	1969	D	73*	60' 00"	20' 00"	6' 00"
	Ray Durocher	TB	1943	D	20*	45' 06"	12' 05"	7' 06"
	Samson II	CS	1959	B	700	90' 00"	50' 00"	7' 02"
	Witch	TB	1950	D	14*	30' 08"	9' 05"	6' 00"
E-1	**EASTERN CANADA TOWING LTD., HALIFAX, NS**							
	Point Carroll	TB	1973	D	366*	127' 00"	30' 05"	14' 05"
	Point Chebucto	TT	1993	D	412*	110' 00"	33' 00"	17' 00"
	Pointe Aux Basques	TB	1972	D	396*	105' 00"	33' 06"	19' 06"
	Pointe Comeau	TT	1976	D	391*	104' 00"	40' 00"	19' 00"
	Pointe Sept-Iles	TB	1980	D	424*	105' 00"	34' 06"	19' 06"
	Point Halifax	TT	1986	D	417*	110' 00"	36' 00"	19' 00"
	Point Valiant {2}	TT	1998	D	302*	80' 00"	30' 01"	14' 09"
	(Launched as Ocean Jupiter {1})							
	Point Vibert	TB	1961	D	236*	96' 03"	28' 00"	14' 06"
	(Foundation Vibert '61 - '73)							
	Point Vigour	TB	1962	D	207*	98' 05"	26' 10"	13' 05"
	(Foundation Vigour '62 - '74)							
	Point Vim	TB	1962	D	207*	98' 05"	26' 10"	13' 05"
	(Foundation Vim '62 - '74)							
E-2	**EASTERN UPPER PENINSULA TRANSIT AUTHORITY, SAULT STE. MARIE, MI**							
	Drummond Islander III	CF	1989	D	96*	108' 00"	37' 00"	12' 03"
	Drummond Islander IV	CF	2000	D		148' 00"	40' 00"	12' 00"
	Neebish Islander II	CF	1946	D	90*	89' 00"	29' 06"	6' 09"
	(Sugar Islander '46 - '95)							
	Sugar Islander II	CF	1995	D	223*	114' 00"	40' 00"	10' 00"

Lee A. Tregurtha prepares to leave the C. Reiss Coal Dock at Duluth, MN, 9 November 2000. (Cedric Woodard)

Passenger liner South American (in service 1914-1967) passes the Great Lakes Steel plant at Detroit in 1937. (All photos this page from the Sid Ferriss Collection)

OLD TIMERS

Crew of the Ford Motor Co. tug Buttercup relax after an icy Lake Michigan trip in November 1939.

John Hulst (1938-1985) ready for launch at Great Lakes Engineering Works, River Rouge, MI. Note the huge christening pennant.

Fleet #.	Fleet Name / Vessel Name	Type of Vessel	Year Built	Type of Engine	Cargo Cap. or Gross*	Overall Length	Breadth	Depth or Draft*
E-3	**EDELWEISS CRUISE DINING, MILWAUKEE, WI**							
	Edelweiss I	ES	1988	D	87*	64' 08"	18' 00"	6' 00"
	Edelweiss II	ES	1989	D	89*	73' 08"	20' 00"	7' 00"
E-4	**EDGEWATER BOAT TOURS, SARNIA, ON**							
	Macassa Bay	ES	1986	D	200*	93' 07"	29' 07"	10' 04"
E-5	**EDWARD E. GILLEN CO., MILWAUKEE, WI**							
	Andrew J.	TB	1950	D	25*	47' 00"	15' 07"	8' 00"
	Edith J.	TB	1962	D	19*	45' 03"	13' 00"	8' 00"
	Edward E. Gillen III	TB	1988	D	95*	75' 00"	26' 00"	9' 06"
	Harbor Builder	DB	1930	B	662*	150' 00"	42' 05"	12' 05"
E-6	**EDWIN M. ERICKSON, BAYFIELD, WI**							
	Outer Island	PK	1942	D	300	112' 00"	32' 00"	8' 06"
E-7	**EGAN MARINE CORP., LEMONT, IL**							
	Alice E.	TB	1950	D	183*	100' 00"	26' 00"	9' 00"
	(L. L. Wright '50 - '55, Martin '55 - '74, Mary Ann '74 - '77, Judi C. '77 - '94)							
	Becky E.	TB	1943	D	146*	81' 01"	24' 00"	9' 10"
	(DPC 51 '43 - '44, WSA 6 '44 - '46, Chas E. Trout '46 - '78, Naomi Marie '78 - '80, South Haven '80 - '90)							
	Crow	TB	1963	D	152*	84' 06"	25' 00"	11' 06"
	Daniel E.	TB	1967	D	70*	70' 00"	18' 06"	6' 08"
	(Foster M. Ford '67 - '84)							
	Denise E.	TB	1912	D	138*	80' 07"	21' 06"	10' 03"
	(Caspian '12 - '48, Trojan '48 - '81, Cherokee {1} '81 - '93)							
	Derek E.	TB	1907	D	85*	72' 06"	20' 01"	10' 06"
	(John Kelderhouse '07 - '13, Sachem '13 - '90)							
	(Foundered in Lake Erie on or about 18 December, 1950 under the name Sachem with the loss of 12 crew. Raised and rebuilt in 1951.)							
	Ethel E.	TB	1913	D	96*	81' 00"	20' 00"	12' 06"
	(Michigan {4} '13 - '78, Ste. Marie II '78 - '81, Dakota '81 - '92)							
	Lisa E.	TB	1963	D	75*	65' 06"	20' 00"	8' 06"
	(Dixie Scout '63 - '90)							
	Robin E.	TB	1889	D	123*	84' 09"	19' 00"	9' 00"
	(Asa W. Hughes 1889 - '13, Triton {1} '13 - '81, Navajo {2} '81 - '92)							
	Susan E.	TB	1921	D	96*	81' 00"	20' 00"	12' 06"
	(Oregon {1} '21 - '78, Ste. Marie I '78 - '81, Sioux {2} '81 - '91)							
E-8	**EMPIRE CRUISE LINES, U. S. A., ST. THOMAS, ON**							
	Marine Star	PA	1945	T	12,773*	520' 00"	71' 06"	43' 06"
	(USNS Marine Star '45 - '55, Aquarama '55 - '94)							
	(Last operated in 1962 — 5 year survey expired May, 1965 — Currently laid up in Lackawanna, NY.)							
E-9	**EMPIRE SANDY, INC., TORONTO, ON**							
	Empire Sandy	3S	1943	W	434*	140' 00"	32' 08"	14' 00"
	(Empire Sandy '43 - '48, Ashford '48 - '52, Chris M. '52 - '79)							
	Wayward Princess	ES	1976	D	325*	92' 00"	26' 00"	10' 00"
	(Cayuga II '76 - '82)							
E-10	**EMPRESS OF CANADA ENTERPRISES LTD., TORONTO, ON**							
	Empress of Canada	ES	1980	D	399*	116' 00"	28' 00"	6' 06"*
	(Island Queen V {2} '80 - '89)							
E-11	**EMPRESS RIVER CASINO, JOLIET, IL**							
	Empress	GA	1992	D	1,136*	214' 00"	66' 00"	6' 07"*
	Empress II	GA	1993	D	1,248*	230' 00"	67' 00"	6' 08"*
	Empress III	GA	1994	D	1,126*	288' 00"	76' 00"	10' 07"*
E-12	**ERIE ISLANDS PETROLEUM, INC., PUT-IN-BAY, OH**							
	Cantankerous	TK	1955	D	323	53' 00"	14' 00"	5' 00"*
E-13	**ERIE SAND & GRAVEL CO., ERIE, PA**							
	J. S. St. John	SC	1945	D	680	174' 00"	32' 02"	15' 00"
	(USS YO-178 '45 - '51, Lake Edward '51 - '67)							
	ERIE NAVIGATION CO. - VESSELS MANAGED BY ERIE SAND & GRAVEL CO.							
	Day Peckinpaugh	CC	1921	D	1,490	254' 00"	36' 00"	14' 00"
	(Interwaterways Line Incorporated 101 '21 - '32, I.L.I. 101 '32 - '36, Richard J. Barnes '36 - '58)							
	(Last operated 9 Sept. 1994 — 5 year survey expired August, 1995 — Currently laid up in Erie, PA.)							
	John R. Emery	SC	1905	D	490	140' 00"	33' 00"	14' 00"
	(Trenton {1} '05 - '25)							
	ERIE SAND STEAMSHIP CO. - VESSEL MANAGED BY ERIE SAND & GRAVEL CO.							
	Richard Reiss	SU	1943	D	14,900	620' 06"	60' 03"	35' 00"
	(Launched as Adirondack, Richard J. Reiss {2} '43 - '86)							
	(The Richard Reiss is a L6-S-B1 class "Maritime" vessel built by Great Lakes Engineering Works.)							

Fleet #.	Fleet Name Vessel Name	Type of Vessel	Year Built	Type of Engine	Cargo Cap. or Gross*	Overall Length	Breadth	Depth or Draft*
F-1	**FAIRMONT SHIPPING (CANADA) LTD., VANCOUVER, BC**							
	Eurasian Charm	BC	1982	D	22,558	539' 02"	75' 02"	44' 06"
	(Sunstars '82 - '85, Castano '85 - '94)							
	Eurasian Cherub	BC	1981	D	22,560	539' 02"	75' 02"	44' 06"
	(Jasper '81 - '83, Maple 2 '83 - '83, Armeria '83 - '88, Ambar '88 - '99)							
	Star Savannah	BC	1983	D	18,764	493' 09"	71' 07"	42' 06"
	(Calliope Maru '83 - '94, Calliope '94 - '97)							
F-2	**FAMILLE DuFOUR CROISIERES, SAINTE-ANNE-DE-BEAUPRE, QC**							
	Famille DuFour	ES	1992	D	451*	132' 00"	29' 00"	11' 00"
	Famille DuFour II	PC	1995	D	465*	127' 06"	34' 09"	10' 06"
	Marie-Clarisse	2S		W	126*	130' 00"	21' 04"	11' 05"*
F-3	**FAUST CORP., DETROIT, MI**							
	Comorant	TB	1991	D	10*	25' 02"	14' 00"	4' 06"
	Linnhurst	TB	1930	D	11*	37' 06"	10' 06"	4' 08"
F-4	**FEDNAV LTD., MONTREAL, QC**							
	CANARCTIC SHIPPING CO. LTD. - A DIVISION OF FEDNAV LTD.							
	Arctic	BC	1978	D	26,440	692' 04"	75' 05"	49' 05"
	Arctic Kalvik	SB	1983	D	4,391	288' 09"	57' 05"	32' 10"
	(Kalvik '83 - '97)							
	FEDERAL TERMINALS LTD. - A DIVISION OF FEDNAV LTD.							
	Brochu	TT	1973	D	390*	100' 00"	36' 00"	14' 06"
	Vachon	TT	1973	D	390*	100' 00"	36' 00"	14' 06"
	FEDNAV INTERNATIONAL LTD. - A DIVISION OF FEDNAV LTD.							
	Federal Asahi {2}	BC	2000	D	36,563	656' 02"	77' 11"	48' 08"
	Federal Baffin	BC	1995	D	43,732	623' 04"	100' 00"	54' 06"
	Federal Franklin	BC	1995	D	43,706	623' 04"	100' 00"	54' 06"
	Federal Hudson {3}	BC	2000	D	35,750	629' 08"	77' 11"	48' 08"
	Federal Kivalina	BC	2000	D	36,563	656' 02"	77' 11"	48' 08"
	Federal Maas {2}	BC	1997	D	34,372	656' 02"	77' 01"	48' 11"
	Federal Oshima	BC	1999	D	35,700	629' 08"	77' 01"	48' 09"
	Federal Rideau	BC	2000	D	36,563	656' 02"	77' 11"	48' 08"
	Federal Rhine {2}	BC	1997	D	34,372	656' 02"	77' 01"	48' 11"
	Federal Saguenay {2}	BC	1996	D	34,372	656' 02"	77' 01"	48' 11"
	Federal Schelde {2}	BC	1997	D	34,372	656' 02"	77' 01"	48' 11"
	Federal St. Laurent {2}	BC	1996	D	34,372	656' 02"	77' 01"	48' 11"
	Federal Sumida {2}	BC	1998	D	72,493	738' 02"	105' 08"	61' 04"
	Federal Welland	BC	2000	D	29,600	629' 08"	77' 11"	48' 08"
	Federal Yukon	BC	2000	D	36,563	656' 02"	77' 11"	48' 08"
	BAY OCEAN MANAGEMENT, INC. - VESSELS CHARTERED BY FEDNAV INTERNATIONAL LTD.							
	Lake Erie	BC	1980	D	35,630	737' 06"	76' 02"	47' 01"
	(Federal Ottawa '80 - '95)							
	Lake Michigan	BC	1981	D	38,294	729' 11"	76' 03"	47' 01"
	(Federal Maas {1} '81 - '95)							
	Lake Ontario	BC	1980	D	35,630	729' 11"	76' 03"	47' 01"
	(Federal Danube '80 - '95)							
	Lake Superior	BC	1981	D	35,630	729' 11"	76' 03"	47' 01"
	(Federal Thames '81 - '95)							
	EIDSIVA REDERI ASA - VESSEL CHARTERED BY FEDNAV INTERNATIONAL LTD.							
	Yarmouth	BC	1985	D	29,462	601' 00"	76' 00"	48' 11"
	(Paolo Pittaluga '85 - '91, Federal Oslo '91 - 2000)							
	MALAYSIA INTERNATIONAL - VESSEL CHARTERED BY FEDNAV INTERNATIONAL LTD.							
	Federal Bergen	BC	1984	D	29,159	593' 00"	76' 00"	47' 00"
	(High Peak '84 - '90, Federal Bergen '90 - '92, Thunder Bay '92 - '93)							
	TEAM SHIP MANAGEMENT AS - VESSELS CHARTERED BY FEDNAV INTERNATIONAL LTD.							
	Federal Fuji	BC	1986	D	29,536	599' 09"	75' 11"	48' 07"
	Federal Polaris	BC	1985	D	29,536	599' 09"	75' 11"	48' 07"
	M & N SHIPPING CORP. - VESSELS CHARTERED BY FEDNAV INTERNATIONAL LTD.							
	Federal Fraser {2}	BC	1983	D	35,315	730' 01"	75' 09"	48' 00"
	(Selkirk Settler '83 - '91, Federal St. Louis '91 - '91)							
	Federal MacKenzie	BC	1983	D	35,315	730' 01"	75' 09"	48' 00"
	(Canada Marquis '83 - '91, Federal Richelieu '91 - '91)							
	Lady Hamilton {2}	BC	1983	D	34,500	730' 01"	75' 09"	48' 00"
	(Saskatchewan Pioneer '83 - '95)							
	VANGUARD ENTERPRISE CO. LTD. - VESSEL CHARTERED BY FEDNAV INTERNATIONAL LTD.							
	Federal Agno	BC	1985	D	29,643	599' 09"	75' 09"	48' 07"
	(Federal Asahi {1} '85 - '89)							

Fleet #.	Fleet Name Vessel Name	Type of Vessel	Year Built	Type of Engine	Cargo Cap. or Gross*	Overall Length	Breadth	Depth or Draft*
F-5	**FERRISS MARINE CONTRACTING CORP., DETROIT, MI**							
	Magnetic	TB	1925	D	30*	55' 00"	14' 00"	6' 06"
	Norma B.	TB	1940	D	14*	43' 00"	15' 00"	4' 00"
F-6	**FRASER SHIPYARDS, INC., SUPERIOR, WI**							
	Brenda L.	TB	1941	D	11*	36' 00"	10' 00"	3' 08"
	(Harbour I '41 - '58, Su-Joy III '58 -'78)							
	Maxine Thompson	TB	1959	D	30*	47' 04"	13' 00"	6' 06"
	(Susan A. Fraser '59 - '78)							
	Murray R.	TB	1946	D	17*	42' 10"	12' 00"	4' 07"
	Phil Milroy	TB	1957	D	41*	47' 11"	16' 08"	8' 04"
	(Barney B. Barstow '57 - '78)							
	Reuben Johnson	TB	1912	D	71*	78' 00"	17' 00"	11' 00"
	(Buffalo {1} '12 - '28, USCOE Churchill '28 - '48, Buffalo {1} '48 - '74, Todd Fraser '74 - '78)							
	Todd L.	TB	1965	D	22*	42' 10"	12' 00"	5' 06"
	(Robert W. Fraser '65 - '78)							
	Troy L. Johnson	TB	1959	D	24*	42' 08"	12' 00"	5' 05"
	(Joyce E. Nelson '59 - ?, Vivian M. Fraser ? - ?)							
	Wally Kendzora	TB	1956	D	24*	43' 00"	12' 00"	5' 06"
	(Byron S. Nelson '56 - '65)							
	Wells Larson	TB	1953	D	22*	42' 10"	12' 00"	5' 06"
	(E. C. Knudsen '53 - '74)							
F-7	**FREDERICK PAINE, SUPERIOR, WI**							
	Spanky Paine	TB	1894	D	124*	94' 06"	22' 00"	11' 00"
	(Tioga 1894 - ?, Calumet ? - ?, John F. Drews ? - '67, William J. Dugan '67 - '91)							
F-8	**FROST ENGINEERING CO., FRANKFORT, MI**							
	Captain George	TB	1929	D	61*	63' 00"	17' 00"	7' 08"
	(USCOE Captain George '29 - '68, Captain George '68 - '73, Kurt R. Luetdke '73 - '91)							
G-1	**GAELIC TUG BOAT CO., GROSSE ILE, MI**							
	Carolyn Hoey	TB	1951	D	146*	90' 00"	25' 00"	11' 00"
	(Atlas '51 - '84 Susan Hoey {1} '84 - '85, Atlas '85 - '87)							
	G.T.B. No. 1	DH	1956	B	2,500	248' 00"	43' 00"	12' 00"
	L.S.C. 236	TK	1946	B	10,000	195' 00"	35' 00"	10' 06"
	Marysville	TK	1973	B	16,000	200' 00"	50' 00"	12' 06"
	(N.M.S. No. 102 '73 - '81)							
	Patricia Hoey {2}	TB	1949	D	146*	88' 06"	25' 00"	11' 00"
	(Propeller '49 - '82, Bantry Bay '82 - '91)							
	Robin Lynn	TB	1952	D	146*	85' 00"	25' 00"	11' 00"
	(Bonita {2} '52 - '85, Susan Hoey {2} '85 - '95, Blackie B. '95 - '98)							
	Roger Stahl	TB	1944	D	148*	110' 00"	26' 05"	15' 05"
	(USCGC Kennebec [WYT-61] '44 - '44, USCGC Kaw [WYT-61] '44 - '80, Kaw '80 - '97)							
	Shannon	TB	1944	D	145*	101' 00"	28' 00"	13' 00"
	(USS Connewango [YT / YTB / YTM-388] '44 - '77)							
	Susan Hoey {3}	TB	1950	D	146*	82' 00"	25' 00"	10' 07"
	(Navajo {1} '50 - '53, Seaval '53 - '64, Mary T. Tracy '64 - '69, Yankee '69 - '70, Minn '70 - '74, William S. Bell '74 - '83, Newcastle '83 - '93, Laura Lynn '93 - '99)							
	William Hoey	TB	1924	D	99*	85' 00"	21' 06"	10' 09"
	(Martha C. '24 - '52, Langdon C. Hardwicke '52 - '82, Wabash {2} '82 - '93, Katie Ann '93 - '99)							
G-2	**GALACTICA 001 ENTERPRISE LTD., TORONTO, ON**							
	Enterprise 2000	ES	1998	D				
	Galactica 001	ES	1957	D	67*	50' 00"	16' 00"	6' 03"
G-3	**GALLAGHER MARINE CONSTRUCTION CO., INC., ESCANABA, MI**							
	Bee Jay	TB	1939	D	19*	45' 00"	13' 00"	7' 00"
G-4	**GANANOQUE BOAT LINE LTD., GANANOQUE, ON**							
	Thousand Islander	ES	1972	D	200*	96' 11"	22' 01"	5' 05"
	Thousand Islander II	ES	1973	D	200*	99' 00"	22' 01"	5' 00"
	Thousand Islander III	ES	1975	D	376*	118' 00"	28' 00"	6' 00"
	Thousand Islander IV	ES	1976	D	347*	110' 09"	28' 04"	10' 08"
	Thousand Islander V	ES	1979	D	246*	88' 00"	24' 00"	5' 00"
G-5	**GANNON UNIVERSITY, ERIE, PA**							
	Environaut	RV	1950	D	17*	55' 00"	13' 06"	3' 10"*
G-6	**GARY ZULAUF, OSHAWA, ON**							
	Rhea	MS	1943	D	245*	136' 00"	24' 06"	10' 00"
	(USS YMS-299 '43 - '47, USS Rhea [AMS-52 / MSCO-52] '47 - '60)							
	(The Rhea earned 3 Battle Stars during World War II as the USS YMS-299.)							
G-7	**GENESEE MARINE, INC.**							
	Spirit of Rochester	ES	1975	D	80*	124' 03"	28' 06"	7' 03"
	(American Eagle '75 - '83, Island Clipper {1} '83 - '94)							

G-8	**GEORGIAN BAY CRUISE CO., PARRY SOUND, ON**							
	Chippewa {5}	PA	1954	D		65' 00"	16' 00"	6' 06"
G-9	**GILLESPIE OIL & TRANSIT, INC., ST. JAMES, MI**							
	American Girl	PK	1922	D	40	64' 00"	14' 00"	8' 03"
	Oil Queen	TK	1949	B	620	65' 00"	16' 00"	6' 00"
G-10	**GODERICH ELEVATORS LTD., GODERICH, ON**							
	Willowglen	R	1943		16,300	620' 06"	60' 00"	35' 00"
	(Launched as Mesabi, Lehigh {3} '43 - '81, Joseph X. Robert '81 - '82)							
	(The Willowglen is a L6-S-B1 class "Maritime" vessel built by Great Lakes Engineering Works.)							
	(Last operated 21 December, 1992 — 5 year survey expired October, 1997.)							
	(Currently in use as a stationary grain storage vessel in Goderich, ON.)							
G-11	**GOODTIME ISLAND CRUISES, INC., SANDUSKY, OH**							
	Goodtime I	ES	1960	D	81*	111' 00"	29' 08"	9' 05"
G-12	**GOODTIME TRANSIT BOATS, INC., CLEVELAND, OH**							
	Goodtime III	ES	1990	D	95*	161' 00"	40' 00"	11' 00"
G-13	**GRAND VALLEY STATE UNIVERSITY, ALLENDALE, MI**							
	ROBERT B. ANNIS WATER RESOURCES INSTITUTE							
	D. J. Angus	RV	1986	D	14*	45' 00"	14' 00"	4' 00"*
	W. G. Jackson	RV	1996	D	80*	64' 10"	20' 00"	5' 00"*
G-14	**GRAVEL & LAKE SERVICES LTD., THUNDER BAY, ON**							
	Donald Mac	TB	1914	D	69*	71' 00"	17' 00"	10' 00"
	F. A. Johnson	TB	1953	B	439*	150' 00"	32' 00"	10' 00"
	(Capt. Charles T. Parker '52 - '54, Rapid Cities '54 - '69, S. P. Renolds '69 - '70)							
	George N. Carleton	TB	1943	D	97*	82' 00"	21' 00"	11' 00"
	(Bansaga '43 - '64)							
	Peninsula	TB	1944	D	261*	111' 00"	27' 00"	13' 00"
	(HMCS Norton [W-31] '44 - '45, W.A.C. 1 '45 - '46)							
	Robert John	TB	1945	D	98*	82' 00"	20' 01"	11' 00"
	(Bansturdy '45 - '66)							
	Wolf River	BC	1956	D	5,880	349' 02"	43' 07"	25' 04"
	(Tecumseh {2} '56 - '67, New York News {3} '67 - '86, Stella Desgagnes '86 - '93, Beam Beginner '94 - '95)							
G-15	**GREAT LAKES ASSOCIATES, INC., ROCKY RIVER, OH**							
	Kinsman Enterprise {2}	BC	1927	T	16,100	631' 00"	65' 00"	33' 00"
	(Harry Coulby {2} '27 - '89)							
	(Last operated 13 Dec. 1995 — 5 year survey expires June, 2003 — Currently laid up in Buffalo, NY.)							
	Kinsman Independent {3}	BC	1952	T	18,800	642' 03"	67' 00"	35' 00"
	(Charles L. Hutchinson {3} '52 - '62, Ernest R. Breech '62 - '88)							
	(The Kinsman Independent {3} was constructed as the Charles L. Hutchinson with the steam turbine of the C1 freighter Alcoa Prospector, damaged in World War II.)							
G-16	**GREAT LAKES DOCK & MATERIALS, MUSKEGON, MI**							
	Fischer Hayden	TB		D				
G-17	**THE GREAT LAKES GROUP, CLEVELAND, OH**							
	THE GREAT LAKES TOWING CO. - A DIVISION OF THE GREAT LAKES GROUP							
	Alabama {2}	TB	1916	D	98*	81' 00"	21' 03"	12' 05"
	Arizona	TB	1931	D	98*	84' 04"	20' 00"	12' 06"
	Arkansas {2}	TB	1909	D	98*	81' 00"	21' 03"	12' 05"
	(Yale '09 - '48)							
	California	TB	1926	D	98*	81' 00"	20' 00"	12' 06"
	Colorado	TB	1928	D	98*	84' 04"	20' 00"	12' 06"
	Delaware {4}	TB	1924	D	98*	81' 00"	20' 00"	12' 06"
	Favorite	FD		B	250	90' 00"	50' 00"	5' 00"
	Florida	TB	1926	D	99*	81' 00"	20' 00"	12' 06"
	(Florida '26 - '83, Pinellas '83 - '84)							
	Idaho	TB	1931	D	98*	84' 00"	20' 00"	12' 06"
	Illinois {2}	TB	1914	D	99*	81' 00"	20' 00"	12' 06"
	Indiana	TB	1911	D	97*	81' 00"	20' 00"	12' 06"
	Iowa	TB	1915	D	98*	81' 00"	20' 00"	12' 06"
	Kansas	TB	1927	D	98*	81' 00"	20' 00"	12' 06"
	Kentucky {2}	TB	1929	D	98*	84' 04"	20' 00"	12' 06"
	Louisiana	TB	1917	D	98*	81' 00"	20' 00"	12' 06"
	Maine {1}	TB	1921	D	96*	81' 00"	20' 00"	12' 06"
	(Maine {1} '21 - '82, Saipan '82 - '83, Hillsboro '83 - '84)							
	Maryland {2}	TB	1925	D	98*	81' 00"	21' 03"	12' 05"
	(Maryland {2} '25 - '82, Tarawa '82 - '83, Pasco '83 - '84)							

Logistic Navigation's Lucien-Paquin in the St. Lawrence Seaway. (Willem VanMaanen)

Fleet #.	Fleet Name Vessel Name	Type of Vessel	Year Built	Type of Engine	Cargo Cap. or Gross*	Overall Length	Breadth	Depth or Draft*
	Milwaukee	DB		B	4,095	172' 00"	40' 00"	11' 06"
	Minnesota {1}	TB	1911	D	98*	81' 00"	20' 00"	12' 06"
	Mississippi	TB	1916	D	98*	81' 00"	20' 00"	12' 06"
	Missouri {2}	TB	1927	D	149*	88' 04"	24' 06"	12' 03"
	(Rogers City {1} '27 - '56, Dolomite {1} '56 - '81, Chippewa {7} '81 - '90)							
	Montana	TB	1929	D	98*	84' 04"	20' 00"	12' 06"
	Nebraska	TB	1929	D	98*	84' 04"	20' 00"	12' 06"
	New Jersey	TB	1924	D	98*	81' 00"	20' 00"	12' 06"
	(New Jersey '24 - '52, Petco-21 '52 - '53)							
	New York	TB	1913	D	98*	81' 00"	20' 00"	12' 06"
	North Carolina {2}	TB	1952	D	145*	87' 09"	24' 01"	10' 07"
	(Limestone '52 - '83, Wicklow '83 - '90)							
	North Dakota	TB	1910	D	97*	81' 00"	20' 00"	12' 06"
	(John M. Truby '10 - '38)							
	Ohio {3}	TB	1903	D	194*	118' 00"	24' 00"	13' 06"
	(M.F.D. No. 15 '03 - '52, Laurence C. Turner '52 - '73)							
	Oklahoma	TB	1913	D	97*	81' 00"	20' 00"	12' 06"
	(T. C. Lutz {2} '13 - '34)							
	Oregon {2}	TB	1952	D	149*	88' 07"	24' 10"	10' 09"
	(Jennifer George '52 - '82, Galway Bay '82 - '90)							
	Pennsylvania {3}	TB	1911	D	98*	81' 00"	20' 00"	12' 06"
	Rhode Island	TB	1930	D	98*	84' 04"	20' 00"	12' 06"
	South Carolina	TB	1925	D	102*	86' 00"	21' 00"	11' 00"
	(Welcome {2} '25 - '53, Joseph H. Callan '53 - '72, South Carolina '72 - '82, Tulagi '82 - '83)							
	Superior {3}	TB	1912	D	147*	97' 00"	22' 00"	12' 00"
	(Richard Fitzgerald '12 - '46)							
	Tennessee	TB	1917	D	98*	81' 00"	20' 00"	12' 06"
	Texas	TB	1916	D	97*	81' 00"	20' 00"	12' 06"
	Triton {2}	TB	1941	D	197*	135' 00"	30' 00"	17' 06"
	(USS Tuscarora [AT-77, YT-341, YTB-341, ATA-245] '41 - '79, Challenger {1} '79 - '86)							
	Vermont	TB	1914	D	98*	81' 00"	20' 00"	12' 06"
	Virginia {2}	TB	1914	D	97*	81' 00"	20' 00"	12' 06"
	Washington {1}	TB	1925	D	97*	81' 00"	20' 00"	12' 06"
	Wisconsin {4}	TB	1897	D	105*	90' 03"	21' 00"	12' 03"
	(America {3} 1897 - '82, Midway '82 - '83)							
	Wyoming	TB	1929	D	104	84' 04"	20' 00"	12' 06"
G-18	**GREAT LAKES MARINE ENGINEERING & SALVAGE, INC., ALPENA, MI**							
	Atlas	RV	1941	D	157*	90' 07"	21' 04"	11' 00"
G-19	**GREAT LAKES MARITIME ACADEMY - NORTHWESTERN MICHIGAN COLLEGE,** **TRAVERSE CITY, MI — (231)-922-1200**							
	Anchor Bay	TV	1953	D	23*	45' 00"	13' 00"	7' 00"*
	GLMA Barge	TV	1960	B	25	80' 00"	20' 00"	7' 00"
	Northwestern {2}	TV	1969	D	12*	55' 00"	15' 00"	6' 06"
	(USCOE North Central '69 - '98)							
G-20	**GREAT LAKES RESPONSE CORP.**							
	Dover Light	EV	1968	B	7,870	146' 05"	50' 00"	13' 07"
	(Jackson Purchase '68 - '83, Eliza S-1877 '83 - '86)							
	(5 year survey expired April, 1995 — Currently laid up in Hamilton, ON.)							
	Sillery	EV	1963	D	9,415	175' 00"	36' 00"	14' 00"
	(Imperial Verdun '63 - '79)							
	S.M.T.B. No. 7	EV	1969	B	7,502	150' 00"	33' 00"	14' 00"
G-21	**GREAT LAKES SCHOONER CO., TORONTO, ON**							
	Challenge	3S	1980	W	76*	96' 00"	16' 06"	8' 00"
	True North of Toronto	2S	1947	W	95*	115' 00"	20' 00"	10' 06"
	(Eenhorn '47 - '86, Unicorn of St. Helier '86 - '96)							
G-22	**GREAT LAKES SHIPWRECK HISTORICAL SOCIETY, SAULT STE. MARIE, MI**							
	Antiquarian	RV		D		40' 00"	12' 00"	4' 00"
	David Boyd	RV	1982	D	23*	47' 00"	17' 00"	3' 00"*
G-23	**GREAT LAKES TRANSPORT LTD. - A DIVISION OF HALIFAX GRAIN ELEVATOR LTD., HALIFAX, NS**							
	Jane Ann IV	TB	1978	D	954*	137' 06"	42' 08"	21' 04"
	(Ouro Fino '78 - '81, Bomare '81 - '93, Tignish Sea '93 - '98)							
	Sarah Spencer	SU	1959	B	23,200	611' 03"	72' 00"	40' 00"
	(Adam E. Cornelius {3} '59 - '89, Capt. Edward V. Smith '89 - '91, Sea Barge One '91 - '96)							
G-24	**GREEN BAY ACQUISTION CO., INC., MENOMINEE, MI**							
	William H. Donner	CS	1914	R	9,400	524' 00"	54' 00"	30' 00"
	(Last operated in 1969 — Currently in use as a stationary cargo transfer vessel in Menominee, MI.)							
H-1	**HALRON OIL CO., INC., GREEN BAY, WI**							
	Mr. Micky	TK	1940	B	10,500	195' 00"	35' 00"	10' 00"

Fleet #.	Fleet Name Vessel Name	Type of Vessel	Year Built	Type of Engine	Cargo Cap. or Gross*	Overall Length	Breadth	Depth or Draft*
H-2	**HAMILTON HARBOUR COMMISSIONERS, HAMILTON, ON**							
	Judge McCombs	TB	1948	D	10*	36' 00"	10' 03"	4' 00"
H-3	**HANK VAN ASPERT, WINDSOR, ON**							
	Queen City {2}	PA	1911	D	248*	116' 00"	23' 00"	12' 07"
	(Polana '11 - '30, Jalobert '30 - '54, Macassa {2} '54 - '65)							
	(Last operated in 1982 — Currently laid up in LaSalle, ON.)							
H-4	**HANNAH MARINE CORP., LEMONT, IL**							
	Daryl C. Hannah {2}	TB	1956	D	268*	102' 00"	28' 00"	8' 00"
	(Cindy Jo '56 - '66, Katherine L. '66 - '93)							
	Donald C. Hannah	TB	1962	D	191*	91' 00"	29' 00"	11' 06"
	Hannah D. Hannah	TB	1955	D	134*	86' 00"	24' 00"	10' 00"
	(Harbor Ace '55 - '61, Gopher State '61 - '71, Betty Gale '71 - '93)							
	Hannah 1801	TK	1967	B	18,550	240' 00"	50' 00"	12' 00"
	(BRI 5 '67 - '88, CT-75 '88 - '92)							
	Hannah 1802	TK	1967	B	18,550	240' 00"	50' 00"	12' 00"
	(BRI 6 '67 - '87, CT-76 '87 - '92)							
	Hannah 2801	TK	1980	B	28,665	275' 00"	54' 00"	17' 06"
	Hannah 2901	TK	1962	B	17,400	264' 00"	52' 06"	12' 06"
	Hannah 2902	TK	1962	B	17,360	264' 00"	52' 06"	12' 06"
	Hannah 2903	TK	1962	B	17,350	264' 00"	52' 06"	12' 06"
	(2903 '62 - '90)							
	Hannah 3601	TK	1972	B	35,360	290' 00"	60' 00"	18' 03"
	Hannah 5101	TK	1978	B	49,660	360' 00"	60' 00"	22' 06"
	James A. Hannah	TB	1945	D	593*	149' 00"	33' 00"	16' 00"
	(U. S. Army LT-280 '45 - '65, Muskegon {1} '65 - '71)							
	Kristin Lee Hannah	TB	1945	D	602*	149' 00"	33' 00"	16' 00"
	(U. S. Army LT-815 '45 - '64, Henry Foss '64 - '84, Kristin Lee '84 - '93)							
	Mark Hannah	TBA	1969	D	191*	127' 05"	32' 01"	14' 03"
	(Lead Horse '69 - '73, Gulf Challenger '73 - '80, Challenger {2} '80 - '93)							
	Mary E. Hannah	TB	1945	D	612*	149' 00"	33' 00"	16' 00"
	(U. S. Army LT-821 '45 - '47, Brooklyn '47 - '66, Lee Reuben '66 - '75)							
	Mary Page Hannah {2}	TB	1972	D	99*	59' 08"	24' 01"	10' 03"
	(Kings Squire '72 - '78, Juanita D. '78 - '79 Katherine L. '79 - '93)							
	No. 25	TK	1949	B	19,500	254' 00"	54' 00"	11' 00"
	No. 26	TK	1949	B	19,500	254' 00"	54' 00"	11' 00"
	No. 28	TK	1957	B	20,725	240' 00"	50' 00"	12' 06"
	(Bay 220 '57 - '62, Tenneco 220 '62 - '70)							
	No. 29 {2}	TK	1952	B	22,000	254' 00"	54' 00"	11' 06"
	Peggy D. Hannah	TB	1920	D	145*	108' 00"	25' 00"	14' 00"
	(William A. Whitney '20 - '92)							
	Susan W. Hannah	TBA	1977	D	174*	121' 06"	34' 06"	18' 02"
	(Lady Elda '77 - '78, Kings Challenger '78 - '78, ITM No. 1 '78 - '81, Kings Challenger '81 - '86)							
	HMC SHIP MANAGEMENT LTD. - AN AFFILIATE OF HANNAH MARINE CORP.							
	C.T.C. No. 1	CC	1943	R	16,300	620' 06"	60' 00"	35' 00"
	(Launched as McIntyre, Frank Purnell {1} '43 - '64, Steelton {3} '64 - '78, Hull No. 3 '78 - '79,							
	Pioneer {4} '79 - '82)							
	(The C.T.C. No. 1 is a L6-S-B1 class "Maritime" vessel built by Great Lakes Engineering Works.)							
	(Last operated 12 Nov. 1981 — in use as a cement storage / transfer vessel in S. Chicago, IL.)							
	Southdown Challenger	CC	1906	S	10,250	552' 01"	56' 00"	31' 00"
	(William P. Snyder '06 - '26, Elton Hoyt II {1} '26 - '52, Alex D. Chisholm '52 - '66, Medusa Challenger '66 - '99)							
	(The Southdown Challenger is the oldest operating bulk carrier on the Great Lakes).							
	Southdown Conquest	CC	1937	D	8,500	437' 06"	55' 00"	28' 00"
	(Red Crown '37 - '62, Amoco Indiana '62 - '87, Medusa Conquest '87 - '99)							
H-5	**HARBOR LIGHT CRUISE LINES, INC., TOLEDO, OH**							
	Sandpiper	ES	1984	D	19*	65' 00"	16' 00"	4' 00"
H-6	**HARBOUR PRINCESS TOURS, PORT DOVER, ONTARIO**							
	Harbour Princess 1	ES		D				
	(Garden City ? - 2000)							
H-7	**HARRAH'S CASINO, EAST CHICAGO, IN**							
	Showboat Mardi Gras	GA	1996	D	12,182*	340' 00"	74' 00"	17' 06"
H-8	**HARRY GAMBLE SHIPYARDS, PORT DOVER, ON**							
	H. A. Smith	TB	1944	D	24*	55' 00"	16' 00"	5' 06"
	J. A. Cornett	TB	1937	D	60*	65' 00"	17' 00"	9' 00"
H-9	**HILTVEIT ASSOCIATES INC., NEW YORK, NY**							
	Martha A	TK	1986	D	103,130	433' 01"	67' 00"	36' 09"
	Rachel B	TK	1987	D	103,520	433' 01"	67' 00"	36' 09"

Listings continued on Page 69

Colors of the Great Lakes & Seaway Smokestacks

A.B.M. Marine
Thunder Bay, ON

Algoma Central Marine Group
Div. of Algoma Central Corp.
St. Catharines, ON

Algoma Tankers Ltd.
Div. of Algoma Central Corp.
Dartmouth, NS

American Canadian Caribbean Line, Inc.
Warren, RI

American Marine Construction
Benton Harbor, MI

American Steamship Co.
Williamsville, NY

Andrie, Inc.
Muskegon, MI

Arnold Transit Co.
Mackinac Island, MI

Atlantic Towing Ltd.
Div. of Irvingdale Shipping Ltd.
St. John, NB

Basic Towing, Inc.
Escanaba, MI

Bay Shipbuilding Co.
Sturgeon Bay, WI

Beaver Island Boat Co.
Charlevoix, MI

Bethlehem Steel Corp.
Chesterton, IN

Bigane Vessel Fueling Co.
Chicago, IL

Billington Contracting Inc.
Duluth, MN

Blue Circle Cement Co.
Detroit, MI
Toronto, ON

Buffalo Public Works Dept.
Buffalo, NY

Busch Marine, Inc.
Carrollton, MI

Canada Steamship Lines, Inc.
Montreal, QC

Canadian Coast Guard
Ottawa, ON

Central Marine Logistics, Inc.
Highland, IN

Chicago Fire Department
Chicago, IL

Cleveland Fire Department
Cleveland, OH

Cleveland Tankers (1991), Inc.
Algoma Tankers, Ltd. Mgr.
Cleveland, OH

Croisieres AML Inc.
Quebec, QC

Croisieres Nordik, Inc.
Div. of Transport Desgagnes, Inc.
Quebec, QC

C.A. Crosbie Shipping Ltd.
Montreal, QC

Dan Minor & Sons, Inc.
Port Colborne, ON

Dean Construction Co.
Belle River, ON

Detroit City Fire Department
Detroit, MI

Diamond Jack's River Tours
Grosse Isle, MI

Durocher Dock & Dredge, Inc.
Cheboygan, MI

Duc D'Orleans Cruise Boat
Corunna, ON

Eastern Canada Towing Ltd.
Halifax, NS

Eastern Upper Peninsula Transportation Authority
Sault Ste. Marie, MI

Erie Sand & Gravel Co.
Erie Sand Steamship Co.
Erie, PA

Essroc Canada, Inc.
Upper Lakes Group, Mgr
Downsville, ON

Fednav Ltd.
Montreal, QC

Ferriss Marine
Contracting Inc.
Detroit, MI

Fraser Shipyards, Inc.
Superior, WI

Gaelic Tug Boat Co.
Grosse Ile, MI

Gananoque Boat Line
Gananoque,ON

Edward E. Gillen Co.
Milwaukee, WI

Goodtime Transit Boats, Inc.
Cleveland, OH

Gravel & Lake Services, Ltd.
Thunder Bay, ON

Great Lakes Associates, Inc.
Rocky River, OH

Great Lakes International
Towing & Salvage Ltd.
Burlington, ON

Great Lakes Maritime Academy
Northwestern Michigan College
Traverse City, MI

Great Lakes Towing Co.
Cleveland, OH

Great Lakes Transport Ltd.
Tug Jane Ann IV
Halifax, NS

HMC Ship Managment
Lemont, IL

Hamilton Marine &
Engineering Ltd.
Div. of ULS Corp.
Port Colborne, ON

Hannah Marine Corp.
Lemont, IL

Holly Marine Towing
Chicago, IL

Inland Bulk Transfer
Cleveland, OH

Inland Lakes Management, Inc.
Alpena, MI

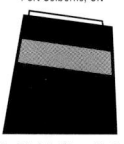

The Interlake Steamship Co.
Lakes Shipping Co.
Richfield, OH

Jacobs Investments
Cleveland, OH

Kadinger Marine Service, Inc.
Milwaukee, WI

Kent Line International Ltd
Div. of Irvingdale Shipping Ltd.
St. John, NB

Keystone Great Lakes, Inc.
Tug Michigan
Bala Cynwyd, PA

Kindra Lake Towing Co.
Downer's Grove, IL

King Company Inc.
Holland, MI

Lafarge Cement Corp.
Toronto, ON
Alpena, MI

Lake Michigan Carferry
Service, Inc.
Ludington, MI

Lake Michigan Contractors, Inc.
Holland, MI

Le Groupe Ocean Inc.
Quebec, QC

Lee Marine, Ltd.
Sombra, ON

Lock Tours Canada
Sault Ste. Marie, ON

Logistec Navigation, Inc.
Transport Igloolik - Mgr.
Montreal, QC

Lower Lakes Towing, Ltd.
Lower Lakes Transportation Ltd.
Port Dover, ON

Luedtke Engineering Co.
Frankfort, MI

M.C.M. Marine Inc.
Sault Ste Marie, MI

MacDonald Marine Ltd.
Goderich, ON

Madeline Island Ferry Line, Inc.
LaPointe, WI

Maid of the Mist
Steamboat Co., Ltd.
Niagara Falls, ON

Malcom Marine
St. Clair, MI

Marine Atlantic, Inc.
Moncton, NB

Mariposa Cruise Line
Toronto, ON

McAllister Towing & Salvage, Inc.
Subsidiary of Le Groupe Ocean, Inc.
Montreal, QC

McKeil Marine Ltd.
Hamilton, ON

Miller Boat Line, Inc.
Put-In-Bay, OH

Museum Ship
CCGC Alexander Henry
Kingston, ON

Museum Tug Edna G
Two Harbors, MN

Museum Ship
HMCS Haida
Toronto, ON

Museum Ship
Keewatin
Douglas, MI

Museum Ships
USS Little Rock
USS The Sullivans
Buffalo, NY

Museum Ship
Meteor
Superior, WI

Museum Ship
City of Milwaukee
Manistee, MI

Museum Ship
Milwaukee Clipper
Muskegon, MI

Museum Ships
Norgoma (Sault Ste. Marie,ON)
Norisle (Manitowaning,ON)

Museum Ship
Valley Camp
Sault Ste. Marie, MI

Museum Ship
William A. Irvin
Duluth, MN

Museum Ships
Willis B. Boyer (Toledo,OH)
William G. Mather (Cleveland,OH)

Muskoka Lakes Navigation
& Hotel Co.
Gravenhurst, ON

N.M. Paterson & Sons Ltd.
Thunder Bay, ON

Nadro Marine Services
Port Dover, ON

Neuman Cruise & Ferry
Line, Inc.
Sandusky, OH

New World Ship Management
Clipper Cruise Line
St. Louis, MO

Oglebay Norton Marine
Services Co.
Cleveland, OH

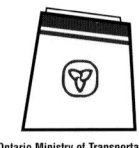

Ontario Ministry of Transportation
& Communication
Kingston, ON

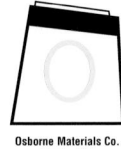

Osborne Materials Co.
Mentor, OH

Owen Sound
Transportation Co. Ltd.
Owen Sound, ON

P & H Shipping
Div. of Parrish & Heimbecker Ltd.
Mississauga, ON

Pelee Island
Transportation Services
Pelee Island, ON

Pere Marquette Shipping Co.
Ludington, MI

Provmar Fuels, Inc.
Div. of ULS Corporation
Toronto, ON

Purvis Marine Ltd.
Sault Ste. Marie, ON

Purvis Marine Ltd.
M/V Yankcanuck
Sault Ste. Marie, ON

Reinauer Transportation
Companies, Inc.
Staten Island, NY

Rigel Shipping Canada, Inc.
Rigel Shipping Co., Inc
Shediac, NB

Roen Salvage Co.
Sturgeon Bay, WI

Sea Fox Thousand
Islands Tours
Kingston, ON

Selvick Marine Towing Corp.
Sturgeon Bay, WI

Shell Canadian Tankers Ltd.
Montreal, QC

Societe des Traversiers du Quebec
Quebec, QC

Society Quebecoise D'Exploration Miniere Algoma Central Corp.-Mgr.
Sault Ste. Marie, ON

Soo Locks Boat Tours
Sault Ste. Marie, MI

St. Lawrence Cruise Lines, Inc.
Kingston, ON

St. Lawrence Seaway Management Corp.
Cornwall, ON

St. Lawrence Seaway Development Corp.
Massena, NY

Three Rivers Boatmen, Inc.
Trois Rivieres, QC

Toronto Metropolitan Park Dept.
Toronto, ON

Transport Desgagnes, Inc.
Quebec, QC

Transport Iglooik, Inc.
Montreal, QC

Trump Indiana, Inc.
Gary, IN

Upper Lakes Group Jackes Shipping, Inc.
Ottawa, ON

United States Army Corps of Engineers Great Lakes and Ohio River Division
Chicago, IL

United States Coast Guard 9th Coast Guard District
Cleveland, OH

United States Environmental Protection Agency
Bay City, MI

United States National Park Service
Houghton, MI

USS Great Lakes Fleet, Inc.
Duluth, MN

U.S.S. Great Lakes Fleet, Inc. M/V Presque Isle
Duluth, MN

University of Michigan Center for Great Lakes & Aquatic Sciences
Ann Arbor, MI

Upper Lakes Towing, Inc.
Escanaba, MI

Colors of Major International Seaway Fleets

Alba Shipping Ltd. A/S
Aalborg, Denmark

Albamar Shipping Co., S.A.
Piraeus, Greece

All-Trust Shipping Co. S.A.
Piraeus, Greece

Atlantis Management, Inc.
Piraeus, Greece

Atlantska Plovidba
Dubrovnik, Croatia

Aurora Shipping, Inc.
Manila, Philippines

Azov Sea Shipping Co.
Mariupol, Ukraine

B&N Bylok & Nordsjofraktas
Oslo, Norway

Bay Ocean Management, Inc
Englewood Cliffs, NJ

Bison Shipmanagement & Chartering Co. Pte. Ltd.
Singapore

Briese Schiffahrts GMBH & Co. KG
Leer, Germany

Canadian Forest Navigation Co. Ltd. Fednav Ltd. Mgr.
Montreal, QC

Canada Maritime Ltd.
Hamilton, Bermuda

Cape Shipping S.A.
Piraeus, Greece

Ceres Hellenic Shipping Enterprises
Piraeus, Greece

Chellaram Shipping Ltd.
Hong Kong, PRC

China Ocean Shipping Group
Bejing, PRC

**Commercial Trading &
Discount Co., Ltd.**
Athens, Greece

**Compagnie des Iles
du Ponant
M/V LeLevant**
Nantes, France

Densan Shipping Co. Ltd.
Istanbul, Turkey

Det Nordenfjeldske D/S AS
Trondheim, Norway

Diana Shipping Agencies S.A.
Piraeus, Greece

Dockendale Shipping Co. Ltd.
Nassau, Bahamas

Donnelly Shipmanagment Ltd.
Limassol, Cyprus

**ER Denizcilik Sanayi Nakliyat
ve Ticaret A.S.**
Istanbul, Turkey

Egon Oldendorff Ltd.
Luebeck, Germany

**Eidsiva Rederi ASA
Fednav Ltd. Mgr.**
Oslo, Norway

Elite Shipping A/S
Copenhagen Denmark

Elmira Shipping & Trading S.A.
Athens, Greece

**Fairmont Shipping
(Canada) Ltd.**
Vancouver, B.C.

Fafalios Shipping S.A.
Piraeus, Greece

Fednav International Ltd.
Montreal, QC

Gourdomichalis Maritime S.A.
Piraeus, Greece

**Great Circle Shipping
Agency Ltd.**
Bangkok, Thailand

**Golden Sun Cruises
M/V Arcadia**
Piraeus, Greece

**Hapag Lloyd Cruises
M/V c. Columbus**
Hamburg, Germany

**Harbor Shipping &
Trading Co. S.A.**
Chios, Greece

**Hilal Shipping, Trading
& Industry Co.**
Istanbul, Turkey

**H.S.S. Holland Ship
Service B.V.**
Rotterdam, Netherlands

**J.G. Roussos (Shipping)
Co. S. A.**
Athens, Greece

**Jugoslavenska Oceanska
Plovidba**
Kotor, Yugoslavia

Jumbo Shipping Co. S.A.
Geneva, Switzerland

Knutsen O.A.S. Shipping
Haugesund, Norway

Laurin Maritime, Inc
Houston, TX

Lithuanian Shipping Co.
Klaipeda, Lithuania

**M.T.M. Ship Management
Pte. Ltd.**
Singapore

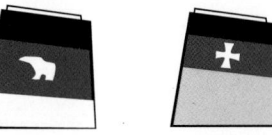
Mammoet Shipping Ltd.
Roosendaahl, Netherlands

Marine Managers, Ltd.
Piraeus, Greece

**Millenium Maritime
Services Ltd.**
Piraeus, Greece

**Metron Shipping &
Agencies, Ltd.**
Piraeus, Greece

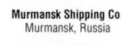
Murmansk Shipping Co.
Murmansk, Russia

Narval Shipping Corp.
Piraeus, Greece

**Navigation Maritime
Bulgare Ltd.**
Varna, Bulgaria

Neste OYJ
Espoo, Finland

**Orient Overseas
Container Line Ltd.**
Hong Kong, PRC

Oceanbulk Maritime S.A.
Athens, Greece

Olympic Shipping and Management S.A.
Athens, Greece

Orion Schiffahrts-Gesellschaft
Hamburg, Germany

P&O Nedlloyd B.V.
Rotterdam, Netherlands

PACC Ship Managers Pte. Ltd.
Singapore, Malaysia

Pacific Basin Agencies Ltd. Fednav Ltd. Mgr.
Hong Kong

Pan Ocean Shipping Co., Ltd.
Seoul, South Korea

Pegasus Denizeilik
Istanbul, Turkey

Polclip (Luxembourg) S.A.
Luxembourg, Luxembourg

Polish Steamship Co.
Szczecin, Poland

Primal Ship Management
Athens, Greece

Prime Orient Shipping S.A.
Panama City, Panama

Prisco (UK) Ltd.
London, England

Reederei Hans-Peter Eckhoft Co., H.G.
Hollenstedt, Germany

Scanscot Shipping Services GmbH
Hamburg, Germany

Seastar Navigation Co. Ltd.
Athens, Greece

Sherimar Management Co. Ltd.
Athens, Greece

Shih Wei Navigation Co. Ltd.
Taipei, Taiwan

Shipping Corp. of India Ltd.
Bombay, India

Shunzan Kaiun Co., Ltd.
Ehime, Japan

Sidemar Servizi Accessori S.p.A.
Genoa, Italy

Societe Anonyme Monegasque d' Administration Maritime et Aerienne
Monte Carlo, Monaco

Sohtorik Denizcilik ve Ticaret A.S.
Istanbul, Turkey

Spar Shipping A.S.
Bergen, Norway

Spliethoff's Bevrachtingskantoor Ltd.
Amsterdam, Netherlands

Split Ship Management, Ltd.
Split, Croatia

Stolt Parcel Tankers
Greenwich, CT

Surrendra Overseas Ltd.
Calcutta, India

Team Ship Management
Bergen, Norway

Teo Shipping Corp.
Piraeus, Greece

Thenamaris Ships Management, Inc.
Athens, Greece

Thoresen & Co. Ltd.
Bangkok, Thailand

Tomasos Brothers, Inc.
Piraeus, Greece

Transman Shipping Enterprises S.A.
Athens, Greece

Triton Bereederungs GMBH & Co.
Leer, Germany

Univan Ship Management Ltd.
Hong Kong

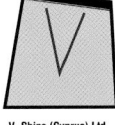
V. Ships (Cyprus) Ltd.
Limassol, Cyprus

Vergos Marine Management
Piraeus, Greece

W. Bockstiegel Reederei KG
Emden, Germany

Wagenborg Shipping B.V.
Delfzijl, Netherlands

House Flags of Great Lakes & Seaway Fleets

**Algoma Central
Marine Group**
Sault Ste. Marie, ON

American Steamship Co.
Williamsville, NY

Atlantic Towing Ltd.
St. John, NB

Bethlehem Steel Corp.
Chesterton, IN

**Canada Steamship
Lines, Inc.**
Montreal, QC

**Cleveland Tankers,
(1991) Inc.**
Cleveland, OH

Erie Sand & Gravel
Erie, PA

Fednav Ltd.
Montreal, QC

Gaelic Tug Boat Co.
Grosse Ile, MI

**Great Lakes
Associates Inc.**
Rocky River, OH

Great Lakes Towing Co.
Cleveland, OH

**Inland Lakes
Management, Inc.**
Alpena, MI

**Interlake Steamship Co.
Lakes Shipping Co.**
Richfield, OH

J.W. Westcott Co.
Detroit, MI

**LaFarge Cement
Corp.**
Montreal, QC

**Lake Michigan
Carferry Service, Inc.**
Ludington, MI

**Lower Lakes
Towing Ltd.**
Port Dover, ON

McKeil Marine Ltd.
Hamilton, ON

**N.M. Paterson
& Sons Ltd.**
Thunder Bay, ON

**Oglebay Norton
Marine Services Co.**
Cleveland, OH

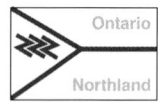

**Owen Sound
Transportation Co. Ltd.**
Owen Sound, ON

P. & H. Shipping
Mississauga, ON

Purvis Marine Ltd.
Sault Ste. Marie, ON

Seaway Marine Transport
Toronto, ON

**Transport
Desgagnes, Inc.**
Quebec, QC

Upper Lakes Group, Inc.
Toronto, ON

**USS Great Lakes
Fleet, Inc.**
Duluth, MN

Wagenborg Shipping B.V.
Delfzijl, Netherlands

Flags of Major Nations in the Marine Trade

Afghanistan

Antigua & Barbuda

Argentina

Australia

Austria

Azerbaijan

Bahamas

Bahrain

Barbados

Belgium

Belize

Bermuda

Bosnia & Herzegovinia

Brazil

Canada

Cayman Islands

Chile

China

Cote D'Ivoire

Croatia

Cyprus

Czech Republic

Denmark

Dominican Republic

Ecuador

Egypt

Estonia

Ethiopia

Fiji

Finland

France

Germany

Ghana

Greece

Guinea

Haiti

Honduras

Hong Kong

Hungary

Iceland

India

Indonesia

Ireland

Isle of Man

Israel

Italy

Japan

Jordan

Korea-South

Latvia

Liberia

Lithuania

Luxembourg

Malaysia

Malta

Marshall Islands

Mexico

Monaco

Morocco

Mozambique

Myanmar

Netherlands

Netherlands Antilles

New Zealand

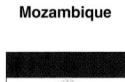
Nicaragua

Nigeria

N. Mariana Islands

Norway

Pakistan

Panama

Peru

Philippines

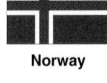
Poland

Portugal

Republic of South Africa

Romania

Russia

Saudi Arabia

Singapore

Solomon Islands

Spain

St. Kitts Nevis

St. Vincent & The Grenadines

Sweden

Switzerland

Syria

Taiwan

Thailand

Trinidad & Tobago

Tunisia

Turkey

Ukraine

United Kingdom

United States

Vanuatu

Venezuela

Vietnam

Yugoslavia

Dangerous Cargo
On Board

Pilot On Board

U.S. Coast Guard
Auxiliary Ensign

U.S. Coast
Guard Ensign

U.S. Army Corps
of Engineers

St. Lawrence Seaway
Development Corp.

St. Lawrence Seaway
Management Corp.

Fleet #.	Fleet Name Vessel Name	Type of Vessel	Year Built	Type of Engine	Cargo Cap. or Gross*	Overall Length	Breadth	Depth or Draft*
H-10	**HOLLY MARINE TOWING, CHICAGO, IL**							
	Chris Ann	TB	1981	D	45*	51' 09"	17' 00"	6' 01"
	(Captain Robbie '81 - '90, Philip M. Pearse '90 - '97)							
	Holly Ann	TB	1926	D	220*	108' 00"	26' 06"	15' 00"
	(Wm. A. Lydon '26 - '92)							
	Margaret Ann	TB	1954	D	131*	82' 00"	24' 06"	11' 06"
	(John A. McGuire '54 - '87, William Hoey '87 - '94)							
	New Mexico {2}	TB	1961	D	96*	65' 06"	24' 00"	9' 00"
H-11	**HORNE TRANSPORTATION, WOLFE ISLAND, ON**							
	William Darrell	CF	1952	D	66*	66' 00"	28' 00"	6' 00"
H-12	**HOWE ISLAND TOWNSHIP, KINGSTON, ON**							
	The Howe Islander	CF	1946	D	13*	53' 00"	12' 00"	3' 00"
H-13	**HULLFORMS (CANADA), INC., WIARTON, ON**							
	Cloud Chaser	ES	1979	D	62*	67' 00"	17' 00"	11' 00"
H-14	**HYDROGRAPHIC SURVEY CO., CHICAGO, IL**							
	Neptune	RV	1970	D		67' 00"	18' 05"	5' 00"
I-1	**ILLINOIS MARINE TOWING, INC., LEMONT, IL**							
	Aggie C	TB	1977	D	89*	81' 00"	26' 00"	6' 10"*
	Albert C	TB	1971	D	47*	61' 02"	18' 00"	5' 08"*
	Chicago Peace	TB	1979	D	101*	61' 04"	26' 00"	8' 00"*
	Eileen C	TB	1982	D	122*	75' 00"	26' 00"	8' 00"*
	Hennepin I	TB	1957	D	35*	48' 04"	16' 00"	4' 00"*
	Mary C	TB	1946	D	34*	56' 02"	18' 00"	5' 00"*
	William C	TB	1968	D	105*	76' 06"	24' 00"	6' 06"*
I-2	**IMPERIAL OIL LTD. - ESSO PETROLEUM CANADA DIVISION, DARTMOUTH, NS**							
	Imperial Dartmouth	RT	1970	D	15,265	205' 06"	40' 00"	16' 00"
	Imperial Lachine {2}	RT	1963	D	9,415	175' 00"	36' 00"	14' 00"
I-3	**INLAND BULK TRANSFER, CLEVELAND, OH**							
	Benjamin Ridgeway	TB	1969	D	51*	53' 00"	18' 05"	7' 05"
	Frank Palladino Jr.	TB	1980	D	89*	100' 00"	32' 00"	13' 00"
	(Lady Ida '80 - '92)							
	Inland 2401	DB	1968	B	2,589	240' 00"	72' 00"	14' 00"
	James Palladino	TB	1999	D	392*	109' 11"	34' 01"	16' 01"
	Kellstone 1	SU	1957	B	9,000	396' 00"	71' 00"	22' 06"
	(M-211 '57 - '81, Virginia '81 - '88, C-11 '88 - '93)							
I-4	**INLAND LAKES MANAGEMENT, INC., ALPENA, MI**							
	Alpena {2}	CC	1942	T	15,550	519' 06"	67' 00"	35' 00"
	(Leon Fraser '42 - '91)							
	E. M. Ford	CC	1898	Q	7,100	428' 00"	50' 00"	28' 00"
	(Presque Isle {1} 1898 - '56)							
	(Built in 1898 and equiped with an engine built in 1897, the E. M. Ford is the oldest Great Lakes cargo vessel.) *(Last operated 16 September, 1996 — 5 year survey expires July, 2001.)* *(Currently in use as a stationary cement storage / transfer vessel in Saginaw, MI.)*							
	J. A. W. Iglehart	CC	1936	T	12,500	501' 06"	68' 03"	37' 00"
	(Pan Amoco '36 - '55, Amoco '55 - '60, H. R. Schemn '60 - '65)							
	Paul H. Townsend	CC	1945	D	8,400	447' 00"	50' 00"	29' 00"
	(USNS Hickory Coll '45 - '46, USNS Coastal Delegate '46 - '52)							
	S. T. Crapo	CC	1927	R	8,900	402' 06"	60' 03"	29' 00"
	(Last operated 4 September, 1996 — 5 year survey expired October, 1997.) *(Currently in use as a stationary cement storage / transfer vessel in Green Bay, WI.)*							
I-5	**INLAND SEAS EDUCATION ASSOCIATION, SUTTONS BAY, MI**							
	Inland Seas	RV	1994	W	41*	61' 06"	17' 00"	7' 00"
I-6	**THE INTERLAKE STEAMSHIP CO., RICHFIELD, OH**							
	Charles M. Beeghly	SU	1959	T	31,000	806' 00"	75' 00"	37' 06"
	(Shenango II '59 - '67)							
	Elton Hoyt 2nd {2}	SU	1952	T	22,300	698' 00"	70' 00"	37' 00"
	Herbert C. Jackson	SU	1959	T	24,800	690' 00"	75' 00"	37' 06"
	James R. Barker	SU	1976	D	63,300	1,004' 00"	105' 00"	50' 00"
	Mesabi Miner	SU	1977	D	63,300	1,004' 00"	105' 00"	50' 00"
	Paul R. Tregurtha	SU	1981	D	68,000	1,013' 06"	105' 00"	56' 00"
	(William J. DeLancey '81 - '90)							
	(At 1,013' 06" long, the Paul R. Tregurtha is the longest cargo vessel operating on the Great Lakes.)							
	INTERLAKE TRANSPORTATION, INC. - A DIVISION OF THE INTERLAKE STEAMSHIP CO.							
	Dorothy Ann	TBA	1999	D	1,600*	124' 03"	44' 00"	24' 00"
	Pathfinder {3}	SU	1953	B	21,260	606' 02"	70' 00"	36' 00"
	(J. L. Mauthe '53 - '97)							
	[Dorothy Ann / Pathfinder {3} overall dimensions together]					700' 00"	70' 00"	36' 00"

Fleet #.	Fleet Name Vessel Name	Type of Vessel	Year Built	Type of Engine	Cargo Cap. or Gross*	Overall Length	Breadth	Depth or Draft*
	(J. L. Mauthe '53 - '97)							
	[Dorothy Ann / Pathfinder {3} overall dimensions together]					700' 00"	70' 00"	36' 00"
	LAKES SHIPPING CO., INC. - A DIVISION OF THE INTERLAKE STEAMSHIP CO.							
	John Sherwin {2}	BC	1958	T	31,500	806' 00"	75' 00"	37' 06"
	(Last operated 16 Nov. 1981 — 5 year survey expired May, 1984 — Currently laid up in Superior, WI.)							
	Kaye E. Barker	SU	1952	T	25,900	767' 00"	70' 00"	36' 00"
	(Edward B. Greene '52 - '85, Benson Ford {3} '85 - '89)							
	Lee A. Tregurtha	SU	1942	T	29,300	826' 00"	75' 00"	39' 00"
	(Laid down as Mobiloil, Launched as Samoset, USS Chiwawa [AO-68] '42 - '46, Chiwawa '46 - '61,							
	Walter A. Sterling '61 - '85, William Clay Ford {2} '85 - '89)							
	(The Lee A. Tregurtha earned 2 Battle Stars and was awarded the <u>American Campaign Medal</u>;							
	<u>American Defense Service Medal</u>; <u>European-African Middle Eastern Campaign with Bronze Star</u>;							
	<u>Asiatic-Pacific Campaign with Bronze Star</u>; <u>World War II Victory Medal</u>; <u>World War II Occupation</u>							
	<u>Medal</u> during World War II as the USS Chiwawa [AO-68].)							
I-7	INTERNATIONAL MARINE SYSTEMS LTD., MILWAUKEE, WI							
	Iroquois {1}	ES	1946	D	57*	61' 09"	21' 00"	6' 04"
I-8	IRVINGDALE SHIPPING LTD., SAINT JOHN, NB							
	ATLANTIC TOWING LTD. - A DIVISION OF IRVINGDALE SHIPPING LTD.							
	ATL 2301	DB	1977	B	3,500	230' 00"	60' 00"	14' 00"
	ATL 2302	DB	1977	B	3,500	230' 00"	60' 00"	14' 00"
	ATL 2401	DB	1981	B	4,310	240' 00"	70' 00"	15' 00"
	ATL 2402	DB	1981	B	4,310	240' 00"	70' 00"	15' 00"
	Atlantic Adler	TB	1982	D	149*	59' 09"	28' 00"	11' 00"
	(Gordon Gill '82 - '97)							
	Atlantic Beech	TB	1983	D	294*	104' 02"	30' 03"	13' 02"
	(Irving Beech '83 - '98)							
	Atlantic Birch	TT	1967	D	827*	162' 03"	38' 02"	19' 08"
	(Irving Birch '67 - '99)							
	Atlantic Cedar	TB	1974	D	708*	148' 04"	35' 07"	21' 06"
	(Sinni '74 - '81, Irving Cedar '81 - '96)							
	Atlantic Eagle	TT	1999	D	3,080*	247' 06"	59' 05"	19' 10"
	Atlantic Elm	TB	1980	D	427*	116' 01"	31' 06"	18' 08"
	(Irving Elm '80 - '98)							
	Atlantic Hawk	TT	2000	D	3,080*	247' 06"	59' 05"	19' 10"
	Atlantic Hemlock	TT	1996	D	290*	101' 00"	36' 06"	12' 06"
	Atlantic Hickory	TB	1973	D	886*	153' 06"	38' 10"	22' 00"
	(Irving Miami '73 - '95)							
	Atlantic Larch	TT	1999	D	360*	101' 01"	36' 07"	17' 01"
	Atlantic Maple	TB	1966	D	487*	125' 08"	32' 04"	17' 06"
	(Irving Maple '66 - '98)							
	Atlantic Oak	TB	1981	D	464*	160' 00"	34' 00"	15' 08"
	(Canmar Tugger '81 - '93)							
	Atlantic Pine	TB	1976	D	159*	70' 00"	24' 00"	7' 08"
	(Grampa Shorty '76 - '76, Irving Pine '76 - '98)							
	Atlantic Poplar	TB	1965	D	195*	96' 06"	30' 00"	14' 00"
	(Amherstburg '66 - '75, Irving Poplar '75 - '96)							
	Atlantic Spruce {2}	TT	1998	D	290*	101' 00"	36' 06"	17' 00"
	Atlantic Teak	TB	1976	D	265*	104' 00"	30' 00"	14' 03"
	(Essar '76 - '79, Irving Teak '79 - '96)							
	Atlantic Willow	TT	1998	D	360*	101' 00"	36' 06"	17' 00"
	Irving Dolphin	TK	1964	B	1,441	200' 00"	50' 00"	13' 00"
	Irving Juniper	TK	1961	D	247*	110' 00"	27' 02"	13' 03"
	(Thorness '61 - '84, Irving Juniper '84 - '98, Atlantic Juniper '98 - '99)							
	Irving Tamarack	TB	1969	D	86*	70' 00"	20' 00"	12' 00"
	Seal VII	TK	1974	B	3,390	223' 06"	51' 03"	14' 00"
	Sealion VII	TK	1969	B	1,548	359' 00"	74' 01"	27' 00"
	Shark VII	TK	1964	B	1,441	200' 00"	50' 00"	13' 00"
	KENT LINE LTD. - A DIVISION OF IRVINGDALE SHIPPING LTD.							
	Irving Arctic	TK	1974	D	292,960	629' 00"	90' 03"	48' 03"
	Irving Canada	TK	1981	D	297,407	628' 06"	90' 02"	48' 03"
	Irving Eskimo	TK	1980	D	292,960	629' 00"	90' 03"	48' 03"
	Irving Timber	RR	1978	D	9,265	415' 00"	66' 03"	38' 05"
	Kent Carrier	GC	1971	B	8,128	363' 00"	82' 02"	22' 03"
	(Saint John Carrier '71 - '79, Nitinat Carrier '79 - '84, Irving Carrier '84 - '92)							
	Kent Express	GC	1999	D	17,500	503' 11"	83' 00"	44' 04"
	Kent Voyageur	GC	1982	D	15,912	488' 10"	78' 01"	42' 00"
	(Reed Voyageur '82 - '88, Daishowa Voyageur '88 - '96)							
	Kent Sprint	GC	2000	D	17,500	503' 11"	83' 00"	44' 04"
	Kent Transport	GC	1971	D	7,366	362' 10"	82' 02"	22' 03"
	(Rothesay Carrier '71 - '97)							

Fleet #.	Fleet Name Vessel Name	Type of Vessel	Year Built	Type of Engine	Cargo Cap. or Gross*	Overall Length	Breadth	Depth or Draft*
I-9	**ISLAND EXPRESS BOAT LINES LTD., SANDUSKY, OH**							
	Island Rocket	PF		D		70' 00"		
	Island Rocket II	PC	1999	D				
I-10	**ISLAND FERRY SERVICES CORP., CHEBOYGAN, MI**							
	Bob Lo Islander	PF	1957	D	31*	68' 00"	21' 00"	5' 00"*
I-11	**IVY LEA 1,000 ISLANDS BOAT TOURS, IVY LEA, ON**							
	Miss Ivy Lea II	ES		D		66' 00"	15' 00"	5' 00"
	Miss Ivy Lea III	ES		D		48' 00"	12' 00"	5' 00"
J-1	**J. M. MARINE TOWING CORP., SYRACUSE, NY**							
	Ariel	TB	1945	D	27*	56' 00"	15' 10"	7' 00"*
	Dynamic	TB	1958	D	19*	34' 11"	12' 00"	4' 08"*
J-2	**J. W. WESTCOTT CO., DETROIT, MI**							
	J. W. Westcott II	MB	1949	D	11*	46' 01"	13' 04"	4' 06"
	Joseph J. Hogan	MB	1957	D	16*	40' 00"	12' 06"	5' 00"
	(Ottawa '57 - '95)							
J-3	**JACOBS INVESTMENTS - JRM, INC., CLEVELAND, OH**							
	Nautica Queen	ES	1981	D	95*	124' 00"	31' 02"	8' 10"
	(Bay Queen '81 - '85, Arawanna Queen '85 - '88, Star of Nautica '88 - '92)							
J-4	**JAMES MAZUREK, HARRISON TWP., MI**							
	West Wind	TB	1941	D	54*	60' 04"	17' 01"	7' 07"
J-5	**JOSEPH G. GAYTON, HARROW, ON**							
	Jenny T. II	TB	1915	D	66*	68' 07"	17' 00"	11' 00"
	(Ashtabula '15 - '55, Tiffin '55 - '69)							
	Princess No. 1	TB	1903	D	87*	77' 00"	20' 04"	7' 11"
	(Radiant '03 - '33, Anna Sheridan '33 - '62, Princess '62 - '77)							
J-6	**JOSEPH MARTIN, BEAVER ISLAND, MI**							
	Shamrock {1}	TB	1933	D	60*	64' 00"	18' 00"	7' 04"
J-7	**JUBILEE QUEEN CRUISES, TORONTO, ON**							
	Jubilee Queen	ES	1986	D	269*	122' 00"		
	(Pioneer Princess III '86 - '89)							
	Pioneer Princess	ES	1984	D	74*	56' 00"		
	Pioneer Queen	ES	1968	D	110*	85' 00"	30' 06"	7' 03"
	(Peche Island III '68 - '71, Papoose IV '71 - '96)							
K-1	**KADINGER MARINE SERVICE, INC., MILWAUKEE, WI**							
	David J. Kadinger Jr.	TB	1969	D	98*	65' 06"	22' 00"	8' 06"
	Jason A. Kadinger	TB	1963	D	60*	52' 06"	19' 01"	7' 04"
	Ruffy J. Kadinger	TB	1981	D	74*	55' 00"	23' 00"	7' 02"
K-2	**KCBX TERMINALS CO., CHICAGO, IL**							
	Matador VI	TB	1971	D	31*	42' 00"	18' 00"	6' 00"*
K-3	**KELLEY'S ISLAND FERRY BOAT LINES, MARBLEHEAD, OH**							
	Erie Isle	CF	1951	D	59*	72' 00"	24' 00"	8' 03"
	(Erie Isle '51 - '92, Marblehead '92 - '93)							
	Kayla Marie	CF	1975	D		122' 00"	40' 00"	
	(R. Bruce Etherige '75 - '97)							
	Shirley Irene	CF	1991	D	68*	160' 00"	46' 00"	9' 00"
K-4	**KEMMA JO WALSH, ZEELAND, MI**							
	Captain Barnaby	TB	1956	D	146*	94' 00"	27' 00"	11' 09"
	(William C. Gaynor '56 - '88)							
K-5	**KEWEENAW EXCURSIONS, INC., HOUGHTON, MI**							
	Keweenaw Star	ES		D		110' 00"		
	(Atlantic Star ? - ?)							
K-6	**KEYSTONE GREAT LAKES, INC., BALA CYNWYD, PA**							
	Great Lakes {2}	TK	1982	B	75,000	414' 00"	60' 00"	30' 00"
	(Amoco Great Lakes '82 - '85)							
	Michigan {10}	TB	1982	D	293*	107' 08"	34' 00"	16' 00"
	(Amoco Michigan '82 - '85)							
	[Great Lakes {2} / Michigan {10} overall dimensions together]					454' 00"	60' 00"	30' 00"
K-7	**KINDRA LAKE TOWING LP., DOWNERS GROVE, IL**							
	Buckley	TB	1958	D	94*	95' 00"	26' 00"	11' 00"
	(Linda Brooks '58 - '67, Eddie B. {2} '67 - '95)							
	Morgan	TB	1974	D	134*	90' 00"	30' 00"	10' 06"
	(Donald O' Toole '74 - '86, Bonesey B. '86 - '95)							
	Old Mission	TB	1945	D	94*	85' 00"	23' 00"	10' 04"
	(U. S. Army ST-880 '45 - '47, USCOE Avondale '47 - '64, Adrienne B. '64 - '95)							

LADY LIBERTY VISITS

One of the highlights of summer 2000 was the visit to the Great Lakes and Seaway by the operational World War II Liberty Ship John W. Brown, based at Boston.

Although the main purpose of the Brown's trip was to have rivet work done by Toledo Shipbuilding Co., a series of 'living history' cruises attracted hundreds of passengers at several ports.

She is shown at right in the Welland Canal, and below passing the Detroit skyline, the tug Patricia Hoey assisting.

(Both photos John C. Meyland)

Fleet #.	Fleet Name Vessel Name	Type of Vessel	Year Built	Type of Engine	Cargo Cap. or Gross*	Overall Length	Breadth	Depth or Draft*
K-8	**KING COMPANY, INC., HOLLAND, MI**							
	Barry J	TB	1943	D	42*	46' 00"	13' 00"	7' 00"
	Carol Ann	TB	1981	D	115*	68' 00"	24' 00"	8' 08"
	Julie Dee	TB	1903	D	59*	63' 03"	17' 05"	9' 00"
	(Bonita {1} '03 - '16, Chicago Harbor No. 4 '16 - '60, Eddie B. {1} '60 - '69, Seneca Queen '69 - '70,							
	Ludington '70 -?)							
	Miss Edna	TB	1935	D	29*	36' 08"	11' 02"	4' 08"
	Muskegon {2}	TB	1973	D	138*	75' 00"	24' 00"	11' 06"
K-9	**KINGSTON 1,000 ISLANDS CRUISES, KINGSTON, ON**							
	Island Belle I	ES	1988	D	150*	65' 00"	22' 00"	8' 00"
	(Spirit of Brockville '88 - '91)							
	Island Queen III	ES	1975	D	300*	96' 00"	26' 00"	11' 00"
	Island Star	ES	1994	D	220*	97' 00"	30' 00"	10' 00"
L-1	**LAFARGE CORP., SOUTHFIELD, MI**							
	J. B. Ford	CC	1904	R	8,000	440' 00"	50' 00"	28' 00"
	(Edwin F. Holmes '04 - '16, E. C. Collins '16 - '59)							
	(Last operated 15 November, 1985 — 5 year survey expired November, 1989.)							
	(Currently in use as a stationary cement storage / transfer vessel in Green Bay, WI.)							
L-2	**LAKE MICHIGAN CARFERRY SERVICE, INC., LUDINGTON, MI**							
	Badger [43] {2}	CF	1953	S	4,244*	410' 06"	59' 06"	24' 00"
	(The Badger [43] {2} is the last operating coal fired Great Lakes cargo vessel.)							
	Spartan [42] {2}	CF	1952	S	4,244*	410' 06"	59' 06"	24' 00"
	(Last operated 20 Jan. 1979 — 5 year survey expired Jan. 1981 — Currently laid up in Ludington, MI.)							
	Wynken, Blynken and Nod	CF	1957	D	73*	61' 01"	28' 10"	8' 06"
	(Rebel '57 - '94)							
L-3	**LAKE MICHIGAN CONTRACTORS, INC., HOLLAND, MI**							
	Art Lapish	TB	1954	D	15*	44' 03"	12' 08"	5' 04"
	Cherokee {3}	DB	1943	B	1,500	155' 00"	50' 00"	13' 00"
	Curly B.	TB	1956	D	131*	84' 00"	26' 00"	9' 02"
	(Waverly '56 - '74, Bother Collins '74 - '80)							
	G. W. Falcon	TB	1936	D	22*	49' 07"	13' 08"	6' 02"
	Illinois {3}	DS	1971	B	521*	140' 00"	50' 00"	9' 00"
	Iroquois {2}	DS	1950	B	495*	120' 00"	30' 00"	7' 00"
	James Harris	TB	1943	D	18*	41' 09"	12' 05"	5' 07"
	John Henry	TB	1954	D	66*	70' 00"	20' 06"	9' 07"
	(U. S. Army ST-2013 '54 - '80)							
	Mohawk	TB	1945	D		65' 00"	19' 00"	10' 06"
	Ojibway {2}	DS	1954	B	517*	120' 00"	50' 00"	10' 00"
	Shirley Joy	TB	1978	D	98*	72' 00"	26' 00"	7' 06"
	(Douglas B. Mackie '78 - '97)							
	Sioux {1}	DS	1954	B	518*	120' 00"	50' 00"	10' 00"
L-4	**LAKE MICHIGAN HARDWOOD CO., LELAND, MI**							
	Glen Shore	PK	1957	D	105	68' 00"	21' 00"	6' 00"
L-5	**LAKE SUPERIOR EXCURSIONS, BEAVER BAY, MN**							
	Grampa Woo III	ES	1978	D		115' 00"	22' 00"	5' 00"*
	(Southern Comfort '78 - '97)							
L-6	**LAKE TOWING, INC., AVON, OH**							
	Jiggs	TB	1911	D	45*	61' 00"	16' 00"	8' 00"
	Johnson	TB	1976	D	287*	140' 06"	40' 00"	15' 06"
	Johnson II	TB	1975	D	311*	194' 00"	40' 00"	17' 00"
	2361	BC	1967	B	3,600	236' 00"	50' 00"	15' 10"
	3403	SU	1963	B	9,500	340' 00"	62' 06"	25' 04"
L-7	**LAKES PILOTS ASSOCIATION, PORT HURON, MI**							
	Huron Belle	PB	1979	D	21*	50' 00"	16' 00"	7' 09"
	Huron Maid	PB	1976	D		46' 00"	16' 00"	
L-8	**LAURIN MARITIME (AMERICA), INC., HOUSTON, TX**							
	Mountain Blossom	TK	1986	D	70,020	527' 07"	74' 11"	39' 04"
	Nordic Blossom	TK	1981	D	152,216	505' 03"	74' 07"	45' 04"
	(Nordic Sun '81 - '89, Nordic '89 - '94)							
	Sunny Blossom	TK	1986	D	92,326	527' 07"	74' 11"	39' 05"
L-9	**LE BATEAU-MOUCHE AU VIEUX, MONTREAL, QC**							
	Le Bateau-Mouche	ES	1992	D	190*	108' 00"	22' 00"	3' 00"
L-10	**LE BRUN NORTHERN CONTRACTING, THUNDER BAY, ON**							
	Henry T.	DB	1932	B	1,000	120' 00"	44' 00"	11' 00"
L-11	**LE GROUPE OCEAN, INC., QUEBEC, QC**							
	Betsiamites	SU	1969	B	11,600	402' 00"	75' 00"	24' 00"

Fleet #.	Fleet Name Vessel Name	Type of Vessel	Year Built	Type of Engine	Cargo Cap. or Gross*	Overall Length	Breadth	Depth or Draft*
	Elmglen {2}	BC	1952	B	21,425	678' 00"	68' 03"	36' 03"
	(John O. McKellar {2} '52 - '84) **(Last operated in 24 June, 1990 — Currently laid up in Quebec, QC.)**							
	H-9901	TT	2000	D	302*	80' 00"	30' 00"	13' 04"
	HMDC No. 4	BC	1967	B	1,200	195' 00"	35' 00"	12' 00"
	HMDC No. 5	BC	1965	B	1,200	195' 00"	35' 00"	12' 00"
	Lac St-Francois	BC	1979	B	1,200	195' 00"	35' 00"	12' 00"
	La Prairie	TB	1975	D	110*	73' 09"	25' 09"	11' 08"
	McAllister No. 3	DB	1956	B	1,000	165' 00"	38' 00"	9' 00"
	Nanook	GC	1946	B	736	225' 00"	38' 00"	12' 06"
	Ocean Abys	DB	1948	B	1,000	140' 00"	40' 00"	9' 00"
	Ocean Bravo	TB	1970	D	320*	110' 00"	28' 06"	17' 00"
	(Takis V. '70 - '80, Donald P '80 - '80, Nimue '80 - '83, Donald P. '83 - '98)							
	Ocean Charlie	TB	1973	D	448*	123' 02"	31' 06"	18' 09"
	(Leonard W. '73 - '98)							
	Ocean Delta	TB	1973	D	722*	136' 08"	35' 08"	22' 00"
	(Sistella '73 - '78, Sandy Cape '78 - '80, Captain Ioannis S. '80 - '99)							
	Ocean Echo II	TBA	1969	D	438*	104' 08"	35' 05"	18' 00"
	(Atlantic '69 - '75, Laval '75 - '96)							
	Ocean Foxtrot	TB	1971	D	700*	184' 05"	38' 05"	16' 07"
	(Polor Shore '71 - '77, Canmar Supplier VII '77 - '95)							
	Ocean Jupiter {2}	TT	1999	D	302*	80' 00"	30' 00"	13' 04"

McALLISTER TOWING & SALVAGE, INC. - A SUBSIDIARY OF LE GROUPE OCEAN, INC.

	Basse-Cote	DB	1932	B	400	201' 00"	40' 00"	12' 00"
	Cathy McAllister	TB	1954	D	225*	101' 10"	26' 00"	13' 08"
	(Charlie S. '54 - '75)							
	Navcomar #1	DB	1955	B	500	135' 00"	35' 00"	9' 00"
	Ocean Alpha	TB	1960	D	202*	91' 06"	27' 03"	12' 06"
	(Jerry G. '60 - '98)							
	Ocean Golf	TB	1959	D	159*	103' 00"	25' 10"	11' 09"
	(Launched as Stranton, Helen M. McAllister '59 - '97)							
	Ocean Hercule	TB	1976	D	448*	120' 00"	32' 00"	19' 00"
	(Stril Pilot '76 - '81, Spirit Sky '81 - '86, Ierland '86 - '89, Ierlandia '89 - '95, Charles Antoine '95 - '97)							
	Ocean Intrepide	TT	1998	D	302*	80' 00"	30' 01"	14' 09"
	Salvage Monarch	TB	1959	D	219*	97' 09"	28' 00"	14' 06"

SOREL TUGBOATS, INC. - A SUBSIDIARY OF McALLISTER TOWING & SALVAGE, INC.

	Omni-Atlas	CS	1913	B	479*	133' 00"	42' 00"	10' 00"
	Omni-Richelieu	TB	1969	D	144*	83' 00"	24' 06"	13' 06"
	(Port Alfred II '69 - '82)							
	Omni Sorel	TB	1962	D	71*	72' 00"	19' 00"	12' 00"
	(Angus M. '62 - '92)							
	Omni St-Laurent	TB	1957	D	161*	99' 02"	24' 09"	12' 06"
	(Diligent '57 - '89)							
L-12	**LEE MARINE LTD., SOMBRA, ON**							
	Hammond Bay	ES	1992	D	43*	54' 00"	16' 00"	3' 00"
	(Scrimp & Scrounge '92 - '95)							
	Nancy A. Lee	TB	1939	D	9*	40' 00"	12' 00"	3' 00"
L-13	**LOCK TOURS CANADA BOAT CRUISES, SAULT STE. MARIE, ON**							
	Chief Shingwauk	ES	1965	D	109*	70' 00"	24' 00"	4' 06"
L-14	**LOWER LAKES TOWING LTD., PORT DOVER, ON**							

BLACK CREEK SHIPPING CO. - OWNER

	Cuyahoga	SU	1943	D	15,675	620' 00"	60' 00"	35' 00"
	(J. Burton Ayers '43 - '95)							
	(The Cuyahoga is a L6-S-A1 class "Maritime" vessel built by American Shipbuilding Co.)							
	Saginaw {3}	SU	1953	T	20,200	639' 03"	72' 00"	36' 00"
	(John J. Boland {3} '53 - '99)							

LOWER LAKES TRANSPORTATION CO. - A SUBSIDARY OF LOWER LAKES TOWING LTD.

	Calcite II	SU	1929	D	12,650	604' 09"	60' 00"	32' 00"
	(William G. Clyde '29 - '61)							
	George A. Sloan	SU	1943	D	15,800	620' 06"	60' 00"	35' 00"
	(Hill Annex '43 - '43)							
	(The George A. Sloan is a L6-S-B1 class "Maritime" vessel built by Great Lakes Engineering Works.)							
	Invincible	TBA	1979	D	180*	100' 00"	35' 00"	22' 06"
	(R. W. Sesler '79 - '91)							
	Myron C. Taylor	SU	1929	D	12,450	603' 09"	60' 00"	32' 00"

LAKE SERVICE SHIPPING CO. - OWNER

	McKee Sons	SU	1945	B	19,900	579' 02"	71' 06"	38' 06"
	(USNS Marine Angel '45 - '52)							

Fleet #.	Fleet Name Vessel Name	Type of Vessel	Year Built	Type of Engine	Cargo Cap. or Gross*	Overall Length	Breadth	Depth or Draft*
L-15	**LUEDTKE ENGINEERING CO., FRANKFORT, MI**							
	Alan K. Luedtke	TB	1944	D	149*	86' 04"	23' 00"	10' 03"
	(U. S. Army ST-527 '44 - '55, USCOE Two Rivers '55 - '90)							
	Chris E. Luedtke	TB	1936	D	18*	45' 00"	12' 03"	6' 00"
	Erich R. Luedtke	TB	1939	D	18*	45' 00"	12' 03"	6' 00"
	Gretchen B.	TB	1943	D	18*	45' 00"	12' 03"	6' 00"
	Karl E. Luedtke	TB	1928	D	32*	59' 03"	14' 09"	8' 00"
	Kurt Luedtke	TB	1956	D	96*	72' 00"	22' 06"	7' 06"
	(Jere C. '56 - '90)							
	Paul L. Luedtke	TB	1935	D	18*	42' 06"	11' 09"	6' 09"
M-1	**M. C. M. MARINE, INC., SAULT STE. MARIE, MI**							
	Drummond Islander II	CF	1961	D	97*	65' 00"	36' 00"	9' 00"
	Mackinaw City	TB	1943	D	23*	38' 00"	11' 05"	4' 07"
	Madison	TB		D				
	T & T DREDGING - OWNER							
	Bonnie G. Selvick	TB	1928	D	95*	86' 00"	21' 00"	12' 00"
	(E. James Fucik '28 - '77)							
	Louise	DR		B				
	Wolverine	TB	1952	D		42' 05"	12' 05"	5' 00"
M-2	**MacDONALD MARINE LTD., GODERICH, ON**							
	Debbie Lyn	TB	1950	D	10*	45' 00"	14' 00"	10' 00"
	(Skipper '50 - '60)							
	Donald Bert	TB	1953	D	11*	45' 00"	14' 00"	10' 00"
	Dover	TB	1931	D	70*	84' 00"	17' 00"	6' 00"
	Ian Mac	TB	1955	D	12*	45' 00"	14' 00"	10' 00"
M-3	**MADELINE ISLAND FERRY LINE, INC., LaPOINTE, WI**							
	Bayfield {2}	CF	1952	D	83*	120' 00"	43' 00"	10' 00"
	(Charlotte '52 - '99)							
	Island Queen {2}	CF	1966	D	90*	75' 00"	34' 09"	10' 00"
	Madeline	CF	1984	D	97*	90' 00"	35' 00"	8' 00"
	Nichevo II	CF	1962	D	89*	65' 00"	32' 00"	8' 09"
M-4	**MAID OF THE MIST STEAMBOAT CO. LTD., NIAGARA FALLS, ON**							
	Maid of the Mist	ES	1987	D	54*	65' 00"	16' 00"	7' 00"
	Maid of the Mist III	ES	1972	D	54*	65' 00"	16' 00"	7' 00"
	Maid of the Mist IV	ES	1976	D	74*	72' 00"	16' 00"	7' 00"
	Maid of the Mist V	ES	1983	D	74*	72' 00"	16' 00"	7' 00"
	Maid of the Mist VI	ES	1990	D	155*	78' 09"	29' 06"	7' 00"
	Maid of the Mist VII	ES	1997	D	160*	80' 00"	30' 00"	7' 00"
M-5	**MALCOLM MARINE, ST. CLAIR, MI**							
	Manitou {2}	TB	1943	D	491*	110' 00"	26' 05"	11' 06"
	(USCGC Manitou [WYT-60] '43 - '84)							
M-6	**MANITOU ISLAND TRANSIT, LELAND, MI**							
	Manitou Isle	PK	1946	D	10	52' 00"	14' 00"	8' 00"
	(Namaycush '46 - '59)							
	Mishe-Mokwa	CF	1966	D	49*	65' 00"	17' 06"	8' 00"
	(LaSalle '66 - '80)							
M-7	**MANSON CONSTRUCTION CO., INC., BUFFALO, NY**							
	Burro	TB	1965	D	19*	36' 00"	13' 03"	5' 01"
	J. G. II	TB	1944	D	16*	42' 03"	13' 00"	5' 06"
	Marcey	TB	1966	D	22*	42' 00"	12' 06"	6' 10"
M-8	**MARINE ATLANTIC, INC., MONCTON, NB**							
	Atlantic Freighter	RR	1978	D	8,661	495' 05"	71' 01"	48' 01"
	(Tor Felicia '78 - '78, Merzario Grecia '78 - '83, Stena Grecia '83 - '86)							
	Caribou	CF	1986	D	27,213*	587' 04"	84' 01"	27' 06"
	Joseph & Clara Smallwood	CF	1989	D	27,614*	587' 03"	84' 01"	22' 02"
M-9	**MARINE CONTRACTING CORP., PORT CLINTON, OH**							
	Pioneerland	TB	1943	D	45*	59' 06"	17' 00"	7' 06"*
	Prairieland	TB	1955	D	29*	50' 00"	15' 07"	6' 05"*
	Timberland	TB	1946	D	19*	44' 00"	13' 05"	6' 11"*
M-10	**MARINE MANAGEMENT, INC., BRUSSELS, WI**							
	Nathan S.	TB	1954	D	76*	66' 00"	19' 00"	9' 00"
	(Sanita '54 - '77, Soo Chief '77 - '81, Susan M. Selvick '81 - '91)							
	Nicole S.	TB	1949	D	146*	88' 07"	24' 10"	10' 09"
	(Evening Star '49 - '86, Protector '86 - '94)							

Thalassa Desgagnes upbound in the Welland Canal south of Lock 1. (Jeff Cameron)

Fleet #.	Fleet Name Vessel Name	Type of Vessel	Year Built	Type of Engine	Cargo Cap. or Gross*	Overall Length	Breadth	Depth or Draft*
M-11	**MARINE SALVAGE CO. LTD., PORT COLBORNE, ON**							
	Sea Castle	CC	1909	B	2,600	260' 00"	43' 00"	25' 03"
	(Kaministiquia {2} '09 - '16, Westoil '16 - '23, J. B. John {1} '23 - '51, John L. A. Galster '51 - '69)							
	(5 year survey expired November, 1983 — Currently laid up in Muskegon, MI.)							
M-12	**MARINE TECH OF DULUTH, INC., DULUTH, MN**							
	B. Yetter	DR	1986	B	338*	120' 00"	48' 00"	7' 00"
	Jason	TB	1945	D	21*	48' 00"	12' 01"	7' 00"
	(Ashland {2} '44 - '72, Charles F. Liscomb '72 - '94)							
	Nancy Ann	TB	1910	D	51*	64' 03"	16' 09"	8' 06"
	(Chattanooga '10 - '79, Howard T. Hagen '79 - '94)							
M-13	**MARINE TOWING, INC., PORT CLINTON, OH**							
	Retriever	TB	1960	D	13*	38' 00"	12' 01"	5' 04"*
M-14	**MARIPOSA CRUISE LINE, TORONTO, ON**							
	Captain Matthew Flinders	ES	1982	D	696*	144' 00"	40' 00"	8' 06"
	Mariposa Belle	ES	1970	D	195*	93' 00"	23' 00"	8' 00"
	(Niagara Belle '70 - '73)							
	Northern Spirit I	ES	1983	D	489*	136' 00"	31' 00"	9' 00"
	(New Spirit '83 - '89, Pride of Toronto '89 - '92)							
	Oriole	ES	1987	D	200*	75' 00"	23' 00"	9' 00"
	Rosemary	ES	1960	D	52*	68' 00"	15' 06"	6' 08"
	Showboat Royal Grace	ES	1988	D	135*	58' 00"	18' 00"	4' 00"
	Torontonian	ES	1962	D	68*	68' 00"	18' 06"	6' 08"
	(Shiawassie '62 - '82)							
M-15	**MARITIME INVESTING LLC., GLADSTONE, MI**							
	Manitowoc	TF	1926	B	27 rail cars	371' 03"	67' 03"	22' 06"
	Roanoke {2}	TF	1930	B	30 rail cars	381' 06"	58' 03"	22' 06"
	(City of Flint 32 '30 - '70)							
	Windsor {2}	TF	1930	B	28 rail cars	370' 05"	65' 00"	21' 06"
	(Above three last operated 1 May, 1994 — Above three currently laid up in Toledo, OH.)							
	Pere Marquette 10	TF	1945	B	27 rail cars	400' 00"	53' 00"	22' 00"
	(Last operated 7 October, 1994 — Currently laid up in Port Huron, MI.)							
M-16	**MARTIN GAS & OIL, BEAVER ISLAND, MI**							
	West Shore {2}	CF	1947	D	94*	64' 10"	30' 00"	9' 03"
M-17	**McASPHALT INDUSTRIES LTD., SCARBOROUGH, ON**							
	McAsphalt 401	TK	1966	B	48,000	300' 00"	60' 00"	23' 00"
	(Pittson 200 '66 - '73, Pointe Levy '73 - '87)							
M-18	**McCUE & OTHERS, CEDAR POINT, ON**							
	Indian Maiden	PF	1987	D	128*	74' 00"	23' 00"	8' 00"
M-19	**McKEIL MARINE LTD., HAMILTON, ON**							
	Albert B.	DS		B	475	120' 00"	32' 00"	8' 00"
	Alice A.	TB	1970	D	564*	135' 00"	34' 09"	19' 04"
	(Warrawee '70 - '76, Seaspan Raider '76 - '87, Raider '87 - '87, Raider IV '87 - '88)							
	Argue Martin	TB	1895	D	71*	69' 00"	19' 06"	9' 00"
	(Ethel 1895 - '38, R. C. Co. Tug No.1 '38 - '58, R. C. L. Tug No. 1 '58 - '62)							
	Atomic	TB	1945	D	96*	82' 00"	20' 00"	10' 00"
	Beaver D.	TB	1955	D	15*	36' 02"	14' 09"	4' 04"
	Billie M.	TB	1897	D	35*	58' 00"	16' 00"	7' 00"
	Black Carrier	DB	1908	B	1,200	200' 06"	43' 01"	10' 00"
	Bonnie B. III	TB	1969	D	308*	100' 03"	32' 00"	17' 00"
	(Esso Oranjestad '69 - '85, Oranjestad '85 - '86, San Nicolas '86 - '87, San Nicolas I '87 - '88)							
	Carrol C I	TB	1969	D	291*	100' 03"	32' 00"	17' 00"
	(Launched as Esso Oranjestad II, Esso San Nicolas '69 - '86, San Nicolas '86 - '87, Carrol C '87 - '88)							
	Colinette	TB	1943	D	64*	65' 00"	16' 00"	7' 00"
	(Ottawa {1} '43 - '57, Lac Ottawa '57 - '66)							
	CSL Trillium	BC	1966	B	18,064	489' 10"	75' 00"	37' 05"
	(Caribbean '66 - '92, Pacnav Princess '92 - '94, CSL Trillium I '94 - '95)							
	Doug McKeil {2}	TB	1943	D	196*	130' 00"	30' 00"	15' 01"
	(U. S. Army LT-643 '44 - '77, Taurus '77 - '90, Gaelic Challenge '90 - '95, Frankie D. '95 - '97, Dawson B. '97 - '98)							
	Erie West	DB	1951	B	1,800	290' 00"	50' 00"	12' 00"
	Escort Protector	TB	1972	D	719*	171' 00"	38' 00"	16' 00"
	(Nordic VI '72 - '73, Federal 6 '73 - '81, Seafed Avalon '81 - '83, Artic Mallik '83 - '90)							
	Evans McKeil	TB	1936	D	284*	110' 07"	25' 06"	11' 06"
	(Alhajuela '36 - '70, Barbara Ann {2} '70 - '89)							
	Florence McKeil	TB	1962	D	207*	98' 05"	26' 00"	9' 07"
	(T. 4 '62 - ?, Foundation Viceroy ? - '72, Feuille D' Erable '72 - '97)							
	Glenbrook	TB	1944	D	91*	81' 00"	20' 00"	9' 07"
	Glenevis	TB	1944	D	91*	80' 06"	20' 00"	9' 07"

Fleet #.	Fleet Name Vessel Name	Type of Vessel	Year Built	Type of Engine	Cargo Cap. or Gross*	Overall Length	Breadth	Depth or Draft*
	Jarrett McKeil	TB	1956	D	197*	91' 08"	27' 04"	13' 06"
	(Robert B. No. 1 '56 - '97)							
	Jean Raymond	DB	1941	B	6,800	409' 00"	57' 00"	18' 00"
	Jerry Newberry	TB	1956	D	244*	98' 00"	28' 02"	14' 04"
	(Foundation Victor '56 - '73, Point Victor '73 - '77, Kay Cole '77 - '95)							
	John Spence	TB	1972	D	719*	171' 00"	38' 00"	15' 01"
	(Mary B. VI '72 - '81, Mary B. '81 - '82, Mary B. VI '82 - '83, Artic Tuktu '83 - '94)							
	Kate B.	TB	1950	D	12*	46' 00"	12' 10"	3' 00"
	King Fish	TB	1955	D	18*	55' 00"	16' 00"	6' 08"
	(Duchess V '55 - 2000)							
	Konigsberg	TB	1960	D	91*	41' 07"	13' 02"	7' 07"
	Lac Como	TB	1944	D	63*	65' 00"	16' 10"	7' 10"
	(Tanac 74 '44 - '64)							
	Lac Erie	TB	1944	D	65*	65' 00"	16' 10"	7' 07"
	(Tanmac '44 - '74)							
	Lac Manitoba	TB	1944	D	65*	65' 00"	16' 10"	7' 07"
	(Tanac 75 '44 - '52, Manitoba '52 - '57)							
	Le Vent	DB	1969	B	13,920	379' 09"	63' 03"	33' 08"
	Manco	TB	1951	D	263*	100' 00"	28' 00"	10' 00"
	Maritime Trader	DB	1969	B	2,636*	250' 00"	76' 01"	16' 01"
	Miss Shawn Simpson	ES		D	30*	55' 02"	13' 02"	5' 00"
	(Currently laid up in Hamilton, ON.)							
	Nunavit Trader	GC	1961	D	5,039	404' 01"	60' 05"	36' 06"
	(French River '61 - '81, Jensen Star '81 - '86, Woodland '86 - '91, Woodlands '91 - '98, Lorena 1 '98 - 2000)							
	Ocean Wrestler	TB	1972	D	807*	170' 01"	36' 02"	19' 00"
	(Wrestler '72- '89, Ocean Wrestler '89 - '96, Hadisangsuria '96 - '98)							
	Paul E. No. 1	TB	1945	D	97*	80' 00"	20' 00"	9' 07"
	(W.A.C. 4 '45 - '46, E. A. Rockett '46 - '76)							
	Peter Kamingoak	DB	1975	B	12,000	351' 03"	91' 00"	20' 08"
	Progress	TB	1948	D	123*	86' 00"	21' 00"	10' 00"
	(P. J. Murer '48 - '81, Michael D. Misner '81 - '93, Thomas A. Payette '93 - '96)							
	Salvager	TB	1961	D	429*	120' 00"	32' 09"	18' 09"
	(M. Moran '61 - '70, Port Arthur '70 - '72, M. Moran '72 - 2000)							
	Salvor	TB	1963	D	426*	120' 00"	32' 09"	18' 09"
	(Esther Moran '63 - 2000)							
	St. Clair {2}	TF	1927	B	27 rail cars	400' 00"	54' 00"	22' 00"
	(Pere Marquette 12 '27 - '70)							
	Stormont	TB	1953	D	108*	80' 00"	20' 00"	9' 07"
	Salty Dog No. 1	TK	1945	B	88,735	313' 00"	68' 03"	26' 07"
	(Fort Hoskins '45 - '66, Ocean Hauler 10 '66 - '79, ATC 610 '79 - '91)							
	Sault au Couchon	DH	1969	B	10,000	422' 11"	74' 10"	25' 07"
	Toledo	TK	1962	B	6,388	135' 00"	34' 00"	9' 00"
	Toni D.	TB	1959	D	15*	50' 00"	16' 00"	5' 00"
	Wyatt McKeil	TB	1950	D	237*	102' 06"	26' 00"	13' 06"
	(Otis Wack '50 - '97)							
	MONTREAL BOATMAN - A SUBSIDARY OF McKEIL MARINE LTD.							
	Aldo H.	TB	1979	D	37*	56' 04"	15' 04"	6' 02"
	Boatman No. 3	TB	1965	D	13*	33' 08"	11' 00"	6' 00"
	Boatman No. 4	TB	1967	D	15*	43' 03"	14' 01"	5' 09"
	Boatman No. 6	TB	1979	D	39*	56' 07"	18' 07"	6' 03"
	Pilot 1	TB	1994	D	14*	32' 01"	5' 08"	2' 06"
	REMORQUEURS & BARGES MONTREAL LTEE - A SUBSIDARY OF McKEIL MARINE LTD.							
	Cavalier	TB	1944	D	18*	40' 00"	10' 05"	4' 08"
	Connie E.	TB	1974	D	9*	30' 00"	11' 00"	6' 00"
	D. C. Everest	CS	1953	D	3,017	259' 00"	43' 06"	21' 00"
	(D. C. Everest '53 - '81, Condarrell '82 - '89)							
	Dufresne M-58	TB	1944	D	40*	58' 08"	14' 08"	6' 02"
	Flo-Mac	TB	1960	D	15*	40' 00"	13' 00"	6' 00"
	Greta V	TB	1951	D	14*	44' 00"	12' 00"	5' 00"
	Lac Vancouver	TB	1943	D	65*	65' 00"	16' 10"	7' 07"
	(Vancouver '43 - '74)							
	Pacific Standard	TB	1967	D	451*	127' 08"	31' 00"	15' 06"
	(Irishman '67 - '76, Kwakwani '76 - '78, Lorna B. '78 - '81)							
	Techno Venture	TB	1939	D	470*	138' 03"	30' 07"	15' 01"
	(Dragonet '39 - '61, Foundation Venture '61 - '73, M.I.L. Venture '73 - '79)							
	Wyn Cooper	TB	1973	D	25*	48' 00"	13' 00"	4' 00"
M-20	**McLEOD BROTHERS MECHANICAL, SAULT STE. MARIE, ON**							
	Kam	TB	1927	D	33*	52' 00"	13' 00"	5' 06"*
	(North Shore Supply '27 - '74)							

Fleet #.	Fleet Name Vessel Name	Type of Vessel	Year Built	Type of Engine	Cargo Cap. or Gross*	Overall Length	Breadth	Depth or Draft*
M-21	**McMULLEN & PITZ CONSTRUCTION CO., MANITOWOC, WI**							
	Dauntless	TB	1937	D	25*	52' 06"	15' 06"	5' 03"
M-22	**McNALLY MARINE, INC., TORONTO, ON**							
	Bagotville	TB	1964	D	65*	65' 00"	18' 06"	10' 00"
	Carl M.	TB	1957	D	21*	47' 00"	14' 06"	6' 00"
	Halton	TB	1942	D	15*	42' 09"	14' 00"	7' 06"
	Oshawa	TB	1971	D	24*	45' 00"	14' 00"	5' 00"
	Paula M.	TB	1959	D	12*	46' 06"	16' 01"	4' 10"
	R.C. L. No. 1	TB	1958	D	20*	42' 09"	14' 03"	5' 09"
	Sandra Mary	TB	1962	D	97*	80' 00"	21' 00"	10' 09"
	(Flo Cooper '62 - 2000)							
	Whitby	TB	1978	D	24*	45' 00"	14' 00"	5' 00"
M-23	**MENASHA TUGBOAT CO., SARNIA, ON**							
	Menasha {2}	TB	1949	D	147*	78' 00"	24' 00"	9' 08"
	(W. C. Harms '49 - '54, Hamilton '54 - '86, Ruby Casho '86 - '88, W. C. Harms '88 - '97)							
M-24	**MERCURY CRUISE LINES, PALATINE, IL**							
	Chicago's First Lady	ES	1991	D	62*	96' 00"	22' 00"	9' 00"
	Chicago's Little Lady	ES	1999	D		68' 00"	23' 00"	8' 06"*
	Skyline Princess	ES	1956	D	56*	59' 04"	16' 00"	4' 08"
	Skyline Queen	ES	1959	D	45*	61' 05"	16' 10"	6' 00"
M-25	**MIDDLE BASS BOAT LINE, MIDDLE BASS, OH**							
	Victory	CF		D		100' 00"		
M-26	**MILLER BOAT LINE, INC., PUT-IN-BAY, OH**							
	Islander {3}	CF	1983	D	92*	90' 03"	38' 00"	8' 03"
	Put-In-Bay {3}	CF	1997	D	95*	96' 00"	38' 06"	9' 06"
	South Bass	CF	1989	D	95*	96' 00"	38' 06"	9' 06"
	Wm. Market	CF	1993	D	95*	96' 00"	38' 06"	8' 09"
M-27	**MILWAUKEE BULK TERMINALS, INC., MILWAUKEE, WI**							
	MBT 10	DH	1994	B	1,960	200' 00"	35' 00"	13' 00"
	MBT 20	DH	1994	B	1,960	200' 00"	35' 00"	13' 00"
	MBT 33	DB	1976	B	3,793	240' 00"	52' 06"	14' 06"*
M-28	**MONTREAL SHIPPING, INC., STEPHENVILLE, NF**							
	Point Viking	TB	1962	D	207*	98' 05"	27' 10"	13' 05"
	(Foundation Viking '62 - '75)							
M-29	**MORTON SALT CO., CHICAGO, IL**							
	Morton Salt 74	DB	1974	B	2,101	195' 00"	35' 00"	12' 00"
M-30	**MUSKOKA LAKES NAVIGATION & HOTEL CO., GRAVENHURST, ON**							
	Segwun	PA	1887	R	168*	128' 00"	24' 00"	7' 06"
	(Nipissing {2} 1887 - '25)							
	Wanda III	ES	1915	R	60*	94' 00"	12' 00"	5' 00"
	Wenonah II	ES	2001	D		127' 00"	28' 00"	6' 00"*
N-1	**N. M. PATERSON & SONS LTD. - MARINE DIVISION, THUNDER BAY, ON**							
	Cartierdoc {2}	BC	1959	D	29,100	730' 00"	75' 09"	40' 02"
	(Ems Ore '59 - '76, Montcliffe Hall '76 - '88)							
	Comeaudoc {2}	BC	1960	D	26,750	730' 00"	75' 06"	37' 09"
	(Murray Bay {2} '60 - '63)							
	(The Comeaudoc was the first 730' long cargo vessel built on the Great Lakes.)							
	(Last operated 4 Dec. 1996 — 5 year survey expires July, 2001 — Laid up in Montreal, QC.)							
	Mantadoc {2}	BC	1967	D	17,650	607' 10"	62' 00"	36' 00"
	Paterson {2}	BC	1985	D	32,600	736' 07"	75' 10"	42' 00"
	(The Paterson {2} was the last straight deck bulk freighter built for Great Lakes service.)							
	Quedoc {3}	BC	1965	D	28,050	730' 00"	75' 00"	39' 02"
	(Beavercliffe Hall '65 - '88)							
	(Last operated 20 December, 1991 — 5 year survey expired June, 1993.) (Laid up in Thunder Bay, ON.)							
	Vandoc {2}	BC	1964	D	16,000	605' 00"	62' 00"	33' 10"
	(Sir Denys Lowson '64 - '79)							
	(Last operated 21 December, 1991 — Currently laid up in Thunder Bay, ON.)							
	Windoc {2}	BC	1959	D	29,100	730' 00"	75' 09"	40' 02"
	(Rhine Ore '59 - '76, Steelcliffe Hall '76 - '88)							
N-2	**NADRO MARINE SERVICES LTD., PORT DOVER, ON**							
	Bert Verge	TB	1959	D	22*	43' 07"	14' 00"	4' 06"
	Intreped	TB	1976	D	39*	66' 00"	17' 00"	7' 06"
	Lois T.	TB	1943	D	32*	63' 00"	16' 06"	7' 06"
	(Kolbe '43 - '86)							
	Miseford	TB	1915	D	116*	85' 00"	20' 00"	10' 06"
	Nadro Clipper	TB	1939	D	64*	70' 00"	23' 00"	6' 06"
	(Stanley Clipper '39 - '94)							

Tug Dorothy Ann and barge Pathfinder unload at a Rouge River dock in Detroit.
(Capt. Albert M. Tielke)

Fleet #.	Fleet Name Vessel Name	Type of Vessel	Year Built	Type of Engine	Cargo Cap. or Gross*	Overall Length	Breadth	Depth or Draft*
	(Stanley Clipper '39 - '94)							
	Offshore Supplier	TB	1979	D	127*	92' 00"	25' 00"	11' 06"
	(Elmore M. Misener '79 - '94)							
	Sea Hound	TB	1941	D	60*	65' 06"	17' 00"	7' 00"
	([Unnamed] '41 - '56, Sea Hound '56 - '80, Carolyn Jo '80 - 2000)							
	Terry S.	TB	1958	D	16*	52' 00"	17' 00"	6' 00"
	Vac	TB	1942	D	37*	65' 00"	21' 00"	6' 06"
N-3	**NELSON CONSTRUCTION CO., LaPOINTE, WI**							
	Eclipse	TB	1937	D	23*	47' 00"	13' 00"	6' 00"
N-4	**NELVANA YACHT CHARTERS, TORONTO, ON**							
	Nelvana {1}	ES	1963	D	61*	55' 10"	16' 00"	5' 00"
N-5	**NEUMAN CRUISE & FERRY LINE, SANDUSKY, OH**							
	Commuter	CF	1960	D	81*	64' 06"	33' 00"	9' 00"
	Endeavor	CF	1987	D	98*	101' 00"	34' 06"	10' 00"
	Kelley Islander	CF	1969	D	95*	100' 00"	34' 03"	8' 00"
N-6	**NEW WORLD SHIP MANAGEMENT LLC, ST. LOUIS, MO**							
	CLIPPER CRUISE LINE							
	Clipper Adventurer	PA	1975	D	4,364*	328' 01"	53' 03"	23' 00"
	(Alla Tarasova '75 - '97)							
	Clipper Odyssey	PA	1989	D	5,200*	337' 10"	50' 07"	20' 04"
	(Oceanic Grace '89- '97, Oceanic Odyssey '97 - '99)							
	Nantucket Clipper	PA	1984	D	96*	207' 00"	37' 00"	11' 06"
	Yorktown Clipper	PA	1988	D	97*	257' 00"	43' 00"	12' 05"
N-7	**NEWFOUNDLAND TRANSSHIPMENT LTD., ST. JOHN, NF**							
	Placentia Hope	TT	1998	D	925*	125' 00"	42' 08"	17' 05"
	Placentia Pride	TT	1998	D	925*	125' 00"	42' 08"	17' 05"
N-8	**NIAGARA STEAMSHIP CO., NIAGARA ON THE LAKE, ON**							
	Pumper	ES	1903	R				
N-9	**NICHOLSON TERMINAL & DOCK CO., RIVER ROUGE, MI**							
	Charles E. Jackson	TB	1956	D	12*	35' 00"	10' 06"	5' 01"
	Detroit {1}	TF	1904	B	22 rail cars	308' 00"	76' 09"	19' 06"
N-10	**NORTH CHANNEL DIVING & MARINE, RICHARD'S LANDING, ON**							
	Opeongo	TB	1947	D	21*	50' 00"	13' 00"	6' 00"*
	Tolsma Bay	TB	1910	D	49*	65' 00"	16' 06"	8' 00"*
	(Willard L '10 - '89)							
N-11	**NORTHERN MARINE TRANSPORTATION, SAULT STE. MARIE, MI**							
	Linda Jean	PB	1950	D	17*	38' 00"	10' 00"	5' 00"
	Soo River Belle	PB	1961	D	25*	40' 00"	14' 00"	6' 00"
N-12	**NORTHUMBERLAND FERRIES LTD. / BAY FERRIES LTD., CHARLOTTETOWN, PEI**							
	Confederation {2}	CF	1993	D	8,060*	374' 08"	61' 07"	17' 09"
	Holiday Island	CF	1971	D	3,037*	325' 00"	67' 06"	16' 06"
	(William Pope '71 - '71)							
	Incat 046	CF	1997	D	5,060*	300' 00"	85' 03"	12' 01"
	(Devil Cat '97 - '98)							
	Princess of Acadia	CF	1971	D	10,051*	480' 01"	66' 00"	12' 06"
O-1	**OAK GROVE MARINE AND TRANSPORTATION, INC., CLAYTON, NY**							
	Maple Grove	PK	1954	D	55	75' 00"	21' 00"	5' 06"*
	Oak Grove	PK	1953	D	18	53' 02"	14' 00"	4' 00"*
O-2	**ODYSSEY CRUISES, CHICAGO, IL**							
	Odyssey II	ES	1993	D	101*	200' 00"	41' 00"	9' 00"*
O-3	**OGLEBAY NORTON MARINE SERVICES CO., CLEVELAND, OH**							
	Armco	SU	1953	T	25,500	767' 00"	70' 00"	36' 00"
	Buckeye {3}	SU	1952	T	22,300	698' 00"	70' 00"	37' 00"
	(Sparrows Point '52 - '90)							
	Columbia Star	SU	1981	D	78,850	1,000' 00"	105' 00"	56' 00"
	Courtney Burton	SU	1953	T	22,300	690' 00"	70' 00"	37' 00"
	(Ernest T. Weir {2} '53 - '78)							
	David Z. Norton {3}	SU	1973	D	19,650	630' 00"	68' 00"	36' 11"
	(William R. Roesch '73 - '95)							
	Earl W. Oglebay	SU	1973	D	19,650	630' 00"	68' 00"	36' 11"
	(Paul Thayer '73 - '95)							
	Fred R. White Jr.	SU	1979	D	23,800	636' 00"	68' 00"	40' 00"
	Joseph H. Frantz	SU	1925	D	13,600	618' 00"	62' 00"	32' 00"
	Middletown	SU	1942	T	26,300	730' 00"	75' 00"	39' 03"

(Laid down as Marquette, USS Neshanic [AO-71] '42 - '47, Gulfoil '47 - '61, Pioneer Challenger '61 - '62)

(The Middletown earned 9 Battle Stars and was damaged by bombs off Saipan during World War II as the USS Neshanic [AO-71].)

Fleet #.	Fleet Name / Vessel Name	Type of Vessel	Year Built	Type of Engine	Cargo Cap. or Gross*	Overall Length	Breadth	Depth or Draft*
	Oglebay Norton	SU	1978	D	78,850	1,000' 00"	105' 00"	56' 00"
	(Launched as Burns Harbor {1}, Lewis Wilson Foy '78 - '90)							
	Reserve	SU	1953	T	25,500	767' 00"	70' 00"	36' 00"
	Wolverine {4}	SU	1974	D	19,650	630' 00"	68' 00"	36' 11"
O-4	**ONTARIO MINISTRY OF TRANSPORTATION & COMMUNICATION, KINGSTON, ON**							
	Amherst Islander {2}	CF	1955	D	184*	106' 00"	38' 00"	10' 00"
	Frontenac II	CF	1962	D	666*	181' 00"	45' 00"	10' 00"
	(Charlevoix {2} '62 - '92)							
	Glenora	CF	1952	D	209*	127' 00"	33' 00"	9' 00"
	(The St. Joseph Islander '52 - '74)							
	The Quinte Loyalist	CF	1954	D	209*	127' 00"	32' 00"	8' 00"
	Wolfe Islander III	CF	1975	D	985*	205' 00"	68' 00"	6' 00"
O-5	**ONTARIO WATERWAY CRUISES, INC., ORILLIA, ON**							
	Kawartha Voyager	PA	1983	D	264*	108' 00"	22' 00"	5' 00"
O-6	**ORILLIA BOAT CRUISES LTD., ORILLIA, ON**							
	Lady Belle II	ES	1967	D	89*	65' 00"	19' 00"	5' 00"
	(Lady Midland '67 - '82)							
	Island Princess {1}	ES	1989	D	194*	65' 00"	27' 00"	5' 00"
O-7	**OSBORNE MATERIALS CO., MENTOR, OH**							
	Emmet J. Carey	SC	1948	D	900	114' 00"	23' 00"	11' 00"
	(Beatrice Ottinger '48 - '63, James B. Lyons '63 - '88)							
	F. M. Osborne {2}	SC	1910	D	500	150' 00"	29' 00"	11' 03"
	(Grand Island {1} '10 - '58, Lesco '58 - '75)							
O-8	**OWEN SOUND TRANSPORTATION CO. LTD., OWEN SOUND, ON**							
	Chi-Cheemaun	CF	1974	D	6,991*	365' 05"	61' 00"	21' 00"
	PELEE ISLAND TRANSPORTATION SERVICES - A DIVISION OF OWEN SOUND TRANS. CO. LTD.							
	Jiimaan	CF	1992	D	2,830*	176' 09"	42' 03"	13' 06"
	Pelee Islander	CF	1960	D	334*	145' 00"	32' 00"	10' 00"
P-1	**P.& H. SHIPPING - A DIVISION OF PARRISH & HEIMBECKER LTD., MISSISSAUGA, ON**							
	Mapleglen {2}	BC	1960	T	26,100	714' 11"	75' 00"	37' 09"
	(Carol Lake '60 - '87, Algocape {1} '87 - '94)							
	Oakglen {2}	BC	1954	T	22,950	714' 06"	70' 03"	37' 03"
	(T. R. McLagan '54 - '90)							
P-2	**PEMBINA EXPLORATION LTD., PORT COLBORNE, ON**							
	Louis J. Coulet	DV	1957	B	2,099*	259' 00"	43' 11"	22' 06"
	(Coniscliffe Hall {2} '57 - '74, Coniscliffe '74 - '75, Telesis '75 - '98)							
	(5 year survey expired November, 1995 — Currently laid up in Port Dover, ON.)							
P-3	**PENETANGUISHENE 30,000 ISLAND CRUISES, PENETANGUISHENE, ON**							
	Georgian Queen	ES	1918	D	249*	119' 00"	36' 00"	16' 06"
	(Victoria '18 - '18, Murray Stewart '18 - '48, David Richard '48 - '79)							
P-4	**PENETANGUISHENE MIDLAND COACH LINE 30,000 ISLAND BOAT CRUISES, MIDLAND, ON**							
	Miss Midland	ES	1974	D	119*	68' 07"	19' 04"	6' 04"
	Serendipity Princess	ES	1982	D	93*	69' 00"	23' 00"	4' 03"*
	(Trent Voyageur '82 - '87, Serendipity Lady '87 - '95)							
P-5	**PERE MARQUETTE SHIPPING CO., LUDINGTON, MI**							
	Pere Marquette 41	SU	1941	B	4,545	403' 00"	58' 00"	23' 06"
	(City of Midland 41 '41 - '97)							
	Undaunted	TBA	1944	D	860*	143' 00"	33' 01"	18' 00"
	(USS Undaunted [ATR-126, ATA-199] '44 - '63, USMA Kings Pointer '63 - '93, Krystal K. '93 - '97)							
	[Pere Marquette 41 / Undaunted overall dimensions together]					493' 06"	58' 00"	23' 06"
P-6	**PICTURED ROCKS CRUISES, INC., MUNISING, MI**							
	Grand Island {2}	ES	1989	D	51*	68' 00"	16' 01"	5' 01"
	Miners Castle	ES	1974	D	72*	68' 00"	17' 00"	5' 00"
	Miss Superior	ES	1984	D	76*	68' 00"	17' 00"	5' 00"
	Pictured Rocks	ES	1972	D	47*	60' 00"	14' 00"	4' 04"
P-7	**PIERRE GAGNE CONTRACTING LTD., THUNDER BAY, ON**							
	M A C Gagne	BC	1964	B	30,500	730' 00"	75' 02"	44' 08"
	(Saguenay {2} '64 - '98) **(Last operated 30 November, 1992 — Currently laid up in Thunder Bay, ON.)**							
P-8	**PLAUNT TRANSPORTATION CO., INC., CHEBOYGAN, MI**							
	Kristen D.	CF	1988	D	83*	64' 11"	36' 00"	6' 05"
P-9	**PORT CITY PRINCESS CRUISES, INC., MUSKEGON, MI**							
	Port City Princess	ES	1966	D	79*	64' 09"	30' 00"	5' 06"
	(Island Queen {1} '66 - '87)							

Fleet #.	Fleet Name / Vessel Name	Type of Vessel	Year Built	Type of Engine	Cargo Cap. or Gross*	Overall Length	Breadth	Depth or Draft*
P-10	**PORT DALHOUSIE PIERS, INC., ST. CATHARINES, ON**							
	Normac	PA	1902	D	462*	124' 06"	25' 00"	18' 00"
	(James R. Elliot '02 - '31)							
	(Former Owen Sound Transportation Commision vessel which last operated in 1968.)							
	(Currently in use as a floating restaurant in Port Dalhousie, ON.)							
P-11	**PORTOFINO ON THE RIVER, WYANDOTTE, MI**							
	Friendship	ES	1968	D	78*	69' 06"	23' 05"	7' 04"
	(Peche Island V '68 - '71, Papoose V '71 - '82)							
P-12	**PRESIDENT RIVERBOAT CASINO, INC., ST. LOUIS, MO**							
	Majestic Star {2}	GA	1997	D	12,805*	330' 00"	76' 00"	20' 00"
P-13	**PROTHERO, TORONTO, ON**							
	Kajama	ES	1930	D/W	263*	128' 09"	23' 01"	12' 00"
P-14	**PURVIS MARINE LTD., SAULT STE. MARIE, ON**							
	Adanac	TB	1913	D	108*	80' 03"	19' 02"	10' 06"
	(Edward C. Whalen '13 - '66, John McLean '66 - '95)							
	Anglian Lady	TB	1953	D	398*	136' 06"	30' 00"	14' 01"
	(Hamtun '53 - '72, Nathalie Letzer '72 - '88)							
	Avenger IV	TB	1962	D	293*	120' 00"	30' 05"	17' 05"
	(Avenger '62 - '85)							
	Charles W. Johnson	DB	1916	B	1,685	245' 00"	43' 00"	14' 00"
	(Iocolite '16 - '47, Imperial Kingston '47 - '61)							
	Chief Wawatam	DB	1911	B	4,500	347' 00"	62' 03"	15' 00"
	G.L.B. No. 1	DB	1953	B	3,215	305' 00"	50' 00"	12' 00"
	(Joe Baugh Jr. '53 - '66, ORG 5503 '66 - '75)							
	G.L.B. No. 2	DB	1953	B	3,215	305' 02"	50' 00"	12' 00"
	(Jane Newfield '53 - '66, ORG 6502 '66 - '75)							
	Goki	TB	1940	D	24*	57' 00"	12' 08"	7' 00"
	Malden	DB	1946	B	1,075	150' 00"	41' 09"	10' 03"
	Martin E. Johnson	TB	1959	D	26*	46' 00"	16' 00"	5' 09"
	McKeller	CS	1935	B	200	90' 00"	33' 00"	8' 00"
	Osprey	TB	1944	D	36*	45' 00"	13' 06"	7' 00"
	P.M.L. Alton	DB	1951	B	150	93' 00"	30' 00"	8' 00"
	P.M.L. Salvager	DB	1945	B	5,200	341' 00"	54' 00"	27' 00"
	([Unnamed] '45 - '55, Balsambranch '55 - '73, M.I.L. Balsam '73 - '77, Techno Balsam '77 - '77, DDS Salvager '77 - '88)							
	P.M.L. 357	DB	1944	B	600	138' 00"	38' 00"	11' 00"
	P.M.L. 2501	TK	1980	B	25,000	302' 00"	52' 00"	17' 00"
	(CTCO 2505 '80 - '96)							
	P.M.L. 9000	DB	1968	B	5,051*	400' 00"	76' 00"	20' 00"
	(Palmer '68 - '2000)							
	Rocket	TB	1901	D	39*	70' 00"	15' 00"	8' 00"
	Sheila P.	TB	1940	D	15*	40' 00"	14' 00"	
	Tecumseh II	DB	1976	B	2,500	180' 00"	54' 00"	12' 00"
	Wilfred M. Cohen	TB	1948	D	284*	104' 00"	28' 00"	14' 06"
	(A. T. Lowmaster '48 - '75)							
	W. I. Scott Purvis	TB	1938	D	206*	96' 06"	26' 04"	10' 04"
	(Orient Bay '38 - '75, Guy M. No. 1 '75 - '90)							
	W. J. Ivan Purvis	TB	1938	D	191*	100' 06"	25' 06"	9' 00"
	(Magpie '38 - '66, Dana T. Bowen '66 - '75)							
	Yankcanuck {2}	CS	1963	D	4,760	324' 03"	49' 00"	26' 00"
P-15	**PUT-IN-BAY BOAT LINE CO., PORT CLINTON, OH**							
	Express Shuttle	PF		D				
	Jet Express	PC	1989	D	93*	92' 08"	28' 06"	8' 04"
	Jet Express II	PC	1992	D	85*	92' 06"	28' 06"	8' 04"
	Jet Express III	PC	2001	D				
R-1	**RAYMOND BURTON BERKSHIRE, PLACENTIA, NF**							
	Paradise Sound	GC	1969	D	430	137' 04"	25' 00"	11' 01"
	(Tower Duchess '69 - '84)							
	Placentia Sound	GC	1969	D	713	173' 11"	29' 00"	12' 01"
	(Apollo 1 '69 - '80, Arklow River '80 - '82, Cynthia June '82 - '86, Tora '86 - '88, Greeba River '88 - '97)							
R-2	**REINAUER TRANSPORTATION COMPANIES, INC., STATEN ISLAND, NY**							
	Austin Reinauer	TB	1978	D	183*	116' 00"	32' 00"	16' 07"
	(Morania No. 20 '78 - '88, Mobil 5 '88 - '93, Tamarac '93 - '95, Morania No. 1 '95 - ?)							
	Bert Reinauer II	TK	1938	D	13,442	293' 07"	43' 01"	17' 04"
	(Paratex '38 - '75)							
	Dace Reinauer	TB	1968	D	84*	130' 00"	31' 00"	14' 06"
	Fulton	TK	1969	B	21,000	242' 07"	43' 05"	14' 10"
	George Morris	TK	1982	B	56,000	325' 00"	60' 00"	22' 00"

Fleet #.	Fleet Name Vessel Name	Type of Vessel	Year Built	Type of Engine	Cargo Cap. or Gross*	Overall Length	Breadth	Depth or Draft*
	George Morris	TK	1982	B	56,000	325' 00"	60' 00"	22' 00"
	Hartford	TK		B	25,200	295' 00"	42' 00"	12' 06"*
	May McGuirl	TB	1973	D	296*	109' 02"	32' 00"	17' 00"
	(Texaco Diesel Chief '73 - '90, Star Diesel Chief '90 - '91, Morania No. 5 '91 - ?)							
	Morgan Reinauer	TB	1981	D	184*	134' 00"	34' 00"	16' 00"
	(Elise M '81 - '88, Exxon Garden State '88 - '93)							
	New London	TK		B	25,200	295' 00"	42' 00"	12' 06"*
	Nicole Leigh Reinauer	TBA	1999	D	1,632*	124' 00"	40' 00"	21' 00"
	Peter R. Hearne	TK	1971	B	20,000	227' 00"	43' 00"	14' 09"
	Putnam	TK	1974	B	42,000	300' 00"	60' 00"	27' 00"
	Richmond	TK	1975	B	42,000	300' 00"	60' 00"	17' 00"
	Rockland	TK	1975	B	67,000	316' 06"	59' 05"	26' 02"
	Stephen Reinauer	TB	1970	D	151*	109' 00"	31' 06"	16' 00"
	(Esso Bay State '70 - '73, Exxon Bay State '73 - '93)							
	Westchester	TK	1975	B	67,000	316' 00"	60' 00"	26' 02"
	Zachery Reinauer	TB	1971	D	271*	100' 00"	28' 00"	14' 11"
	(Mobil 1 '71 - '91, Tioga '91 - '93)							
R-3	**RIGEL SHIPPING CANADA, INC., SHEDIAC, NB**							
	Diamond Star	TK	1992	D	68,019	405' 11"	58' 01"	34' 09"
	(Elbestern '92 - '93)							
	Emerald Star	TK	1992	D	68,019	405' 11"	58' 01"	34' 09"
	(Emsstern '92 - '92)							
	Jade Star	TK	1993	D	68,019	405' 11"	58' 01"	34' 09"
	(Jadestern '93 - '94)							
R-4	**ROBERT PARR, SAULT STE. MARIE, ON**							
	Mink Isle	TB	1947	D		50' 00"	13' 00"	6' 07"*
R-5	**ROCKPORT BOAT LINE (1994) LTD., ROCKPORT, ON**							
	Ida M.	ES	1970	D	29*	55' 00"	14' 00"	3' 00"
	Ida M. II	ES	1973	D	116*	63' 02"	22' 02"	5' 00"
R-6	**ROEN SALVAGE CO., STURGEON BAY, WI**							
	Chas Asher	TB	1967	D	10*	50' 00"	18' 00"	8' 00"
	John R. Asher	TB	1943	D	93*	70' 00"	20' 00"	8' 06"
	(U. S. Army ST-71 '43 - '46, Russell 8 '46 - '64, Reid McAllister '64 - '67, Donegal '67 - '85)							
	Louie S.	TB	1956	D	43*	37' 00"	12' 00"	5' 00"
	Spuds	TB	1944	D	19*	42' 00"	12' 06"	6' 00"
	Stephen M. Asher	TB	1954	D	60*	65' 00"	19' 01"	5' 04"
	(Captain Bennie '54 - '82, Dumar Scout '82 - '87)							
	Timmy A.	TB	1953	D	12*	33' 06"	10' 08"	5' 02"
R-7	**RUSSELL ISLAND TRANSIT CO., ALGONAC, MI**							
	Islander {2}	CF	1982	D		41' 00"	15' 00"	3' 06"
R-8	**RYBA MARINE CONSTRUCTION CO., CHEBOYGAN, MI**							
	Alcona	TB	1957	D	18*	40' 00"	12' 06"	5' 06"
	Amber Mae	TB	1922	D	67*	65' 00"	14' 01"	10' 00"
	(E. W. Sutton '22 - '52, Venture '52 - ?)							
	Harbor Master	CS	1979	B	100*	70' 00"	27' 00"	4' 00"
	Kathy Lynn	TB	1944	D	140*	85' 00"	24' 00"	9' 06"
	(U. S. Army ST-693 '44 - '79, Sea Islander '79 - '91)							
	Jarco 1402	CS	1981	B	473*	140' 00"	39' 00"	9' 00"
	Relief	CS	1924	B	1,000	160' 00"	40' 00"	9' 00"
	Rochelle Kaye	TB	1963	D	52*	51' 06"	19' 04"	7' 00"
	(Jaye Anne '63 - ?, Katanni ? - '97)							
	Tonawanda	CS	1935	B	600	120' 00"	45' 00"	8' 00"
S-1	**SANKORE MARINE IMMERSION HIGH SCHOOL, DETROIT, MI**							
	Huron Lady	ES	1961	D	55*	65' 00"	17' 00"	5' 00"
	(Falcon '61 - '65, Bucky '65 - '68, Holiday '68 - '72, Speedy IV '72 - '74, Capt. Bill Van '74 - '76, Pilot II '76 - '77, Capt. Eddie B. '77 - '94)							
S-2	**SAWMILL CREEK RESORT, HURON, OH**							
	Dispatch	ES	1953	D		65' 00"	17' 00"	4' 00"
	(Cedar Point II '53 - '89)							
S-3	**SCIO SHIPPING, INC., NEW YORK, NY**							
	Island Gem	BC	1984	D	28,005	584' 08"	76' 02"	48' 05"
	Island Skipper	BC	1984	D	28,031	584' 08"	76' 02"	48' 05"
S-4	**SEA FOX THOUSAND ISLANDS BOAT TOURS, KINGSTON, ON**							
	Sea Fox II	ES	1988	D	55*	39' 08"	20' 00"	2' 00"*
	Limestone Clipper	ES	1968	D	110*	85' 00"	30' 06"	7' 03"
	(Peche Island II '68 - '71, Papoose III '71 - '96)							
S-5	**SEA SERVICE L. L. C., DULUTH / SUPERIOR**							

Fleet #.	Fleet Name / Vessel Name	Type of Vessel	Year Built	Type of Engine	Cargo Cap. or Gross*	Overall Length	Breadth	Depth or Draft*
	Sea Falcon	PB		D				
	Sea Ox	DB		B				
	Sea Pilot	PB		D	18*	48' 00"	14' 00"	5' 06"*
	Sea Sparrow	TB		D				
	Sea Wolf	TB		D				
S-6	**SEARS OIL CO., ROME, NY**							
	Midstate I	TB	1942	D	106*	86' 00"	24' 00"	12' 00"
	Midstate II	TB	1945	D	137*	89' 00"	24' 00"	12' 06"
S-7	**SEAWAY MARINE TRANSPORT, ST. CATHARINES, ON**							

PARTNERSHIP BETWEEN ALGOMA CENTRAL CORP. AND UPPER LAKES GROUP, INC.

ALGOMA CENTRAL CORP.	UPPER LAKES GROUP, INC.		
Agawa Canyon	Algorail {2}	Canadian Century	Canadian Trader
Algobay	Algoriver	Canadian Enterprise	Canadian Transfer
Algocape {2}	Algosoo {2}	Canadian Leader	Canadian Transport {2}
Algocen {2}	Algosound	Canadian Mariner	Canadian Venture
Algogulf {2}	Algosteel {2}	Canadian Miner	Canadian Voyager
Algoisle	Algoville	Canadian Navigator	Gordon C. Leitch {2}
Algolake	Algoway {2}	Canadian Olympic	James Norris
Algomarine	Algowest	Canadian Progress	Montrealais
Algonorth	Algowood	Canadian Prospector	Quebecois
Algontario	Capt. Henry Jackman	Canadian Provider	Seaway Queen
Algoport	John B. Aird	Canadian Ranger	

Fleet #.	Fleet Name / Vessel Name	Type of Vessel	Year Built	Type of Engine	Cargo Cap. or Gross*	Overall Length	Breadth	Depth or Draft*
S-8	**SELVICK MARINE TOWING CORP., STURGEON BAY, WI**							
	Baldy B.	TB	1932	D	36*	62' 00"	16' 01"	7' 00"
	Carla Anne Selvick	TB	1908	D	191*	96' 00"	23' 00"	11' 02"
	(S.O. Co. No. 19 '08 - '16, S.T. Co. No. 19 '16 - '18, Socony 19 '18 - '47, Esso Tug No. 4 '47 - '53, McAllister 44 '53 - '55, Roderick McAllister '55 - '84)							
	Escort	TB	1955	D	26*	50' 00"	15' 00"	7' 03"
	John M. Selvick	TB	1898	D	256*	118' 00"	24' 00"	12' 07"
	(Illinois {1} 1898 - '41, John Roen III '41 - '74)							
	Joseph Medill {2}	FB	1949	D	350*	92' 06"	24' 00"	11' 00"
	Mary Page Hannah {1}	TB	1950	D	461*	143' 00"	33' 01"	14' 06"
	(U. S. Army ATA-230 '49 - '72, G. W. Codrington '72 - '73, William P. Feeley {2} '73 - '73, William W. Stender '73 - '78)							
	Moby Dick	DB	1952	B	835	121' 00"	33' 02"	10' 06"
	Sharon M. Selvick	TB	1945	D	28*	45' 06"	13' 00"	7' 01"
	Susan L.	TB	1944	D	163*	86' 00"	23' 00"	10' 04"
	(U. S. Army ST-709 '44 - '47, USCOE Stanley '47 - '99)							
	Timmy L.	TB	1939	D	148*	110' 00"	25' 00"	13' 00"
	(USCGC Naugatuck [WYT / WYTM-92] '39 - '80, Timmy B. '80 - '84)							
	William C. Selvick	TB	1944	D	142*	85' 00"	22' 11"	10' 04"
	(U. S. Army ST-500 '44 - '49, Sherman H. Serre '49 - '77)							
S-9	**SHAKER CRUISE LINES, TORONTO, ON**							
	Sunrise V	HY	1990	D		90' 07"	20' 04"	6' 07"*
	(Sunrise I '90 - '96)							
	Sunrise VI	HY	1990	D		90' 07"	20' 04"	6' 07"*
	(Sunrise II '90 - '96)							
S-10	**SHAMROCK CHARTERING CO., GROSSE POINT, MI**							
	Helene	ES	1927	D	109*	106' 00"	17' 00"	6' 06"*
S-11	**SHELL CANADIAN TANKERS LTD., MONTREAL, QC**							
	Horizon Montreal	RT	1958	D	32,900	315' 00"	45' 07"	24' 07"
	(Tyee Shell '58 - '69, Arctic Trader '69 - '83, Rivershell {4} '83 - '95)							
S-12	**SHEPHERD BOATS LTD., TORONTO, ON**							
	Glenmont	TB	1943	D	102*	82' 00"	20' 01"	9' 00"
S-13	**SHEPLER'S MACKINAC ISLAND FERRY SERVICE, MACKINAW CITY, MI**							
	Capt. Shepler	PF	1986	D	71*	78' 00"	21' 00"	7' 10"
	Felicity	PF	1972	D	84*	65' 00"	18' 01"	8' 03"
	Sacre Bleu	PK	1959	D	92*	94' 10"	31' 00"	9' 09"
	(Put-In-Bay {2} '59 - '94)							
	The Hope	PF	1975	D	87*	77' 00"	20' 00"	8' 03"
	The Welcome	PF	1969	D	66*	60' 06"	16' 08"	8' 02"
	Wyandot	PF	1979	D	99*	77' 00"	20' 00"	8' 00"
S-14	**SHIPWRECK TOURS, INC., MUNISING, MI**							
	Miss Munising	ES	1967	D	50*	60' 00"	14' 00"	4' 04"
S-15	**SHORELINE MARINE CO., CHICAGO, IL**							
	Cap Streeter	ES		D				

SELF-UNLOADERS

A self-unloader is just what its name implies – a vessel able to discharge its own cargo using a system of conveyor belts and gates beneath the cargo holds and a movable boom, usually located on deck, that can be swung over either side of the ship. No dockside assistance is required; the average unloading rate is between 6,000-10,000 tons an hour.

Boom-type self-unloaders first made an appearance in the early 1900s and became the mainstay of the coal and stone trades during the next few decades. (Petroleum and cement carriers are also technically self-unloaders, but use a different system for unloading.) **Wyandotte** of 1908 is given credit for being the first Great Lakes vessel built as a self-unloader. But it was not until the 1970s, as older vessels became obsolete, newer ships were built and easy-to-handle pelletized taconite became the mainstay of the iron ore trade, that the more versatile self-unloader began to edge out traditional "straight-deck" bulk carriers that for years had been in the majority.

During the 1970s and early 1980s, many older straight-deckers were converted to self-unloaders, however, other vessels thought to have years of service ahead of them went to the scrapyard. A depressed Great Lakes shipping economy in the mid-1980s prohibited more self-unloader conversions, hastening the demise of vessels such as the1960-built **Arthur B. Homer**, lengthened to 826 feet in 1976, but scrapped just 10 years later.

Today, no U.S.-flag, straight-deck bulk carriers survive in the ore trade. One U.S. straight-decker, the **Kinsman Independent**, carries grain, and she is the last of her kind.

Canadian-flag owners operate around two dozen straight-deckers, many of them in the grain trade (although some backhaul ore after delivering a grain cargo). The newer of these vessels are slowly being converted to self-unloaders, while many of the older ones see service only a portion of the season, usually during the spring and fall grain rush. It is probably only a matter of time before virtually all Great Lakes bulk cargo will be carried on self-unloaders.

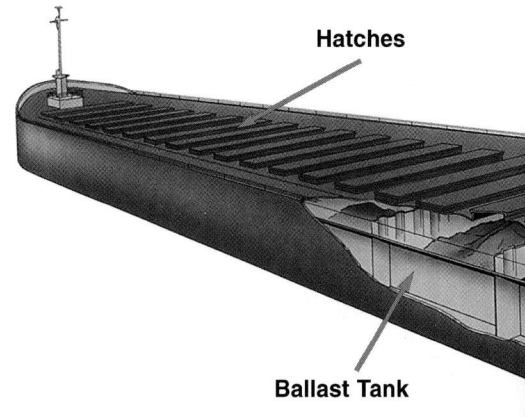

Hatches

Ballast Tank

Self-unloader drawing courtesy Oglebay Norton Marine Services Co.

Indiana Harbor offloads coal at Essexville, MI, via her topside boom. (Ryan Kenny)

In contrast, the Canadian-flag straight-decker Mantadoc lacks her own self-unloading gear.
(Steve Hogler)

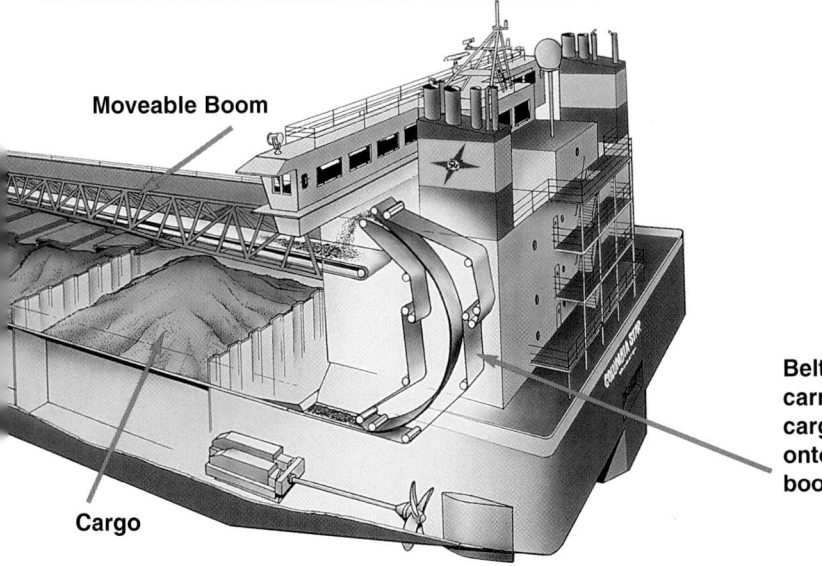

Moveable Boom

Belts carry cargo onto boom

Cargo

Fleet #.	Fleet Name / Vessel Name	Type of Vessel	Year Built	Type of Engine	Cargo Cap. or Gross*	Overall Length	Breadth	Depth or Draft*
	Cap Streeter	ES		D				
	Marlyn	ES	1961	D	85*	65' 00"	25' 00"	7' 00"*
	Shoreline II	ES	1987	D	89*	75' 00"	26' 00"	7' 01"
	Star of Chicago {2}	ES	1999	D		64' 10"	22' 08"	7' 05"
S-16	**SIVERTSON'S GRAND PORTAGE - ISLE ROYALE TRANSPORTATION LINES, INC., SUPERIOR, WI**							
	A. E. Clifford	TB	1946	D	33*	45' 00"	15' 00"	7' 00"
	Hiawatha {1}	TB	1938	D	63*	58' 00"	15' 00"	8' 00"
	(Apostle Islands '38 - '60)							
	Provider	TB	1959	D		46' 00"	13' 05"	5' 05"
	Sharon Jon	TB	1943	D	17*	32' 04"	11' 06"	5' 00"
	Voyageur II	ES	1970	D		63' 00"	18' 00"	5' 00"
	Wenonah	ES	1960	D	91*	70' 07"	19' 04"	9' 07"
	(Jamacia '60 - '64)							
S-17	**SOCIETE DES TRAVERSIERS DU QUEBEC, QUEBEC, QC**							
	Alphonse des Jarnins	CF	1971	D	1,741*	214' 00"	71' 06"	20' 00"
	Armand Imbeau	CF	1980	D	1,285*	203' 07"	72' 00"	18' 04"
	Camille Marcoux	CF	1974	D	6,122*	310' 09"	62' 09"	39' 00"
	Catherine-Legardeur	CF	1985	D	1,348*	205' 09"	71' 10"	18' 10"
	Felix-Antoine-Savard	CF	1997	D	2,489*	272' 00"	70' 00"	
	Grue Des Iles	CF	1981	D	447*	155' 10"	41' 01"	12' 06"
	Jos Deschenes	CF	1980	D	1,287*	203' 07"	72' 00"	18' 04"
	Joseph Savard	CF	1985	D	1,445*	206' 00"	71' 10"	18' 10"
	Lomer Gouin	CF	1971	D	1,741*	214' 00"	71' 06"	20' 00"
	Lucien L.	CF	1967	D	867*	220' 10"	61' 06"	15' 05"
	Radisson {1}	CF	1954	D	1,043*	164' 03"	72' 00"	10' 06"
S-18	**SOCIETE DU PORT DE MONTREAL, MONTREAL, QC**							
	Maisonneuve	TB	1972	D	103*	63' 10"	20' 07"	9' 03"
S-19	**SOO LOCKS BOAT TOURS, SAULT STE. MARIE, MI**							
	AMERICAN AND CANADIAN LOCK TOURS, INC. - OWNER							
	Bide-A-Wee {3}	ES	1955	D	99*	64' 07"	23' 00"	7' 11"
	Hiawatha {2}	ES	1959	D	99*	64' 07"	23' 00"	7' 11"
	Holiday	ES	1957	D	99*	64' 07"	23' 00"	7' 11"
	FAMOUS SOO LOCK CRUISES, INC. - OWNER							
	LeVoyageur	ES	1959	D	70*	65' 00"	25' 00"	7' 00"
	Nokomis	ES	1959	D	70*	65' 00"	25' 00"	7' 00"
S-20	**SPECIALTY RESTAURANTS CORP., ANAHEIM, CA**							
	Lansdowne	TF	1884	B	1,571*	319' 00"	41' 03"	13' 00"
	(Last operated in 1974 — Currently laid up in Erie, PA.)							
S-21	**SPIRIT LAKE MARINE, INC., DULUTH, MN**							
	John V. III	TB	1942	D	12*	40' 00"	10' 00"	3' 05"
S-22	**ST. LAWRENCE CRUISE LINES, INC., KINGSTON, ON**							
	Canadian Empress	PA	1981	D	463*	108' 00"	30' 00"	8' 00"
S-23	**ST. LAWRENCE SEAWAY DEVELOPMENT CORP., MASSENA, NY**							
	Eighth Sea	TB	1958	D	17*	40' 00"	12' 06"	4' 00"
	Performance	TB	1997	D		50' 00"	16' 07"	7' 06"
	Robinson Bay	TB	1958	D	213*	103' 00"	26' 10"	14' 06"
S-24	**ST. LAWRENCE SEAWAY MANAGEMENT CORP., CORNWALL, ON**							
	VM/S Hercules	GL	1962	D	2,107	200' 00"	75' 00"	18' 08"
	VM/S Iroquois	TB	1974	D	20*			
	VM/S Massinouve	SV		D				
	VM/S St. Lambert	TB	1974	D	20*	63' 00"		
	VM/S St. Louis III	TB		D		107' 08"		
S-25	**STAR LINE MACKINAC ISLAND FERRY, ST. IGNACE, MI**							
	Cadillac {5}	PF	1990	D	73*	64' 07"	20' 00"	7' 07"
	Joliet {3}	PF	1993	D	83*	64' 08"	22' 00"	8' 03"
	La Salle {4}	PF	1983	D	55*	65' 00"	20' 00"	7' 05"
	Marquette {5}	PF	1979	D	55*	62' 03"	22' 00"	7' 01"
	Nicolet {2}	PF	1985	D	51*	65' 00"	20' 00"	7' 05"
	Radisson {2}	PF	1988	D	97*	80' 00"	23' 06"	7' 00"
S-26	**STAR SHIP MANAGEMENT LTD., CORAL GABLES, FL**							
	Feederteam	RR	1973	D	4,658	372' 05"	63' 02"	41' 04"
	Florence Star	GC	1979	D	12,665	492' 02"	69' 01"	37' 01"
	Gulf Star	GC	1979	D	3,458	271' 07"	52' 09"	29' 07"
	Kaylin Star	RR	1969	D	2,540	426' 10"	64' 05"	42' 09"
S-27	**STEVEN WALLACE, PENETANGUISHENE, ON**							
	Georgian Storm	TB	1931	D	167*	91' 00"	24' 02"	12' 00"

Fleet #.	Fleet Name / Vessel Name	Type of Vessel	Year Built	Type of Engine	Cargo Cap. or Gross*	Overall Length	Breadth	Depth or Draft*
S-28	**STOLT PARCEL TANKERS, INC., GREENWICH, CT**							
	Stolt Alliance	TK	1985	D	88,147	404' 06"	65' 08"	36' 09"
	(Shoun Trader '85 - '89)							
	Stolt Aspiration	TK	1987	D	90,305	422' 11"	66' 04"	36' 01"
	Stolt Kent	TK	1998	D	122,025	487' 00"	75' 06"	42' 06"
T-1	**TECHNO-NAVIGATION LTEE., SILLERY, QC**							
	Petrel V	SV	1947	D	955*	195' 00"	30' 01"	16' 00"
	(Akurey '47 - '67, Akeroy '67 - '68, Petrel '68 - '76) **(Currently laid up in Quebec, QC.)**							
	Techno St-Laurent	TB	1944	D	261*	111' 00"	27' 00"	13' 00"
	(HMCS Riverton [W-47 / ATA-528] '44 - '79)							
T-2	**TEE DEE ENTERPRISES, INC., CHICAGO, IL**							
	Anita Dee	ES	1972	D	97*	90' 00"	21' 00"	8' 10"
	(M/V Happy Dolphin '72 - '84, Spirit of Toledo '84 - ?)							
	Anita Dee II	ES	1990	D	81*	140' 00"	33' 00"	8' 06"
T-3	**THE ISLE ROYALE LINE, COPPER HARBOR, MI**							
	Isle Royale Queen III	PK	1959	D	15	85' 00"	18' 04"	9' 05"
T-4	**THOMAS W. MARSHALL, TORONTO, ON**							
	Still Watch	SV	1960	D	390*	134' 02"	28' 00"	13' 09"
	(CCGS Ville Marie '60 - '85, Heavenbound '85 - '95) **(Currently laid up in Toronto, ON.)**							
T-5	**THORNTON CONSTRUCTION CO., INC., HANCOCK, MI**							
	Shannon 66-5	TB	1950	D	21*	49' 00"	16' 00"	5' 00"*
T-6	**THREE RIVERS BOATMEN LTD., TROIS-RIVIERES, QC**							
	Andre H.	TB	1963	D	317*	126' 00"	28' 06"	15' 06"
	(Foundation Valiant '63 - '73, Point Valiant {1} '73 - '95)							
	Avantage	TB	1969	D	367*	116' 10"	32' 09"	16' 03"
	(Sea Lion '69 - '97)							
	Duga	TB	1977	D	403*	111' 00"	33' 00"	16' 01"
	Escorte	TT	1964	D	120*	85' 00"	23' 08"	11' 00"
	(USS Menasha [YTB / YTM-773, YTM-761] '64 - '92, Menasha {1} '92 - '95)							
	R. F. Grant	TB	1969	D	78*	71' 00"	17' 00"	8' 00"
	Robert H.	TB	1944	D	261*	111' 00"	27' 00"	13' 00"
	(HMCS Heatherton [W-22 / ATA-527] '44 - '77)							
T-7	**THUNDER BAY MARINE SERVICE LTD., THUNDER BAY, ON**							
	Agoming	CS	1926	B	155*	100' 00"	34' 00"	9' 00"
	Coastal Cruiser	TB	1939	D	29*	65' 00"	18' 00"	12' 00"
	Glenada	TB	1944	D	107*	80' 06"	25' 00"	10' 01"
	Robert W.	TB	1949	D	48*	60' 00"	16' 00"	8' 06"
	Rosalee D.	TB	1943	D	22*	55' 00"	16' 00"	10' 00"
T-8	**THUNDER BAY TUG SERVICES LTD., THUNDER BAY, ON**							
	Point Valour	TB	1958	D	246*	97' 08"	28' 02"	13' 10"
	(Foundation Valour '58 - '83)							
T-9	**TORONTO DRYDOCK CORP., TORONTO, ON**							
	Menier Consol	FD	1962	B	2,575*	304' 07"	49' 06"	25' 06"
	(Last operated 13 September, 1984 — Currently in use as a floating drydock in Toronto, ON.)							
T-10	**TORONTO FIRE DEPARTMENT, TORONTO, ON**							
	Wm. Lyon Mackenzie	FB	1964	D	102*	81' 01"	20' 00"	10' 00"
T-11	**TORONTO HARBOUR COMMISSIONERS, TORONTO, ON**							
	Fred Scandrett	TB	1963	D	52*	62' 00"	17' 00"	8' 00"
	(C. E. "Ted" Smith '63 - '70)							
	J. G. Langton	TB	1934	D	15*	45' 00"	12' 00"	5' 00"
	Maple City	CF	1951	D	135*	70' 06"	36' 04"	5' 11"
	Ned Hanlan II	TB		D				
	William Rest	TB	1961	D	62*	65' 00"	18' 06"	10' 06"
	Windmill Point	CF	1954	D	118*	65' 00"	36' 00"	10' 00"
T-12	**TORONTO METROPOLITAN PARK DEPARTMENT, TORONTO, ON**							
	Ongiara	PF	1963	D	180*	78' 00"	36' 00"	9' 09"
	Sam McBride	PF	1939	D	412*	129' 00"	34' 11"	6' 00"
	Thomas Rennie	PF	1950	D	419*	129' 00"	32' 11"	6' 00"
	Trillium	PF	1910	R	611*	150' 00"	30' 00"	8' 04"
	William Inglis	PF	1935	D	238*	99' 00"	24' 10"	6' 00"
	(Shamrock {2} '35 - '35)							
T-13	**TRANSPORT DESGAGNES, INC., QUEBEC, QC**							
	CROISIERES NORDIK, INC. - A DIVISION OF TRANSPORT DESGAGNES, INC.							
	Nordik Passeur	RR	1962	D	627	285' 04"	62' 00"	20' 01"
	(Confederation {1} '62 - '93, Hull 28 '93 - '94)							
	(5 year survey expired April, 1994 — Currently laid up in Quebec, QC.)							

Fleet #.	Fleet Name / Vessel Name	Type of Vessel	Year Built	Type of Engine	Cargo Cap. or Gross*	Overall Length	Breadth	Depth or Draft*
	DESGAGNES SHIPPING INTERNATIONAL, INC. - A DIVISION OF TRANSPORT DESGAGNES, INC.							
	Anna Desgagnes	RR	1986	D	17,850	565' 00"	75' 00"	45' 00"
	(Truskavets '86 - '96, Anna Desgagnes '96 - '98, PCC Panama '98 - '99)							
	DESGAGNES TANKER, INC. - A DIVISION OF TRANSPORT DESGAGNES, INC.							
	Maria Desgagnes	TK	1999	D	95,607	393' 08"	68' 11"	40' 04"
	(Kilchem Asia '99 - '99)							
	Petrolia Desgagnes	TK	1975	D	97,725	441' 05"	56' 06"	32' 10"
	(Jorvan '75 - '79, Lido '79 - '84, Ek-Sky '84 - '98)							
	Thalassa Desgagnes	TK	1976	D	104,667	441' 05"	56' 06"	32' 10"
	(Joasla '76 - '79, Orinoco '79 - '82, Rio Orinoco '82 - '93)							
	GROUP DESGAGNES, INC. - A DIVISION OF TRANSPORT DESGAGNES, INC.							
	Alcor	BC	1977	D	27,536	584' 08"	75' 01"	48' 03"
	(Patricia V '77 - '83, Mekhanik Dren '83 - '97)							
	Amelia Desgagnes	GC	1976	D	7,126	355' 00"	49' 00"	30' 06"
	(Soodoc {2} '76 - '90)							
	Catherine Desgagnes	GC	1962	D	8,350	410' 03"	56' 04"	31' 00"
	(Gosforth '62 - '72, Thorold {4} '72 - '85)							
	Cecelia Desgagnes	GC	1971	D	7,875	374' 10"	54' 10"	34' 06"
	(Carl Gorthon '71 - '81, Federal Pioneer '81 - '85)							
	Jacques Desgagnes	GC	1960	D	1,250	208' 10"	36' 00"	14' 00"
	(Loutre Consol '60 - '77)							
	Mathilda Desgagnes	GC	1959	D	6,920	360' 00"	51' 00"	30' 02"
	(Eskimo '59 - '80)							
	Melissa Desgagnes	GC	1975	D	7,000	355' 00"	49' 00"	30' 06"
	(Ontadoc {2} '75 - '90)							
	Nordik Express	CF	1974	D	1,697	219' 11"	44' 00"	16' 01"
	(Theriot Offshore IV '74 - '77, Scotoil 4 '77 - '79, Tartan Sea '79 - '87)							
T-14	**TRANSPORT IGLOOLIK, INC., MONTREAL, QC**							
	Aivik	HL	1980	D	4,860	359' 08"	63' 08"	38' 09"
	(Mont Ventoux '80 - '90, Aivik '90 - '91, Unilifter '91 - '92)							
	LOGISTEC NAVIGATION, INC. - VESSEL MANAGED BY TRANSPORT IGLOOIK, INC.							
	Lucien-Paquin	GC	1969	D	12,802	459' 05"	70' 06"	42' 01"
	(Boreland '69 - '79, Sunemerillon '79 - '82, Mesange '82 - '85)							
T-15	**TRANSPORT NANUK, INC., MONTREAL, QC**							
	Umiavut	GC	1988	D	9,682	371' 02"	63' 01"	37' 00"
	(Completed as Newca, Kapitan Silin '88 - '92, Lindengracht '92 - 2000)							
T-16	**TRAVERSE TALL SHIP CO., TRAVERSE CITY, MI**							
	Manitou {1}	2S	1983	W	78*	114' 00"	21' 00"	9' 00"
	Westwind	2S		W		66' 00"		
T-17	**TRUMP INDIANA, INC., GARY, IN**							
	Trump Casino	GA	1996	D	7,256*	288' 00"	76' 00"	17' 06"
T-18	**30,000 ISLANDS CRUISE LINES, INC., PARRY SOUND, ON**							
	Island Queen V {3}	ES	1990	D	526*	130' 00"	35' 00"	6' 06"
U-1	**UNCLE SAM BOAT TOURS, ALEXANDRIA, NY**							
	Alexandria Belle	ES	1988	D	72*	104' 00"	32' 00"	7' 08"*
	Island Duchess	ES	1988	D	60*	110' 00"	27' 08"	8' 08"*
	Island Wanderer	ES	1971	D	57*	62' 05"	22' 00"	7' 02"
	Uncle Sam Jr.	ES	1958	D	30*	50' 00"	10' 00"	4' 00"*
	Uncle Sam II	ES	1958	D	75*	63' 00"	17' 06"	5' 04"
	Uncle Sam VII	ES	1976	D	55*	60' 04"	22' 00"	7' 01"
U-2	**UNISPEED GROUP, INC., WESTMOUNT, QC**							
	Phoenician Trader	GC	1969	D	12,898	496' 09"	66' 09"	39' 02"
	(Professor Nikolay Baranskiy '69 - '96)							
U-3	**UNITED STATES ARMY CORPS OF ENGINEERS GREAT LAKES AND OHIO RIVER DIVISION, CHICAGO, IL**							
	BUFFALO DISTRICT							
	Buffalo	TB	1953	D	23*	45' 00"	13' 00"	7' 00"*
	Cheraw	TB	1970	D	356*	109' 00"	30' 06"	16' 03"
	(USS Cheraw [YTB-802] '70 - '96)							
	Koziol	TB	1973	D	356*	109' 00"	30' 06"	16' 03"
	(USS Chetek [YTB-827] '73 - '96, Chetek '96 - 2000)							
	McCauley	CS	1948	B		112' 00"	52' 00"	3' 00"*
	Simonsen	CS	1954	B		142' 00"	58' 00"	5' 00"*
	Wheeler	DR	1982	B	10,353	384' 00"	78' 00"	39' 00"
	CHICAGO DISTRICT							
	Kenosha	TB	1954	D	82*	70' 00"	20' 00"	9' 08"

Fleet #.	Fleet Name / Vessel Name	Type of Vessel	Year Built	Type of Engine	Cargo Cap. or Gross*	Overall Length	Breadth	Depth or Draft*
	Manitowoc	CS	1976	B		132' 00"	44' 00"	8' 00"*
	Racine	TB	1931	D	61*	66' 03"	18' 05"	7' 08"
	DETROIT DISTRICT							
	D. L. Billmaier	TB	1968	D	345*	109' 00"	30' 06"	16' 03"
	(USS Natchitoches [YTB-799] '68 - '95)							
	Duluth	TB	1954	D	82*	70' 00"	20' 00"	9' 08"
	(U. S. Army ST-2015 '54 - '62)							
	Fairchild	TB	1953	D	23*	45' 00"	13' 00"	7' 00"*
	Forney	TB	1944	D	163*	86' 00"	23' 00"	10' 04"
	(U. S. Army ST-707 '44 - '60)							
	Hammond Bay	TB	1953	D	23*	45' 00"	13' 00"	7' 00"*
	Harvey	CS	1961	B		122' 00"	40' 00"	4' 10"*
	H. J. Schwartz	CS	1995	B		150' 00"	48' 00"	11' 00"
	Huron	CS	1954	B		100' 00"	34' 00"	4' 06"*
	James M. Bray	SV	1924	D	194*	128' 00"	31' 00"	8' 00"
	(Deck Cargo Barge 20 '24 - '85)							
	Michigan	CS	1971	B		120' 00"	33' 00"	3' 06"*
	Nicolet	CS	1971	B		120' 00"	42' 00"	5' 00"*
	Owen M. Frederick	TB	1942	D	56*	65' 00"	17' 00"	7' 06"
	Paj	SV	1955	D	151*	120' 06"	34' 02"	6' 05"
	(Deck Cargo Barge No. 30 '55 - '86)							
	Paul Bunyan	GL	1945	B		150' 00"	65' 00"	12' 06"
	Shelter Bay	TB	1953	D	23*	45' 00"	13' 00"	7' 00"*
	Tawas Bay	TB	1953	D	23*	45' 00"	13' 00"	7' 00"*
	Veler	CS	1991	B	613*	150' 00"	46' 00"	10' 06"
	Whitefish Bay	TB	1953	D	23*	45' 00"	13' 00"	7' 00"*
U-4	**UNITED STATES COAST GUARD - 9TH COAST GUARD DISTRICT, CLEVELAND, OH**							
	Acacia **[WLB-406]**	BT	1944	D	1,025*	180' 00"	37' 00"	17' 04"
	(Launched as USCGC Thistle [WAGL-406]) **(To be decommissioned in 2004.)**							
	Adler **[WLB-216]**	BT	2004	D	2,000*	225' 09"	46' 00"	19' 08"
	(To be commissioned in January 2004 and stationed at Charlevoix, MI.)							
	Biscayne Bay **[WTGB-104]**	IB	1979	D	662*	140' 00"	37' 06"	12' 00"*
	Bramble **[WLB-392]**	BT	1944	D	1,025*	180' 00"	37' 00"	17' 04"
	(To be decommissioned in 2003.)							
	Bristol Bay **[WTGB-102]**	IB	1979	D	662*	140' 00"	37' 06"	12' 00"*
	Buckthorn **[WLI-642]**	BT	1963	D	200*	100' 00"	24' 00"	4' 08"*
	CGB-12000 **[CGB-12000]**	BT	1991	B	700*	120' 00"	50' 00"	6' 00"*
	CGB-12001 **[CGB-12001]**	BT	1991	B	700*	120' 00"	50' 00"	6' 00"*
	Hollyhock **[WLB-215]**	BT	2003	D	2,000*	225' 09"	46' 00"	19' 08"
	(To be commissioned in September 2003 and stationed at Port Huron, MI.)							
	Katmai Bay **[WTGB-101]**	IB	1978	D	662*	140' 00"	37' 06"	12' 00"*
	Mackinaw **[WAGB-83]**	IB	1944	D	5,252*	290' 00"	74' 00"	29' 00"
	(Launched as USCGC Manitowoc [WAG-83]) **(To be decommissioned in 2006.)**							
	Mobile Bay **[WTGB-103]**	IB	1979	D	662*	140' 00"	37' 06"	12' 00"*
	Neah Bay **[WTGB-105]**	IB	1980	D	662*	140' 00"	37' 06"	12' 00"*
	Sundew **[WLB-404]**	BT	1944	D	1,025*	180' 00"	37' 00"	17' 04"
	NEW BUILDING AT MARINETTE, WI, FOR UNITED STATES COAST GUARD - "JUNIPER" CLASS							
	Spar **[WLB-206]**	BT	2001	D	2,000*	225' 09"	46' 00"	19' 08"
	(To be commissioned in Jan. 2001 and stationed at Kodiak, AK in the 17th Coast Guard District.)							
	Maple **[WLB-207]**	BT	2001	D	2,000*	225' 09"	46' 00"	19' 08"
	(To be commissioned in April 2001 and stationed at Sitka, AK in the 17th Coast Guard District.)							
	Aspen **[WLB-208]**	BT	2001	D	2,000*	225' 09"	46' 00"	19' 08"
	(To be commissioned June 2001 and stationed at San Francisco, CA in the 11th Coast Guard District.)							
	Sycamore **[WLB-209]**	BT	2001	D	2,000*	225' 09"	46' 00"	19' 08"
	(To be commissioned in Sept. 2001 and stationed at Cordova, AK in the 17th Coast Guard District.)							
	Cypress **[WLB-210]**	BT	2002	D	2,000*	225' 09"	46' 00"	19' 08"
	(To be commissioned in January 2002 and stationed at Mobile, AL in the 8th Coast Guard District.)							
	Oak **[WLB-211]**	BT	2002	D	2,000*	225' 09"	46' 00"	19' 08"
	(To be commissioned in June 2002 and stationed at Miami, FL in the 7th Coast Guard District.)							
	Hickory **[WLB-212]**	BT	2002	D	2,000*	225' 09"	46' 00"	19' 08"
	(To be commissioned in Sept. 2002 and stationed at Homer, AK in the 17th Coast Guard District.)							
	Fir **[WLB-213]**	BT	2003	D	2,000*	225' 09"	46' 00"	19' 08"
	(To be commissioned in Jan. 2003 and stationed at Astoria, OR in the 13th Coast Guard District.)							
	Sequoia **[WLB-214]**	BT	2003	D	2,000*	225' 09"	46' 00"	19' 08"
	(To be commissioned in June 2003 and stationed at Apra Harbor, Guam in the 14th Coast Guard District.)							
U-5	**UNITED STATES DEPT. OF THE INTERIOR - U. S. FISH & WILDLIFE SERVICE, ANN ARBOR, MI**							
	Cisco	RV	1951	D		60' 06"	16' 08"	7' 08"
	Grayling	RV	1977	D		75' 00"	22' 00"	9' 10"
	Kaho	RV	1961	D		64' 10"	17' 10"	9' 00"
	Kiyi	RV	1999	D		107' 00"	27' 00"	12' 00"

The 65-foot U.S. Army Corps of Engineers' harbor tug Owen M. Frederick breaks spring ice in the vicinity of the Soo Locks. (Charles 'PR' Reed)

Former saltwater tug Jane Ann IV, brought to the lakes to push the barge Sarah Spencer, inbound in the Welland Canal. (Jimmy Sprunt)

Fleet #.	Fleet Name Vessel Name	Type of Vessel	Year Built	Type of Engine	Cargo Cap. or Gross*	Overall Length	Breadth	Depth or Draft*
	Musky II	RV	1960	D	25*	45' 00"	14' 04"	5' 00"
	Siscowet	RV	1946	D	54*	57' 00"	14' 06"	7' 00"
U-6	**UNITED STATES ENVIRONMENTAL PROTECTION AGENCY - REGION 5, CHICAGO, IL**							
	Lake Explorer	RV	1962	D	69*	82' 10"	17' 07"	5' 11"*
	(USCGC Point Roberts [WPB-82332] '62 - '92)							
	Lake Guardian	RV	1989	D	282*	180' 00"	40' 00"	11' 00"
	(Marsea Fourteen '81 - '90)							
U-7	**UNITED STATES NATIONAL PARK SERVICE - ISLE ROYALE NATIONAL PARK, HOUGHTON, MI**							
	Beaver	GC	1952	B	550	110' 00"	32' 00"	6' 05"
	Charlie Mott	PF	1953	D	28*	56' 00"	14' 00"	4' 07"
	Greenstone	TK	1977	B	30	81' 00"	24' 00"	6' 01"
	J. E. Colombe	TB	1953	D	25*	45' 00"	12' 05"	5' 03"
	Ranger III	PK	1958	D	140	165' 00"	34' 00"	15' 03"
U-8	**UNITED STATES NAVAL SEA CADET CORPS - FC SHERMAN DIVISION, PORT HURON, MI**							
	Grey Fox **[TWR-825]**	TV	1985	D	213*	120' 00"	25' 00"	12' 00"*
	(USS TWR-825 '85 - '97)							
	Pride of Michigan **[YP-673]**	TV	1977	D	70*	80' 06"	17' 08"	5' 03"*
	(USS YP-673 '77 - '89)							
U-9	**UNIVERSITE DU QUEBEC, RIMOUSKI, QC**							
	Alcide C. Horth	RV	1965	D	135*	89' 02"	22' 09"	11' 00"
	(Villmont No. 2 '65 - '83, Raymond Moore '83 - '90)							
U-10	**UNIVERSITY OF MICHIGAN - CENTER FOR GREAT LAKES AND AQUATIC SCIENCES, ANN ARBOR, MI**							
	Laurentian	RV	1977	D	129*	80' 00"	21' 06"	11' 00"
U-11	**UNIVERSITY OF MINNESOTA, DULUTH, DULUTH, MN**							
	Blue Heron	RV	1985	D	175*	119' 06"	28' 00"	15' 06"
U-12	**UNIVERSITY OF WISCONSIN, MILWAUKEE - GREAT LAKES WATER INSTITUTE, MILWAUKEE, WI**							
	Neeskay	RV	1952	D	75*	71' 00"	17' 06"	7' 06"*
U-13	**UNIVERSITY OF WISCONSIN, SUPERIOR, SUPERIOR, WI**							
	L. L. Smith Jr.	RV	1950	D	38*	57' 06"	16' 06"	6' 06"
U-14	**UPPER CANADA STEAMBOATS, INC., BROCKVILLE, ON**							
	Miss Brockville	ES		D		48' 00"	10' 00"	4' 00"
	Miss Brockville IV	ES		D		45' 00"	10' 00"	5' 00"
	Miss Brockville V	ES		D		62' 00"	13' 00"	5' 00"
	Miss Brockville VI	ES		D		38' 00"	8' 00"	3' 00"
	Miss Brockville VII	ES		D		66' 00"	15' 00"	5' 00"
	Miss Brockville VIII	ES		D		48' 00"	12' 00"	5' 00"
U-15	**UPPER LAKES BARGE LINE, INC., BARK RIVER, MI**							
	Olive M. Moore	TB	1928	D	301*	125' 00"	27' 01"	13' 09"
	(John F. Cushing '28 - '66, James E. Skelly '66 - '66)							
U-16	**UPPER LAKES GROUP, INC., TORONTO, ON**							
	HAMILTON MARINE & ENGINEERING LTD. - A DIVISION OF UPPER LAKES GROUP, INC.							
	James E. McGrath	TB	1963	D	90*	77' 00"	20' 00"	10' 09"
	JACKES SHIPPING, INC. - A DIVISION OF UPPER LAKES GROUP, INC.							
	Canadian Trader	BC	1969	D	28,300	730' 00"	75' 00"	39' 08"
	(Ottercliffe Hall '69 - '83, Royalton {2} '83 - '85, Ottercliffe Hall '85 - '88, Peter Misener '88 - '94)							
	Canadian Venture	BC	1965	D	28,050	730' 03"	75' 00"	39' 02"
	(Lawrencecliffe Hall {2} '65 - '88, David K. Gardiner '88 - '94)							
	Gordon C. Leitch {2}	BC	1968	D	29,700	730' 00"	75' 00"	42' 00"
	(Ralph Misener '68 - '94)							
	PROVMAR FUELS, INC. - A DIVISION OF UPPER LAKES GROUP, INC.							
	Hamilton Energy	TK	1965	D	8,622	201' 05"	34' 01"	14' 09"
	(Partington '65 - '79, Shell Scientist '79 - '81, Metro Sun '81 - '85)							
	Provmar Terminal	TK	1959	B	60,000	403' 05"	55' 06"	28' 05"
	(Varangnes '59 - '70, Tommy Wiborg '70 - '74, Ungava Transport '74 - '85)							
	(Last operated in 1984 —Currently in use as a stationary fuel storage barge in Hamilton, ON.)							
	Provmar Terminal II	TK	1948	D	73,740	408' 08"	53' 00"	26' 00"
	(Imperial Sarnia {2} '48 - '89)							
	(Last operated 13 Dec. 1986 — Currently in use as a stationary fuel storage barge in Hamilton, ON.)							
	ULS CORPORATION - A DIVISION OF UPPER LAKES GROUP, INC.							
	Canadian Century	SU	1967	D	31,600	730' 00"	75' 00"	45' 00"
	Canadian Enterprise	SU	1979	D	35,100	730' 00"	75' 08"	46' 06"
	Canadian Leader	BC	1967	T	28,300	730' 00"	75' 00"	39' 08"
	(Feux - Follets '67 - '72)							
	(The Canadian Leader is the last steam powered Great Lakes cargo vessel built.)							

Fleet #.	Fleet Name Vessel Name	Type of Vessel	Year Built	Type of Engine	Cargo Cap. or Gross*	Overall Length	Breadth	Depth or Draft*
	Canadian Mariner	BC	1963	T	27,700	730' 00"	75' 00"	39' 03"
	(Newbrunswicker '63 - '68, Grande Hermine '68 - '72)							
	Canadian Miner	BC	1966	D	28,050	730' 00"	75' 00"	39' 01"
	(Maplecliffe Hall '66 - '88, Lemoyne {2} '88 - '94)							
	Canadian Navigator	SU	1967	D	30,925	728' 11"	75' 10"	40' 06"
	(Demeterton '67 - '75, St. Lawrence Navigator '75 - '80)							
	Canadian Olympic	SU	1976	D	35,100	730' 00"	75' 00"	46' 06"
	Canadian Progress	SU	1968	D	32,700	730' 00"	75' 00"	46' 06"
	Canadian Prospector	BC	1964	D	30,500	730' 00"	75' 10"	40' 06"
	(Carlton '64 - '75, Federal Wear '75 - '75, St. Lawrence Prospector '75 - '79)							
	Canadian Provider	BC	1963	T	27,450	730' 00"	75' 00"	39' 02"
	(Murray Bay {3} '63 - '94)							
	Canadian Ranger	GU	1943	D	25,900	729' 10"	75' 00"	39' 03"
	([Fore Section] Grande Ronde '43 - '48, Kate N. L. '48 - '61, Hilda Marjanne '61 - '84)							
	([Stern Section] Chimo '67 - '83)							
	Canadian Transfer	GU	1943	D	22,204	650' 00"	60' 00"	35' 00"
	([Fore Section] J. H. Hillman Jr. '43 - '74, Crispin Oglebay {2} '74 - '95, Hamilton '95 - '96,							
	Hamilton Transfer '96 - '98) ([Stern Section] Cabot {1} '65 - '83, Canadian Explorer '83 - '98)							
	(The Canadian Transfer is a L6-S-B1 class "Maritime" vessel built by Great Lakes Engineering Works.)							
	Canadian Transport {2}	SU	1979	D	35,100	730' 00"	75' 08"	46' 06"
	Canadian Voyager	BC	1963	T	27,050	730' 00"	75' 00"	39' 02"
	(Black Bay '63 - '94)							
	Everlast	TB	1977	D	1,361*	143' 04"	44' 04"	21' 04"
	(Bilibino '77 - '96)							
	James Norris	SU	1952	U	18,600	663' 06"	67' 00"	35' 00"
	Montrealais	BC	1962	T	27,800	730' 00"	75' 00"	39' 00"
	(Launched as Montrealer)							
	Quebecois	BC	1963	T	27,800	730' 00"	75' 00"	39' 00"
	Seaway Queen	BC	1959	T	24,300	713' 03"	72' 00"	37' 00"
	ESSROC ITALCEMENTI GROUP - VESSELS MANAGED BY UPPER LAKES GROUP, INC.							
	Metis	CC	1956	B	5,800	331' 00"	43' 09"	26' 00"
	(Last operated 19 Aug. 1993 — In use as a stationary cement storage barge in Windsor, ON.)							
	Stephen B. Roman	CC	1965	D	7,600	488' 09"	56' 00"	35' 06"
	(Fort William '65 - '83)							
U-17	**UPPER LAKES TOWING, INC., ESCANABA, MI**							
	Joseph H. Thompson	SU	1944	B	21,200	706' 06"	71' 06"	38' 06"
	(USNS Marine Robin '44 - '52)							
	(The Joseph H. Thompson partcipated in the Normandy Invasion on 6 June, 1944 during							
	World War II as the USNS Marine Robin.)							
	Joseph H. Thompson Jr.	TBA	1990	D	841*	146' 06"	38' 00"	35' 00"
U-18	**USS GREAT LAKES FLEET, INC. - A DIVISION OF THE TRANSTAR CO., DULUTH, MN**							
	Arthur M. Anderson	SU	1952	T	25,300	767' 00"	70' 00"	36' 00"
	Cason J. Callaway	SU	1952	T	25,300	767' 00"	70' 00"	36' 00"
	Edgar B. Speer	SU	1980	D	73,700	1,004' 00"	105' 00"	56' 00"
	Edwin H. Gott	SU	1979	D	74,100	1,004' 00"	105' 00"	56' 00"
	John G. Munson {2}	SU	1952	T	25,550	768' 03"	72' 00"	36' 00"
	Ojibway {1}	SB	1945	D	65*	53' 00"	28' 00"	7' 00"
	Philip R. Clarke	SU	1952	T	25,300	767' 00"	70' 00"	36' 00"
	Roger Blough	SU	1972	D	43,900	858' 00"	105' 00"	41' 06"
	GLF GREAT LAKES CORP. - A DIVISION OF USS GREAT LAKES FLEET, INC.							
	Presque Isle {2}	TBA	1973	D	1,578*	153' 03"	54' 00"	31' 03"
	Presque Isle {2}	SU	1973	B	57,500	974' 06"	104' 07"	46' 06"
	[Presque Isle {2} overall dimensions together]			1,000' 00"	104' 07"	46' 06"		
V-1	**V. M. SHIPPING L.L.C., BARK RIVER, MI**							
	Great Lakes Trader	SU	2000	B	39,600	740' 00"	78' 00"	45' 00"
	Joyce L. Van Enkevort	TBA	1998	D	1,179*	135' 04"	50' 00"	26' 00"
	[Great Lakes Trader / Joyce L. Van Enkevort overall dimensions together]			844' 10"	78' 00"	45' 00"		
V-2	**VERREAULT NAVIGATION, INC., LES MACHINS, QC**							
	I.V. No. 9	GC	1936	D	320	110' 00"	23' 10"	8' 05"
	(A.C.D. '36 - '69)							
	I.V. No. 10	GC	1936	D	320	110' 00"	23' 10"	8' 05"
	(G.T.D. '36 - '69)							
	I.V. No. 14	GC	1937	D	229	113' 00"	22' 05"	8' 06"
	(Kermic '37 - '74)							
	Nindawayma	CF	1976	D	6,197*	333' 06"	55' 00"	36' 06"
	(Monte Cruceta '76 - '76, Monte Castillo '76 - '78, Manx Viking '78 - '87, Manx '87 - '88, Skudenes '88 - '89,							
	Ontario No.1 {2} '89 - '89) **(Last operated in 1992 — 5 year survey expired January, 1996.)**							
V-3	**VINCENT KLAMERUS EXCAVATING, DRUMMOND ISLAND, MI**							
	Lime Island	TB	1957	D	21*	42' 10"	12' 00"	12' 00"

Walter J. McCarthy Jr. sails upbound past Detroit. *(Richard I. Weiss)*

WALTER J. McCARTHY JR.

Vessel Spotlight

McCARTHY JR.	
Length	1,000'
Beam	105'
Depth	56'
Built	1977
Tonnage	78,850

Of the 13 1,000-foot-class vessels on the lakes, one of the most familiar is the **Walter J. McCarthy Jr.** Operated by the American Steamship Co., the McCarthy can most often be seen hauling low-sulfur western coal from the Superior Midwest Energy Terminal (SMET) in Superior, WI., to the Detroit Edison Belle River Power Plant at St. Clair (Recors Point), MI, or to Detroit Edison a few miles further downstream at Monroe, MI.

Built in two sections by Bay Shipbuilding Co. at Sturgeon Bay, WI, the self-unloading vessel was christened **Belle River** on 12 July 1977. She was the first 1000-footer built at Bayship, and her design was later adopted for the construction of the 1000-footers **Burns Harbor**, **Columbia Star**, **Indiana Harbor**, and **Oglebay Norton**. Her maiden voyage was one for the record books – the 62,802 net tons of coal she carried on board was the largest such cargo ever carried on the Great Lakes.

In 1990, the Belle River was renamed Walter J. McCarthy Jr., in honor of the retired chairman of the board and chief executive officer of the Detroit Edison company. Her seven cargo holds are able to carry 78,850 tons at her maximum mid-summer draft of 34 feet. The McCarthy's 250-foot, stern-mounted unloading boom can be swung 92 degrees to port or starboard and can discharge coal at a rate of up to 10,000 tons per hour. At that speed, the McCarthy is doing more than her share to keep the lights on and air-conditioners running!

– George Wharton

Fleet #.	Fleet Name / Vessel Name	Type of Vessel	Year Built	Type of Engine	Cargo Cap. or Gross*	Overall Length	Breadth	Depth or Draft*
V-4	**VISTA FLEET, DULUTH, MN**							
	Vista King	ES	1978	D	60*	78' 00"	28' 00"	5' 02"
	Vista Star	ES	1987	D	95*	91' 00"	24' 09"	7' 08"
	(Island Empress '87 - '88)							
V-5	**VOIGHT'S MARINE SERVICES, ELLISON BAY, WI**							
	Bounty	ES	1968	D		40' 00"	14' 00"	3' 03"
	Island Clipper {2}	ES	1987	D	149*	65' 00"	20' 00"	5' 00"
	Yankee Clipper	ES	1971	D		54' 00"	17' 00"	5' 00"
V-6	**VOYAGEUR CRUISES, INC., CHARLEVOIX, MI**							
	Voyageur	ES	1981	D	72*	105' 00"	21' 06"	6' 00"*
W-1	**WAGNER CHARTER CO., INC., CAROL STREAM, IL**							
	Buccaneer	ES	1925	D	98*	100' 00"	23' 00"	14' 06"
	(USCGC Dexter '25 - '35, USS Dexter [YP-67] '35 - '46, Kingfisher '46 - '61, Jamica II '61 - '61, Trinidad {1} '61 - '94)							
	Jamica	ES	1967	D	88*	105' 00"	25' 00"	10' 06"
	Trinidad {2}	ES	1926	D	98*	100' 00"	23' 00"	14' 06"
W-2	**WASHINGTON ISLAND FERRY LINE, INC., WASHINGTON ISLAND, WI**							
	C. G. Richter	CF	1950	D	82*	70' 06"	25' 00"	9' 05"
	Eyrarbakki	CF	1970	D	95*	87' 00"	36' 00"	7' 06"
	Robert Noble	CF	1979	D	97*	90' 04"	36' 00"	8' 03"
	Voyager	CF	1960	D	98*	65' 00"	35' 00"	8' 00"
	Washington {2}	CF	1989	D	93*	100' 00"	37' 00"	9' 00"
W-3	**WENDELLA SIGHTSEEING CO., CHICAGO, IL**							
	Queen of Andersonville	ES	1962	D	23*	40' 00"	15' 00"	3' 05"
	Wendella Clipper	ES	1958	D	41*	67' 00"	20' 00"	4' 00"
	Wendella Limited	ES	1992	D	66*	68' 00"	20' 00"	4' 09"
	Wendella Sunliner	ES	1961	D	35*	68' 00"	17' 00"	6' 05"

VESSEL ENGINE DATA

Vessel Name	Engine Manufacturer & Model #	Engine Type	Total Engines	Total Cylinders	Rated HP	Total Props	Speed MPH

❑ **bhp** = brake horsepower, a measure of diesel engine output power measured at the crankshaft before entering gear box or any other power take-out device

❑ **ihp** = indicated horsepower, based on an internal measurement of mean cylinder pressure, piston area, piston stroke and engine speed. Used for reciprocating engines

❑ **shp** = shaft horsepower, a measure of engine output at the propeller shaft at the output of the reduction gear box. Used for steam and diesel-electric engines

❑ **cpp** = controllable pitch propeller

Vessel Name	Engine Manufacturer & Model #	Engine Type	Total Engines	Total Cylinders	Rated HP	Total Props	Speed MPH
Adam E. Cornelius	General Motors - EMD 20-645-E7B	Diesel	2	20	7,200 bhp	1 cpp	16.1
Agawa Canyon	Fairbanks Morse 10-38D8-1/8	Diesel	4	10	6,662 bhp	1 cpp	13.8
Aivik	Pielstick 8PA6L-280	Diesel	2	8	5,199 bhp	1 cpp	15.0
Alcor	Sulzer 6RND68M	Diesel	1	6	11,480 bhp	1	19.9
Algobay	Pielstick 10PC2-3V-400	Diesel	2	10	10,699 bhp	1 cpp	13.8
Algocape	Sulzer 6RND76	Diesel	2	6	9,599 bhp	1	17.3
Algocatalyst	Pielstick 12PC2-V-400	Diesel	4	12	6,000 bhp	1 cpp	17.3
Algocen	Fairbanks Morse 10-38D8-1/8	Diesel	2	10	7,999 bhp	1 cpp	13.8
Algoeast	B&W 6K45GF	Diesel	2	6	5,299 bhp	1 cpp	15.8
Algofax	M.A.N. K5Z70/120	Diesel	2	5	6,410 bhp	1	15.5
Algogulf	General Electric Co.	Turbine	2	*	9,900 shp	1	17.3
Algoisle	M.A.N. K6Z78/155	Diesel	1	6	9,000 bhp	1 cpp	19.3
Algolake	Pielstick 10PC2-2V-400	Diesel	2	10	9,000 bhp	1 cpp	17.3
Algomarine	Sulzer 6RND76	Diesel	1	6	9,599 bhp	1 cpp	17.0
Algonorth	Werkspoor 9TM410	Diesel	2	9	11,999 bhp	1 cpp	16.1
Algonova	Fairbanks Morse 12-38D8-1/8	Diesel	2	12	4,000 bhp	1 cpp	15.0
Algontario	B&W 7-74VTBF-160	Diesel	1	7	8,750 bhp	1 cpp	14.4

96

Vessel Name	Engine Manufacturer & Model #	Engine Type	Total Engines	Total Cylinders	Rated HP	Total Props	Speed MPH
Algoport	Pielstick 10PC2-3V-400	Diesel	2	10	10,699 bhp	1 cpp	13.8
Algorail	Fairbanks Morse 10-38D8-1/8	Diesel	2	10	8,065 bhp	1 cpp	13.8
Algoriver	General Electric Co. Turbine	Turbine	2	*	9,900 shp	1	17.0
Algosar	M.A.N. K5Z70/120E	Diesel	1	5	6,500 bhp	1 cpp	17.3
Algoscotia	B&W 7-50VT2BF-110	Diesel	1	7	5,326 bhp	1	15.5
Algosea	Sulzer 4RLB76	Diesel	1	4	8,796 bhp	1 cpp	16.8
Algosoo	Pielstick 10PC2-V-400	Diesel	2	10	9,000 bhp	1 cpp	15.0
Algosound	Canadian General Electric Co. Ltd.	Turbine	2	*	9,900 shp	1	17.3
Algosteel	Sulzer 6RND76	Diesel	1	6	9,599 bhp	1	17.0
Algoville	M.A.N. K6Z78/155	Diesel	1	6	9,900 bhp	1 cpp	17.8
Algoway	Fairbanks Morse 10-38D8-1/8	Diesel	4	10	8,065 bhp	1 cpp	13.8
Algowest	MaK 6M552AK	Diesel	2	6	10,199 bhp	1 cpp	13.8
Algowood	MaK 6M552AK	Diesel	2	6	10,199 bhp	1 cpp	13.8
Alpena	De Laval Steam Turbine Co.	Turbine	2	*	4,400 shp	1	14.1
Amelia Desgagnes	Allen 12PVBCS12-F	Diesel	2	12	4,000 bhp	1 cpp	16.1
American Mariner	General Motors - EMD 20-645-E7	Diesel	2	20	7,200 bhp	1 cpp	15.0
American Republic	General Motors - EMD 20-645-E7	Diesel	2	20	7,200 bhp	2 cpp	15.0
Anna Desgagnes	M.A.N. K5SZ70/125B	Diesel	1	5	10,332 bhp	1	17.8
Arctic	M.A.N. 14V52/55A	Diesel	1	14	14,770 bhp	1 cpp	17.8
Armco	Westinghouse Elec. Corp.	Turbine	2	*	7,700 shp	1	19.0
Arthur K. Atkinson	Nordberg	Diesel	2	12	5,610 bhp	2 cpp	
Arthur M. Anderson	Westinghouse Elec. Corp.	Turbine	2	*	7,700 shp	1	16.1
Atlantic Erie	Sulzer 6RLB66	Diesel	1	6	11,100 bhp	1 cpp	16.1
Atlantic Huron	Sulzer 6RLB66	Diesel	1	6	11,094 bhp	1 cpp	17.3
Badger	Skinner Engine Co.	Unaflow	2	4	8,000 ihp	2	18.4
Buckeye	Bethlehem Steel Co.	Turbine	2	*	7,700 shp	1	17.3
Buffalo	General Motors - EMD 20-645-E7	Diesel	2	20	7,200 bhp	1 cpp	16.1
Burns Harbor	General Motors - EMD 20-645-E7	Diesel	4	20	14,400 bhp	2 cpp	18.4
Calcite II	Nordberg FS-1312-H5C	Diesel	1	12	3,240 bhp	1	11.5
Canadian Century	B&W 5-74VT2BF-160	Diesel	1	5	7,500 bhp	1 cpp	16.1
Canadian Enterprise	M.A.N. 7L40/45	Diesel	2	7	8,804 bhp	1 cpp	13.8
Canadian Leader	Canadian General Electric Co. Ltd.	Turbine	2	*	9,900 shp	1	19.0
Canadian Mariner	General Electric Co.	Turbine	2	*	9,900 shp	1	19.0
Canadian Miner	Fairbanks Morse 12-38D8-1/8	Diesel	4	12	8,000 bhp	1 cpp	15.0
Canadian Navigator	Doxford Engines Ltd. 76J4	Diesel	1	4	9,680 bhp	1	16.8
Canadian Olympic	M.A.N. 8L40/54A	Diesel	2	8	10,001 bhp	1 cpp	15.0
Canadian Progress	Caterpillar 3612-TA	Diesel	2	12	9,000 bhp	1 cpp	15.5
Canadian Prospector	Gotaverken 760/1500VGS6U	Diesel	1	6	7,500 bhp	1	16.1
Canadian Provider	John Inglis Co. Ltd.	Turbine	2	*	10,000 shp	1	17.3
Canadian Ranger	Sulzer 5RND68	Diesel	1	5	6,100 bhp	1 cpp	19.6
Canadian Trader	Mirrlees Blackstone Ltd. KMR6	Diesel	3	6	8,308 bhp	1 cpp	16.4
Canadian Transfer	Sulzer 5RND68	Diesel	1	5	6,100 bhp	1 cpp	18.4
Canadian Transport	M.A.N. 8L40/45	Diesel	2	8	10,001 bhp	1 cpp	13.8
Canadian Venture		Diesel			9,400 bhp	1 cpp	19.6
Canadian Venture (Total)		Diesel			9,400 bhp	1 cpp	19.6
Canadian Venture (Main)	Fairbanks Morse 12-38D8-1/8	Diesel	4	12	8,000 bhp		
Canadian Venture (2ndary)	Caterpillar D398-TA	Diesel	2	12	1,400 bhp		
Canadian Voyager	Canadian General Electric Co. Ltd.	Turbine	2	*	9,000 shp	1	17.8
Capt. Henry Jackman	MaK 6M552AK	Diesel	2	6	9,465 bhp	1 cpp	17.3
Cartierdoc	B&W 7-74VTBF-160	Diesel	1	7	8,750 bhp	1 cpp	17.3
Cason J. Callaway	Westinghouse Elec. Corp.	Turbine	2	*	7,700 shp	1	16.1
Catherine Desgagnes	Sulzer 6SAD60	Diesel	1	6	3,841 bhp	1	15.5
Cecelia Desgagnes	B&W 6S50LU	Diesel	1	6	5,100 bhp	1 cpp	17.3
Charles M. Beeghly	General Electric Co.	Turbine	2	*	9,350 shp	1	17.8
Chi-Cheemaun	Ruston Paxman 16RKCM	Diesel	2	16	7,000 bhp	2	18.7
Columbia	Detroit Shipbuilding Co.	Triple Exp.	1	3	1,217 ihp	1	
Columbia Star	General Motors - EMD 20-645-E7B	Diesel	4	20	14,400 bhp	2 cpp	17.3
Comeaudoc	MaK 6M601AK	Diesel	1	6	8,158 bhp	1	15.0
Courtney Burton	General Electric Co.	Turbine	2	*	7,700 shp	1	16.8
CSL Niagara	Pielstick 10PC2-2V-400	Diesel	2	10	9,000 bhp	1 cpp	15.0
Cuyahoga	Caterpillar 3608	Diesel	1	8	3,000 bhp	1	
David Z. Norton	Alco 16V251E	Diesel	2	16	5,600 bhp	1	16.1
Day Peckinpaugh	Detroit Diesel Allison 6-110	Diesel	2	6	480 bhp	2	9.2
Diamond Star	B&W 6L35MC	Diesel	1	6	5,030 bhp	1 cpp	14.4
Dorothy Ann / (Tug & barge)							
Pathfinder	General Motors - EMD 20-645-E7B	Diesel	2	20	7,200 bhp	Z Drive	16.1
E. M. Ford	Cleveland Ship Building Co.	Quad. Exp.	1	4	1,500 ihp	1	11.5
Earl W. Oglebay	Alco 16V251E	Diesel	2	16	5,600 bhp	1	16.1
Edgar B. Speer	Pielstick 18PC2-3V-400	Diesel	2	18	19,260 bhp	2 cpp	17.0
Edward L. Ryerson	General Electric Co.	Turbine	2	*	9,900 shp	1	19.0
Edwin H. Gott	Enterprise DMRV-16-4	Diesel	2	16	19,500 bhp	2 cpp	16.8

Fred R. White Jr. shows off the power of her 7,200 horsepower diesels just north of the Blue Water Bridge. (Patrick Lapinski)

Vessel Name	Engine Manufacturer & Model #	Engine Type	Total Engines	Total Cylinders	Rated HP	Total Props	Speed MPH
Elton Hoyt 2nd	Bethlehem Steel Co.	Turbine	2	*	7,700 shp	1	17.3
Emerald Star	B&W 6L35MC	Diesel	1	6	5,030 bhp	1 cpp	14.4
Emmet J. Carey	Detroit Diesel Allison 6-71N	Diesel	2	6	400 bhp	2	
English River	Werkspoor TMAB-390	Diesel	1	8	1,850 bhp	1 cpp	13.8
F. M. Osborne	Caterpillar D334	Diesel	2	6	410 bhp	1	
Federal Agno	Sulzer 6RTA58	Diesel	1	6	9,500 bhp	1	16.8
Federal Asahi	B&W 6S46MC-C	Diesel	1	6	10,710 bhp	1	16.1
Federal Baffin	B&W 6L60MC	Diesel	1	6	15,600 bhp	1	18.0
Federal Bergen	B&W 6L60MCE	Diesel	1	6	9,500 bhp	1	16.4
Federal Franklin	B&W 6L60MC	Diesel	1	6	15,600 bhp	1	18.0
Federal Fraser	Sulzer 4RLB76	Diesel	1	4	10,880 bhp	1 cpp	13.8
Federal Fuji	Sulzer 6RTA58	Diesel	1	6	9,500 bhp	1	19.6
Federal Hudson	B&W 6S46MC-C	Diesel	1	6	10,710 bhp	1	16.1
Federal Kivalina	B&W 6S46MC-C	Diesel	1	6	10,710 bhp	1	16.1
Federal Maas	B&W 6S50MC	Diesel	1	6	10,476 bhp	1	16.1
Federal MacKenzie	Sulzer 4RLB76	Diesel	1	4	10,880 bhp	1 cpp	13.8
Federal Oshima	B&W 6S46MC-C	Diesel	1	6	10,710 bhp	1	16.1
Federal Polaris	Sulzer 6RTA58	Diesel	1	6	9,500 bhp	1	16.8
Federal Rhine	B&W 6S50MC	Diesel	1	6	10,476 bhp	1	16.1
Federal Rideau	B&W 6S46MC-C	Diesel	1	6	10,710 bhp	1	16.1
Federal Saguenay	B&W 6S50MC	Diesel	1	6	10,476 bhp	1	16.1
Federal Schelde	B&W 6S50MC	Diesel	1	6	11,640 bhp	1	16.1
Federal St. Laurent	B&W 6S50MC	Diesel	1	6	10,476 bhp	1	16.1
Federal Welland	B&W 6S46MC-C	Diesel	1	6	10,710 bhp	1	16.1
Federal Yukon	B&W 6S46MC-C	Diesel	1	6	10,710 bhp	1	16.1
Ferbec	Sulzer 6RD90	Diesel	1	6	14,999 bhp	1	17.3
Fred R. White Jr.	General Motors - EMD 20-645-E7	Diesel	2	20	7,200 bhp	1 cpp	16.1
Frontenac	Sulzer 6RND76	Diesel	1	6	9,599 bhp	1 cpp	17.0
Gemini	Alco 16V251E	Diesel	2	16	5,150 bhp	2	14.4
George A. Sloan	Caterpillar 3612-TA	Diesel	1	12	4,500 bhp	1 cpp	
George A. Stinson	Pielstick 16PC2-2V-400	Diesel	2	16	16,000 bhp	2	17.3
Gordon C. Leitch	Sulzer 6RND76	Diesel	1	6	9,599 bhp	1 cpp	17.3
H. Lee White	General Motors - EMD 20-645-E7B	Diesel	2	20	7,200 bhp	1 cpp	15.0
Halifax	John Inglis Co. Ltd.	Turbine	2	*	10,000 shp	1	19.6
Herbert C. Jackson	General Electric Co.	Turbine	2	*	6,600 shp	1	
Indiana Harbor	General Motors - EMD 20-645-E7	Diesel	4	20	14,400 bhp	2 cpp	16.1
Invincible / (Tug & Barge)							
McKee Sons	General Motors - EMD 16-645-E7B	Diesel	2	16	5,750 bhp	2	13.8
J. A. W. Iglehart	De Laval Steam Turbine Co.	Turbine	2	*	4,400 shp	1	15.0
J. B. Ford	American Ship Building Co.	Triple Exp.	1	3	1,500 ihp	1	
J. S. St. John	General Motors - EMD 8-567	Diesel	1	8	850 bhp	1	11.5
Jacklyn M. / (Tug & Barge)							
Integrity	Caterpillar 3608-DITA	Diesel	2	8	6,008 bhp	2	17.3
Jacques Desgagnes	Lister Blackstone Marine Ltd.	Diesel	2	8	1,200 bhp	2	12.1
Jade Star	B&W 6L35MC	Diesel	1	6	5,030 bhp	1 cpp	14.4
James Norris	Canadian Vickers Ltd.	Uniflow	1	5	4,000 ihp	1	16.1
James R. Barker	Pielstick 16PC2-2V-400	Diesel	2	16	16,000 bhp	2 cpp	15.5
Jane Ann IV / (Tug & Barge)							
Sarah Spencer	Pielstick 8PC2-2L-400	Diesel	2	8	8,000 bhp	2	15.8
Jean Parisien	Pielstick 10PC2-2V-400	Diesel	2	10	9,000 bhp	1 cpp	15.0
Jiimaan	Ruston Paxman Diesels Ltd. 6RK215	Diesel	2	6	2,839 bhp	2 cpp	15.0
John B. Aird	MaK 6M552AK	Diesel	2	6	9,459 bhp	1 cpp	13.8
John G. Munson	General Electric Co.	Turbine	2	*	7,700 shp	1	17.3
John J. Boland	General Motors - EMD 20-645-E7B	Diesel	2	20	7,200 bhp	1 cpp	15.0
John R. Emery	Detroit Diesel Allison 6-110	Diesel	2	6	550 bhp	2	
John Sherwin	De Laval Steam Turbine Co.	Turbine	2	*	9,350 shp	1	16.8
Joseph H. Frantz	Enterprise DMRV-12-4	Diesel	1	12	4,000 bhp	1 cpp	13.2
Joseph H. Thompson Jr. / (Tug & Barge)							
Joseph H. Thompson	General Electric Co. 7FDM16	Diesel	3	16	7,500 bhp	1	
Joseph L. Block	General Motors - EMD 20-645-E7	Diesel	2	20	7,200 bhp	1 cpp	17.3
Joyce L. Van Enkevort / (Tug & Barge)							
Great Lakes Trader	Caterpillar 3612	Diesel	2	12	10,200 bhp	2 cpp	
Kaye E. Barker	De Laval Steam Turbine Co.	Turbine	2	*	7,700 shp	1	17.3
Kinsman Enterprise	De Laval Steam Turbine Co.	Turbine	2	*	5,500 shp	1	
Kinsman Independent	Bethlehem Steel Co.	Turbine	2	*	4,400 shp	1	
L. E. Block	Westinghouse Elec. Corp.	Turbine	2	*	4,950 shp	1	
Lady Hamilton	Sulzer 4RLB76	Diesel	1	4	10,880 bhp	1 cpp	15.5
Lake Carling	Sulzer 4RTA58	Diesel	1	4	6,662 bhp	1	16.1
Lake Champlain	Sulzer 4RTA58	Diesel	1	4	6,662 bhp	1	16.1
Lake Charles	Sulzer 4RTA58	Diesel	1	4	6,662 bhp	1	16.1
Lake Erie	B&W 6K67GF	Diesel	1	6	11,600 bhp	1	16.1

Vessel Name	Engine Manufacturer & Model #	Engine Type	Total Engines	Total Cylinders	Rated HP	Total Props	Speed MPH
Lake Michigan	B&W 6K67GF	Diesel	1	6	11,600 bhp	1	16.1
Lake Ontario	B&W 6K67GF	Diesel	1	6	11,600 bhp	1	16.1
Lake Superior	B&W 6K67GF	Diesel	1	6	11,600 bhp	1	16.1
Lee A. Tregurtha	Bethlehem Steel Co.	Turbine	2	*	7,700 shp	1	16.8
Louis R. Desmarais	Pielstick 10PC2-2V-400	Diesel	2	10	9,000 bhp	1 cpp	16.1
Lucien-Paquin	Pielstick 10PC2-V-400	Diesel	2	10	8,799 bhp	1 cpp	19.3
M. H. Baker III	Sulzer 6RLA66	Diesel	1	6	11,095 bhp	1 cpp	17.3
Manitoulin **(Total)**		Diesel			9,400 bhp	1 cpp	17.3
Manitoulin **(Main)**	Fairbanks Morse 12-38D8-1/8	Diesel	4	12	8,000 bhp		
Manitoulin **(2ndary)**	Caterpillar D398B	Diesel	2	12	1,400 bhp		
Mantadoc	Fairbanks Morse 8-38D8-1/8	Diesel	4	8	5,332 bhp	1 cpp	16.1
Mapleglen	General Electric Co.	Turbine	2	*	9,350 shp	1	17.8
Maria Desgagnes	B&W 6S42MC	Diesel	1	6	8,361 bhp	1 cpp	16.1
Marine Star	General Electric Co.	Turbine	2	*	10,001 shp	1	21.9
Mathilda Desgagnes	Fairbanks Morse 10-38D8-1/8	Diesel	2	10	3,200 bhp	2	
Melissa Desgagnes	Allen 12PVBCS12-F	Diesel	2	12	4,000 bhp	1 cpp	13.8
Mesabi Miner	Pielstick 16PC2-2V-400	Diesel	2	16	16,000 bhp	2 cpp	15.5
Middletown	Bethlehem Steel Co.	Turbine	2	*	7,700 shp	1	16.1
Montrealais	Canadian General Electric Co. Ltd.	Turbine	2	*	9,900 shp	1	19.0
Myron C. Taylor	Nordberg	Diesel	1	16	4,234 bhp	1	12.1
Nanticoke	Pielstick 10PC2-2V-400	Diesel	2	10	10,699 bhp	1 cpp	13.8
Nunavit Trader	Werkspoor TMAB-390	Diesel	1	8	1,850 bhp	1 cpp	12.7
Oakglen	Westinghouse Elec. Corp.	Turbine	2	*	8,500 shp	1	17.3
Oglebay Norton	General Motors - EMD 20-645-E7	Diesel	4	20	14,400 bhp	2 cpp	18.4
Ojibway	Caterpillar 3306	Diesel	1	6	190 bhp	1	
Paterson	MaK 6M601AK	Diesel	1	6	8,158 bhp	1 cpp	15.5
Paul H. Townsend	Nordberg	Diesel	1	6	2,150 bhp	1	12.1
Paul R. Tregurtha	Pielstick 16PC2-3V-400	Diesel	2	16	17,120 bhp	2 cpp	15.5
Petrolia Desgagnes	B&W 8K42EF	Diesel	1	8	5,000 bhp	1 cpp	16.4
Philip R. Clarke	Westinghouse Elec. Corp.	Turbine	2	*	7,700 shp	1	16.1
Pioneer	Doxford Engines Ltd. 76J4C	Diesel	1	4	9,000 bhp	1	16.8
Presque Isle	Mirrlees Blackstone Ltd. KVMR-16	Diesel	2	16	14,840 bhp	2 cpp	
Quebecois	Canadian General Electric Co. Ltd.	Turbine	2	*	9,900 shp	1	19.0
Quedoc **(Total)**		Diesel			9,400 bhp	1 cpp	19.6
Quedoc **(Main)**	Fairbanks Morse 12-38D8-1/8	Diesel	4	12	8,000 bhp		
Quedoc **(2ndary)**	Caterpillar D398-TA	Diesel	2	12	1,400 bhp		
Reserve	Westinghouse Elec. Corp.	Turbine	2	*	7,700 shp	1	19.0
Richard Reiss	General Motors - EMD 20-645-E6	Diesel	1	20	2,950 bhp	1	
Roger Blough	Pielstick 16PC2V-400	Diesel	2	16	14,200 bhp	1 cpp	16.8
Rt. Hon. Paul J. Martin	Pielstick 10PC2-V-400	Diesel	2	10	9,000 bhp	1 cpp	15.0
S. T. Crapo	Great Lakes Engineering Works	Triple Exp.	1	3	1,800 ihp	1	13.2
Saginaw	De Laval Steam Turbine Co.	Turbine	2	*	7,700 shp	1	16.1
Sam Laud	General Motors - EMD 20-645-E7	Diesel	2	20	7,200 bhp	1 cpp	16.1
Saturn	General Motors - EMD 12-645-E6	Diesel	2	12	3,000 bhp	2	11.0
Sauniere	MaK 6M552AK	Diesel	2	6	8,799 bhp	1 cpp	15.0
Seaway Queen	John Inglis Co. Ltd.	Turbine	2	*	8,250 shp	1	17.8
Southdown Challenger	Skinner Engine Co.	Unaflow	1	4	3,500 ihp	1	
Spartan	Skinner Engine Co.	Unaflow	2	4	8,000 ihp	2	18.4
St. Clair	General Motors - EMD 20-645-E7	Diesel	3	20	10,800 bhp	1 cpp	16.8
Ste. Claire	Toledo Ship Building Co.	Triple Exp.	1	3	1,083 ihp	1	
Stephen B. Roman **(Total)**		Diesel			5,996 bhp	1 cpp	18.4
Stephen B. Roman **(Center)**	Fairbanks Morse 10-38D8-1/8	Diesel	2	10	3,331 bhp		
Stephen B. Roman **(Wing)**	Fairbanks Morse 8-38D8-1/8	Diesel	2	8	2,665 bhp		
Stewart J. Cort	General Motors - EMD 20-645-E7	Diesel	4	20	14,400 bhp	2 cpp	18.4
Susan W. Hannah / **(Tug & Barge)**							
Southdown Conquest	General Motors - EMD 12-645-E5	Diesel	2	12	4,320 bhp	2	11.5
Tadoussac	Sulzer 6RND76	Diesel	1	6	9,599 bhp	1	17.0
Thalassa Desgagnes	B&W 8K42EF	Diesel	1	8	5,000 bhp	1 cpp	16.4
Undaunted / **(Tug & Barge)**							
Pere Marquette 41	GM - Cleveland Diesel 12-278A	Diesel	1	12	2,400 bhp	1	
Vandoc	Fairbanks Morse 8-38D8-1/8	Diesel	4	8	5,998 bhp	1 cpp	14.4
Walter J. McCarthy Jr.	General Motors - EMD 20-645-E7B	Diesel	4	20	14,400 bhp	2 cpp	16.1
Wellington Kent	MaK 9M552AK	Diesel	1	9	7,504 bhp	1 cpp	
Wilfred Sykes	Westinghouse Elec. Corp.	Turbine	2	*	7,700 shp	1	16.1
Windoc	B&W 7-74VTBF-160	Diesel	1	7	8,750 bhp	1 cpp	14.4
Wolf River	Fairbanks Morse 10-38D8-1/8	Diesel	1	10	1,880 bhp	1	10.4
Wolverine	Alco 16V251E	Diesel	2	16	5,600 bhp	1	17.8
Yankcanuck	Cooper-Bessemer Corp.	Diesel	1	8	1,860 bhp	1	11.5

International Fleets

Verdon below the Welland Canal Flight Locks.
(Roger LeLievre)

Space does not permit listing every potential international visitor to the Great Lakes and Seaway. At the end of 1997, the world fleet totaled 85,494 vessels more than 100 gross tons, according to Lloyd's Register of Shipping. Therefore we have included only those fleets and vessels that make regular transits of the St. Lawrence Seaway and Great Lakes system, according to reports compiled by the St. Lawrence Seaway Authority. We have also included some vessels that are too large to transit the Seaway but are frequent visitors to St. Lawrence River ports.

Fleet #. Fleet Name Vessel Name	Type of Vessel	Year Built	Type of Engine	Cargo Cap. or Gross*	Overal Length	Breadth	Depth or Draft*
IA-1 **A/S BILLABONG, BERGEN, NORWAY**							
Santiago	GC	1997	D	3,525	280' 10"	42' 00"	23' 04"
Star Eagle	GC	1981	D	39,749	589' 03"	96' 07"	53' 04"
IA-2 **ACOMARIT (U.K.) LTD., GLASGOW, SCOTLAND**							
Echo Pioneer	GC	1981	D	11,464	479' 09"	70' 08"	37' 01"
IA-3 **AEGEUS SHIPPING S.A., PIREAUS, GREECE**							
George	GC	1977	D	16,875	530' 00"	70' 03"	43' 00"
Nini	GC	1976	D	16,291	529' 10"	70' 03"	43' 00"
IA-4 **AKMAR SHIPPING & TRADING CO., INC., ISTANBUL, TURKEY**							
Ayse Ana	BC	1979	D	25,452	607' 08"	75' 05"	46' 05"
IA-5 **ALBA SHIPPING LTD. A/S, AALBORG, DENMARK**							
Kasla	TK	1974	D	8,639	427' 07"	57' 10"	26' 03"
IA-6 **ALBAMAR SHIPPING CO. S.A., PIREAUS, GREECE**							
Yria	BC	1977	D	26,425	564' 04"	75' 02"	47' 03"
Zephyros	BC	1974	D	22,593	539' 02"	75' 02"	44' 06"
IA-7 **ALL TRUST SHIPPING CO. S.A., PIRAEUS, GREECE**							
Aghia Marina	BC	1978	D	16,868	481' 03"	75' 02"	40' 01"
Akrathos	BC	1981	D	25,817	605' 08"	75' 05"	46' 05"
Dora	BC	1978	D	30,350	622' 07"	76' 05"	47' 05"
IA-8 **ALVARGONZALEZ S.A., GIJON, SPAIN**							
Flag Adrienne	BC	1968	D	18,289	518' 11"	71' 05"	42' 08"
IA-9 **AMASUS SHIPPING B.V., FARMSUM, NETHERLANDS**							
Aldebaran	GC	1997	D	2,270	270' 06"	37' 05"	13' 02"
Antares	GC	1984	D	1,576	258' 08"	33' 02"	13' 10"
Auriga	GC	1978	D	1,670	276' 04"	35' 03"	17' 03"
Bolder	GC	1986	D	1,500	266' 06"	34' 03"	15' 02"
Christiaan	GC	1984	D	2,280	261' 09"	36' 05"	17' 01"
Compaen	GC	1975	D	1,458	262' 09"	29' 07"	14' 05"
Daan	GC	1979	D	1,163	204' 11"	30' 11"	13' 01"
Diamant	GC	1985	D	1,497	255' 09"	32' 08"	13' 10"
Eemshorn	GC	1995	D	4,250	293' 10"	43' 03"	23' 04"
Elisabeth G	GC	1978	D	1,163	204' 11"	32' 06"	13' 01"
Gitana	GC	1970	D	830	219' 10"	26' 08"	12' 03"
Laurina Neeltje	GC	1995	D	2,310	279' 04"	35' 05"	17' 07"
Morgenstond	GC	1967	D	530	203' 10"	23' 06"	10' 00"
Njord	GC	1985	D	1,490	258' 06"	34' 09"	13' 10"
Quo-Vadis	GC	1983	D	1,564	259' 03"	32' 08"	14' 10"
IA-10 **ANANGEL SHIPPING ENTERPRISES S.A., PIRAEUS, GREECE**							
Anangel Ares	GC	1980	D	17,154	477' 04"	68' 11"	43' 00"
Anangel Endeavor	GC	1978	D	23,130	539' 02"	75' 00"	44' 06"
Anangel Fidelity	BC	1979	D	22,000	539' 02"	75' 00"	44' 06"
Anangel Honesty	BC	1983	D	31,774	598' 07"	77' 05"	50' 06"
Anangel Honour	BC	1976	D	22,600	539' 02"	75' 00"	44' 06"
Anangel Hope	BC	1974	D	22,670	539' 02"	75' 00"	44' 06"
Anangel Horizon	BC	1977	D	27,090	580' 10"	75' 02"	46' 03"
Anangel Liberty	BC	1976	D	22,668	539' 02"	75' 00"	44' 06"
Anangel Might	BC	1978	D	23,130	539' 02"	75' 00"	46' 06"
Anangel Prosperity	BC	1976	D	22,314	539' 02"	75' 00"	44' 06"
Anangel Sky	GC	1979	D	17,199	477' 04"	68' 11"	43' 00"
Anangel Spirit	GC	1978	D	22,109	539' 02"	75' 00"	44' 06"
Anangel Triumph	BC	1976	D	22,311	539' 02"	75' 00"	44' 06"
Anangel Victory	GC	1979	D	17,188	477' 04"	68' 11"	44' 06"
Anangel Wisdom	BC	1974	D	22,353	539' 02"	75' 02"	44' 05"
Maria Angelicoussi	GC	1978	D	16,934	477' 05"	69' 00"	43' 00"
Pistis	BC	1973	D	22,627	539' 02"	75' 02"	44' 06"

Fleet #.	Fleet Name Vessel Name	Type of Vessel	Year Built	Type of Engine	Cargo Cap. or Gross*	Overall Length	Breadth	Depth or Draft*
IA-11	**ARGOSY SHIPMANAGEMENT, INC. LIBERIA, PIRAEUS, GREECE**							
	Alba Sierra	GC	1979	D	14,990	472' 05"	73' 07"	38' 07'
IA-12	**ARION SHIPPING LTD., PIRAEUS, GREECE**							
	Zoitsa S	BC	1978	D	26,991	564' 04"	75' 02"	47' 03"
IA-13	**ATLANTIS MANAGEMENT, INC., PIRAEUS, GREECE**							
	Atlantis Charm	BC	1982	D	22,558	539' 02"	75' 02"	44' 06"
	Atlantis Joy	BC	1977	D	18,216	511' 11"	73' 10"	39' 05"
	Atlantis Spirit	BC	1977	D	19,019	497' 10"	75' 00"	42' 00"
IA-14	**ATLANTSKA PLOVIDBA D.D., DUBROVNIK, CROATIA**							
	Kupari	HL	1979	D	2,720	266' 05"	48' 09"	21' 08"
	Lapad	HL	1978	D	1,970	307' 11"	52' 07"	24' 00"
	Mljet	BC	1982	D	29,643	622' 01"	74' 11"	49' 10"
	Orsula	BC	1996	D	34,198	656' 02"	77' 01"	48' 11"
	Plitvice	HL	1979	D	2,720	266' 05"	48' 09"	21' 08"
	Ruder Boskovic	BC	1974	D	27,020	599' 05"	73' 09"	46' 07"
	Slano	HL	1978	D	2,811	289' 04"	51' 02"	24' 10"
IA-15	**AURORA SHIPPING, INC., MANILA, PHILIPPINES**							
	Aurora Gold	GC	1976	D	10,027	419' 10"	60' 02"	32' 06"
	Aurora Jade	BC	1979	D	13,206	436' 04"	67' 08"	37' 09"
	Aurora Topaz	BC	1982	D	28,268	639' 09"	75' 10"	46' 11"
IA-16	**AZOV SHIPPING CO., MARIUPOL, UKRAINE**							
	Avdeevka	BC	1977	D	26,398	570' 11"	75' 03"	47' 07"
	Dobrush	BC	1982	D	28,160	644' 06"	75' 10"	46' 11"
	General Blazhevich	GC	1981	D	7,805	399' 09"	67' 00"	27' 03"
	Makeevka	BC	1982	D	28,136	644' 06"	75' 07"	46' 11"
	Mekhanik Aniskin	GC	1973	D	8,264	426' 04"	58' 06"	32' 02"
	Sumy	BC	1978	D	22,904	540' 00"	75' 00"	45' 00"
IB-1	**B & N, BYLOCK & NORDSJOFRAKT AS, OSLO, NORWAY**							
	Bergon	GC	1978	D	5,449	330' 10"	54' 02"	26' 03"
	Bremon	GC	1976	D	8,650	393' 10"	54' 06"	33' 04"
	Concord	GC	1985	D	6,994	404' 11"	65' 08"	34' 05"
	Corner Brook	GC	1976	D	7,173	445' 06"	61' 00"	40' 01"
	Holmon	GC	1978	D	10,900	442' 11"	59' 06"	32' 10"
	Humber Arm	GC	1976	D	7,173	426' 07"	61' 00"	40' 01"
	Macado	GC	1985	D	9,650	404' 11"	65' 09"	34' 06"
	Neva Trader	GC	1977	D	7,884	370' 09"	63' 00"	28' 07"
	Norcove	RR	1977	D	6,671	466' 07"	63' 02"	47' 08"
	Storon	BC	1975	D	10,880	470' 02"	61' 00"	33' 04"
	Swallow	GC	1996	D	4,251	296' 09"	43' 04"	23' 11"
	Tofton	GC	1980	D	14,883	522' 02"	70' 03"	41' 04"
	Tor Belgia	RR	1979	D	8,400	558' 07"	69' 00"	42' 00"
	Weston	GC	1979	D	14,938	522' 02"	70' 03"	41' 04"
IB-2	**B+H EQUIMAR SINGAPORE PTE. LTD., SINGAPORE, SINGAPORE**							
	Narragansett	BC	1977	D	35,910	729' 11"	76' 00"	47' 00"
IB-3	**BALTIMAR APS LTD., HUMLEBAEK, DENMARK**							
	Baltimar Boreas	GC	1989	D	2,742	299' 07"	49' 03"	25' 00"
	Baltimar Euros	GC	1991	D	3,181	299' 04"	49' 04"	24' 11"
	Baltimar Neptune	GC	1988	D	2,742	299' 05"	49' 05"	25' 00"
	Baltimar Nereus	CO	1986	D	4,250	349' 09"	52' 11"	27' 11"
	Baltimar Notos	GC	1988	D	3,168	299' 05"	50' 10"	24' 11"
	Baltimar Orion	GC	1990	D	3,168	299' 04"	49' 05"	24' 11"
	Baltimar Saturn	GC	1991	D	2,700	299' 03"	49' 05"	24' 11"
	Baltimar Sirius	GC	1991	D	3,181	299' 04"	49' 07"	24' 11"
	Baltimar Venus	GC	1990	D	2,700	299' 04"	49' 03"	25' 00"
IB-4	**BARU DELTA MARITIME, INC., PIRAEUS, GREECE**							
	Ocean D	BC	1977	D	26,779	580' 10"	75' 04"	47' 07"
IB-5	**BARU KAHA, INC., PIRAEUS, GREECE**							
	Elite B	BC	1979	D	19,009	509' 07"	74' 10"	41' 01"
	Iron B	GC	1981	D	21,889	584' 08"	75' 03"	46' 00"
	Runner B	GC	1983	D	14,930	532' 06"	72' 10"	44' 00"
	Star B	GC	1986	D	16,781	476' 01"	68' 03"	43' 03"
IB-6	**BELUGA SHIPPING GMBH, BREMEN, GERMANY**							
	Beluga Obsession	GC	1982	D	5,327	270' 03"	51' 11"	29' 06"
	Beluga Performer	GC	1982	D	6,081	303' 04"	53' 02"	33' 06"
IB-7	**BIRLIK DENIZCILIK ISLETMECILIGI SANAYI VE TICARET A.S., ISTANBUL, TURKEY**							
	Haci Hilmi Bey	BC	1977	D	24,354	607' 07"	75' 00"	46' 05"
	Riza Sonay	GC	1989	D	8,219	380' 07"	56' 06"	32' 02"

Fleet #.	Fleet Name Vessel Name	Type of Vessel	Year Built	Type of Engine	Cargo Cap. or Gross*	Overall Length	Breadth	Depth or Draft*
IB-8	**BISON SHIPMANAGEMENT & CHARTERING CO. PTE. LTD., SINGAPORE, SINGAPORE**							
	Olga	BC	1996	D	18,319	486' 01"	74' 10"	40' 00"
IB-9	**BLUE MARINE S.A. LIBERIA, PIRAEUS, GREECE**							
	Anthony	GC	1981	D	15,883	532' 09"	73' 00"	44' 02"
IB-10	**BLUE PLANET SHIPPING LTD., PIRAEUS, GREECE**							
	Evmar	BC	1976	D	29,212	593' 02"	76' 00"	47' 07"
IB-11	**BLUE SAPPHIRE SHIPPING CORP., MONROVIA, LIBERIA**							
	Toro	BC	1983	D	28,126	584' 08"	75' 11"	48' 05"
IB-12	**BOTANY BAY MANAGEMENT SERVICES PTY. LTD., SYDNEY, AUSTRALIA**							
	Botany Tradewind	TK	1986	D	87,719	404' 06"	65' 09"	36' 09"
	Botany Trust	TK	1998	D	57,238	370' 09"	61' 08"	31' 08"
	Marinor	TK	1992	D	53,464	368' 01"	59' 02"	31' 02"
IB-13	**BRIESE SCHIFFAHRTS GMBH & CO. KG, LEER, GERMANY**							
	Bavaria	GC	1996	D	3,500	288' 09"	42' 00"	23' 04"
	BBC America	GC	1999	D	4,806	330' 01"	54' 06"	26' 07"
	BBC Brazil	GC	1997	D	4,900	330' 01"	55' 01"	26' 07"
	BBC Canada	GC	1999	D	4,798	330' 01"	54' 06"	26' 07"
	BBC Finland	GC	2000	D	8,760	353' 06"	59' 09"	33' 02"
	BBC Norway	GC	2000	D	7,800	353' 06"	59' 09"	33' 02"
	Bremer Flagge	GC	1985	D	3,840	326' 01"	46' 05"	23' 06"
	Frigga	GC	1987	D	3,938	330' 01"	46' 06"	24' 02"
	Helgoland	GC	1998	D	6,375	344' 06"	53' 02"	29' 06"
	Industrial Accord	GC	1999	D	4,806	330' 01"	54' 06"	26' 07"
	Sjard	GC	1989	D	8,224	352' 06"	63' 02"	34' 09"
IB-14	**BURMA NAVIGATION CORP., YANGON, UNION OF MYANMAR**							
	Great Laker	BC	1987	D	28,358	590' 07"	75' 10"	48' 07"
	Sea Eagle	BC	1984	D	17,330	519' 03"	75' 09"	44' 00"
IC-1	**CANADA MARITIME LTD., HAMILTON, BERMUDA**							
	Canmar Conquest	CO	1979	D	18,643	580' 09"	88' 10"	44' 03"
	Canmar Courage	CO	1996	D	34,330	709' 01"	105' 10"	62' 04"
	Canmar Fortune	CO	1995	D	34,330	709' 01"	105' 10"	62' 04"
	Canmar Glory	CO	1979	D	18,964	580' 10"	88' 09"	44' 04"
	Canmar Honour	CO	1998	D	40,879	803' 10"	105' 08"	35' 05"*
	Canmar Pride	CO	1998	D	40,879	803' 10"	105' 08"	35' 05"*
	Canmar Spirit	CO	1971	D	16,963	548' 02"	84' 02"	50' 01"
	Canmar Triumph	CO	1978	D	18,606	580' 10"	88' 10"	44' 04"
	Canmar Valour	CO	1979	D	18,643	580' 09"	88' 10"	44' 03"
	Canmar Venture	CO	1971	D	16,963	548' 02"	84' 02"	50' 00"
	Canmar Victory	CO	1979	D	18,381	580' 09"	88' 10"	44' 04"
	Cast Performance	CO	1983	D	32,424	727' 02"	105' 08"	49' 03"
	Cast Privilege	CO	1978	D	33,869	717' 02"	101' 11"	54' 03"
	Contship Success	CO	1982	D	32,207	730' 00"	105' 10"	61' 08"
IC-2	**CAPE SHIPPING S.A., PIRAEUS, GREECE**							
	Cape Syros	GC	1978	D	14,948	470' 06"	65' 01"	40' 06"
	Monterey	GC	1978	D	15,078	470' 06"	65' 01"	40' 06"
	Radnor	GC	1975	D	14,970	470' 06"	65' 01"	40' 06"
	Shannon	GC	1976	D	14,829	470' 06"	65' 01"	40' 06"
IC-3	**CAPELLE CHARTERING EN TRADING B.V., CAPELLE A / D IJSSEL, NETHERLANDS**							
	Blue Moon	GC	1975	D	1,559	216' 00"	35' 06"	16' 09"
	Irene	GC	1978	D	1,548	216' 00"	36' 05"	16' 09"
	Wijmers	GC	1984	D	5,050	301' 05"	49' 08"	26' 07"
IC-4	**CARISBROOKE SHIPPING PLC, COWES, ISLE OF WIGHT**							
	Anja C	GC	1991	D	3,222	327' 03"	41' 00"	20' 10"
	Cheryl C	GC	1983	D	2,367	230' 01"	42' 11"	19' 09"
	Eliza	GC	1971	D	2,823	278' 11"	41' 10"	20' 04"
	Emily C	GC	1996	D	4,650	294' 07"	43' 02"	23' 05"
	Janet C	GC	1998	D	4,570	294' 11"	43' 04"	23' 06"
	Johanna C	GC	1998	D	4,570	294' 11"	43' 04"	23' 06"
	Klazina C	GC	1983	D	2,554	266' 09"	39' 04"	17' 09"
	Mark C	GC	1996	D	4,620	294' 11"	43' 04"	23' 06"
	Mary C	GC	1977	D	2,440	216' 10"	42' 11"	20' 05"
	Minka C	GC	1975	D	2,657	258' 00"	40' 10"	20' 00"
	Nordstrand	GC	1991	D	2,800	289' 08"	41' 00"	21' 04"
	Tina C	GC	1974	D	2,591	258' 02"	40' 10"	20' 00"
	Vanessa C	GC	1974	D	3,165	262' 11"	44' 08"	22' 01"
	Vectis Falcon	GC	1978	D	3,564	285' 06"	45' 01"	22' 04"
	Vectis Isle	GC	1990	D	3,222	327' 02"	41' 00"	20' 10"

Fleet #.	Fleet Name Vessel Name	Type of Vessel	Year Built	Type of Engine	Cargo Cap. or Gross*	Overall Length	Breadth	Depth or Draft*
IC-5	**CARSTEN REHDER SCHIFFSMAKLER UND REEDEREI GMBH & CO., HAMBURG, GERMANY**							
	Almania	GC	1983	D	5,900	327' 09"	58' 06"	29' 04"
	Arosette	GC	1971	D	1,968	244' 06"	35' 06"	19' 09"
	Cabot Strait	GC	1983	D	9,300	416' 11"	65' 03"	35' 02"
	Industrial Advantage	GC	1984	D	17,330	519' 03"	75' 08"	44' 00"
IC-6	**CATSAMBIS SHIPPING LTD., PIRAEUS, GREECE**							
	Adimon	BC	1977	D	30,880	644' 11"	75' 04"	47' 06"
IC-7	**CERES HELLENIC SHIPPING ENTERPRISES LTD., PIRAEUS, GREECE**							
	George L.	BC	1975	D	27,419	597' 01"	75' 02"	48' 03"
	Kalliopi L.	BC	1974	D	26,998	585' 08"	75' 01"	47' 06"
	Marka L.	BC	1975	D	27,418	597' 01"	75' 02"	48' 03"
	Mini Lace	GC	1969	D/W	3,217	214' 11"	50' 03"	21' 08"
	Pantazis L.	BC	1974	D	27,434	597' 02"	75' 02"	48' 03"
	Tatiana L.	GC	1978	D	16,251	482' 00"	72' 04"	39' 05"
IC-8	**CHANGJIANG NATIONAL SHIPPING CORP., SHEKOU, PEOPLE'S REPUBLIC OF CHINA**							
	Gold River	TK	1999	D	94,028	477' 09"	64' 04"	34' 11"
IC-9	**CHARTWORLD SHIPPING CORP., PIRAEUS, GREECE**							
	Akebono Star	GC	1980	D	8,071	475' 07"	61' 04"	38' 09"
	Ariake Star	GC	1980	D	8,076	475' 07"	61' 06"	38' 10"
	Capricorn	GC	1973	D	12,180	575' 03"	75' 00"	44' 04"
	Fuji Star	GC	1979	D	8,084	475' 07"	61' 06"	38' 09"
	Golden Sky	BC	1975	D	30,449	625' 06"	75' 00"	47' 11"
	Golden Sun	BC	1977	D	22,647	539' 03"	75' 01"	44' 06"
	Pelagos	GC	1973	D	10,973	511' 02"	70' 01"	41' 08"
	Perseus	GC	1972	D	10,974	511' 02"	70' 01"	41' 08"
	Tokachi Star	GC	1985	D	3,621	367' 04"	53' 11"	31' 06"
IC-10	**CHEKKA SHIPPING S.A., ATHENS, GREECE**							
	Alexander K.	BC	1978	D	30,353	622' 07"	76' 05"	47' 05"
IC-11	**CHELLARAM SHIPPING LTD., HONG KONG, PEOPLE'S REPUBLIC OF CHINA**							
	Darya Devi	BC	1985	D	28,019	584' 08"	75' 11"	48' 05"
	Darya Ma	BC	1983	D	30,750	617' 04"	76' 00"	47' 07"
	Darya Shaan	BC	1977	D	19,158	486' 03"	75' 02"	42' 08"
IC-12	**CHEMICO NAVIGATION LTD., ATHENS, GREECE**							
	Gulfbreeze	TK	1982	D	85,191	416' 08"	65' 09"	36' 09"
	Gulfstream	TK	1975	D	167,231	561' 04"	73' 08"	42' 06"
IC-13	**CHEMOIL INTERNATIONAL LTD., ATHENS, GREECE**							
	Bahamas	TK	1970	D	150,864	560' 01"	72' 00"	43' 02"
	Martinique	TK	1974	D	46,470	360' 11"	54' 07"	28' 01"
	Queen of Evian	TK	1984	D	10,064	228' 05"	36' 02"	16' 05"
IC-14	**CHINA OCEAN SHIPPING (GROUP) CO., BEIJING, PEOPLE'S REPUBLIC OF CHINA**							
	An Guang Jiang	GC	1987	D	14,913	491' 02"	71' 06"	41' 00"
	An Kang Jiang	GC	1985	D	15,852	487' 02"	74' 07"	43' 04"
	An Qing Jiang	GC	1985	D	14,913	491' 02"	71' 06"	41' 00"
	An Ze Jiang	GC	1987	D	14,913	491' 02"	71' 06"	41' 00"
	Aptmariner	BC	1979	D	31,000	619' 03"	75' 11"	47' 07"
	Da Hua	GC	1998	D	16,957	502' 00"	75' 08"	46' 03"
	Hai Ji Shun	GC	1978	D	15,189	462' 07"	67' 05"	38' 06"
	Handymariner	BC	1978	D	31,200	619' 03"	75' 11"	47' 07"
	Hui Fu	BC	1978	D	35,887	734' 02"	76' 08"	47' 05"
	Hun Jiang	GC	1981	D	15,265	474' 11"	67' 01"	38' 07"
	Jing Hong Hai	BC	1976	D	28,863	594' 01"	76' 01"	47' 07"
	Ocean Priti	BC	1982	D	27,019	599' 05"	75' 04"	46' 08"
	Rong Cheng	GC	1977	D	18,687	484' 07"	75' 00"	42' 08"
	Tong Fu	BC	1977	D	35,887	729' 11"	76' 00"	47' 00"
	Yick Hua	BC	1984	D	28,086	584' 08"	75' 11"	48' 05"
IC-15	**CLIPPER GREECE LTD., ATHENS, GREECE**							
	Clipper Spirit	BC	1985	D	17,825	481' 08"	74' 10"	40' 01"
IC-16	**COMMERCIAL TRADING & DISCOUNT CO. LTD., ATHENS, GREECE**							
	Ira	BC	1979	D	26,697	591' 02"	75' 10"	45' 08"
	Ivi	BC	1979	D	26,697	591' 04"	75' 10"	45' 08"
IC-17	**COMMON PROGRESS COMPANIA NAVIERA S.A., PIRAEUS, GREECE**							
	Altis P	BC	1976	D	22,636	539' 02"	75' 02"	44' 06"
	Angelia P	BC	1979	D	22,549	539' 02"	75' 02"	44' 06"
	Athinais P	BC	1973	D	22,631	539' 02"	75' 02"	44' 06"
	Danais P	BC	1978	D	22,670	539' 02"	75' 02"	44' 06"
	Ellinis P	BC	1974	D	22,669	539' 02"	75' 02"	44' 06"

Fleet #.	Fleet Name / Vessel Name	Type of Vessel	Year Built	Type of Engine	Cargo Cap. or Gross*	Overall Length	Breadth	Depth or Draft*
	Kastor P	BC	1983	D	22,713	528' 03"	75' 07"	45' 07"
	Nereis P	BC	1974	D	22,631	539' 02"	74' 11"	44' 05"
	Polydefkis P	BC	1982	D	22,713	528' 03"	75' 07"	45' 07"
IC-18	**COMPAGNIE DES ILES DU PONANT, NANTES, FRANCE**							
	Le Levant	PA	1998	D	3,504*	326' 09"	45' 11"	11' 06"*
	Le Ponant	PA	1991	D/W	1,489*	290' 06"	39' 01"	17' 00"
IC-19	**COMPAGNIE TUNISIENNE DE NAVIGATION S.A., TUNIS, TUNISIA**							
	Bizerte	GC	1979	D	8,312	450' 06"	64' 01"	34' 05"
	El Kef	BC	1982	D	26,355	599' 10"	75' 08"	46' 00"
	Habib	RR	1978	D	3,372	478' 01"	77' 02"	27' 05"
	Kairouan	GC	1979	D	8,345	450' 06"	64' 01"	34' 05"
ID-1	**DALEX SHIPPING CO. S.A., PIRAEUS, GREECE**							
	Arabian Express	GC	1977	D	17,089	483' 05"	72' 04"	39' 01"
	Caribbean Express I	GC	1977	D	17,057	483' 05"	72' 04"	39' 01"
	Platytera	GC	1980	D	14,930	462' 06"	67' 00"	38' 07"
	Pol Daisy	GC	1982	D	17,279	509' 03"	74' 10"	43' 04"
	Pol Iris	GC	1982	D	16,467	509' 03"	74' 10"	43' 04"
	Pol Pansy	GC	1982	D	17,279	509' 03"	74' 10"	43' 04"
	Pol Primrose	GC	1984	D	17,279	509' 03"	74' 10"	43' 04"
ID-2	**DALNAVE NAVIGATION, INC., ATHENS, GREECE**							
	DS Pioneer	DS	1978	D	29,696	584' 00"	75' 04"	48' 03"
	Winner	BC	1975	D	27,223	579' 10"	74' 11"	46' 03"
ID-3	**DENSAN SHIPPING CO. LTD., ISTANBUL, TURKEY**							
	Gunay A	BC	1981	D	30,900	617' 04"	76' 00"	47' 07"
	Necat A	BC	1981	D	28,645	655' 06"	75' 00"	45' 11"
ID-4	**DESMOS MARITIME S.A., PIRAEUS, GREECE**							
	Axion	BC	1976	D	30,242	621' 06"	75' 00"	47' 11"
ID-5	**DET NORDENFJELDSKE D/S AS, TRONDHEIM, NORWAY**							
	Consensus Reefer	GC	1991	D	9,157	452' 04"	60' 08"	41' 03"
ID-6	**DIANA SHIPPING AGENCIES S.A., PIRAEUS, GREECE**							
	Elm	BC	1984	D	21,978	509' 02"	75' 01"	44' 07"
	Maple	BC	1977	D	19,020	497' 10"	75' 00"	42' 00"
	Oak	BC	1981	D	21,951	509' 02"	75' 02"	44' 07"
ID-7	**DILMUN SHIPPING CO. LTD., MANAMA, BAHRAIN**							
	Dilmun Fulmar	TK	1980	D	10,150	361' 04"	60' 02"	32' 10"
	Dilmun Shearwater	TK	1983	D	19,217	486' 06"	69' 00"	38' 03"
	Dilmun Tern	TK	1980	D	21,770	496' 05"	74' 10"	39' 05"
ID-8	**DOBSON FLEET MANAGEMENT LTD., LIMASSOL, CYPRUS**							
	Evangeline	GC	1975	D	4,250	316' 07"	52' 07"	28' 11"
	Fetish	GC	1977	D	4,240	309' 09"	50' 08"	27' 03"
	Ice Bird	GC	1990	D	3,043	304' 10"	50' 05"	34' 05"
	Ice Crystal	GC	1991	D	3,043	304' 10"	50' 05"	34' 05"
	Ice Star	GC	1990	D	3,039	304' 10"	50' 05"	34' 05"
	Jenny D	BC	1972	D	19,306	508' 11"	74' 11"	41' 06"
	Nicola D	BC	1977	D	9,267	439' 01"	59' 03"	29' 06"
	Scarab	GC	1983	D	4,240	309' 01"	50' 07"	27' 03"
ID-9	**DOCKENDALE SHIPPING CO. LTD., NASSAU, BAHAMAS**							
	Attica	GC	1984	D	20,412	503' 07"	74' 08"	45' 04"
	Clipper Arita	GC	1984	D	17,247	477' 05"	69' 00"	43' 01"
	Express Progress	GC	1985	D	17,247	477' 05"	69' 01"	43' 00"
	Okim	GC	1989	D	23,270	539' 02"	75' 01"	46' 05"
	Sakura	GC	1987	D	23,209	539' 02"	75' 00"	46' 05"
ID-10	**DONNELLY SHIPMANAGEMENT LTD., LIMASSOL, CYPRUS**							
	Finnsnes	BC	1978	D	12,394	441' 04"	67' 11"	37' 09"
	Fonnes	BC	1978	D	5,753	346' 09"	50' 07"	26' 03"
	Frines	BC	1978	D	12,358	441' 04"	67' 11"	37' 09"
	Fullnes	BC	1979	D	12,274	441' 04"	67' 11"	37' 09"
	Garnes	GC	1980	D	5,995	351' 01"	49' 04"	28' 09"
	Rafnes	BC	1976	D	6,351	339' 09"	52' 06"	28' 11"
	Risnes	BC	1976	D	5,699	339' 09"	52' 10"	28' 11"
	Rollnes	BC	1976	D	5,789	334' 09"	52' 00"	28' 09"
	Vigsnes	BC	1979	D	6,105	352' 04"	49' 03"	28' 09"
ID-11	**DYNASTY SHIPPING CO. LTD., ATHENS, GREECE**							
	Seaglory	BC	1978	D	29,212	593' 03"	75' 11"	47' 07"
IE-1	**E. P. SHIPPING & TRADING B.V., ROCKANJE, NETHERLANDS**							
	Storm	GC	1983	D	2,175	241' 10"	37' 05"	17' 01"

Fleet #.	Fleet Name Vessel Name	Type of Vessel	Year Built	Type of Engine	Cargo Cap. or Gross*	Overall Length	Breadth	Depth or Draft*
IE-2	**EGON OLDENDORFF LTD., LUEBECK, GERMANY**							
	Anna Oldendorff	BC	1994	D	18,355	486' 05"	74' 10"	40' 00"
	Antonie Oldendorff	BC	1999	D	20,427	488' 10"	75' 11"	44' 03"
	Elise Oldendorff	BC	1998	D	20,100	488' 10"	75' 11"	44' 03"
	Erna Oldendorff	BC	1994	D	18,355	486' 05"	74' 10"	40' 00"
	Helena Oldendorff	BC	1984	D	28,354	644' 06"	75' 10"	46' 11"
	Jobst Oldendorff	GC	1983	D	14,279	462' 06"	67' 01"	38' 06"
	Johann Oldendorff	GC	1999	D	20,567	502' 07"	77' 05"	44' 03"
	Maria Oldendorff	GC	1988	D	20,586	595' 06"	77' 01"	44' 00"
	Mathilde Oldendorff	BC	1999	D	20,427	488' 10"	75' 11"	44' 03"
	Regina Oldendorff	BC	1986	D	28,031	639' 09"	75' 10"	46' 11"
	Rixta Oldendorff	BC	1986	D	28,031	639' 09"	75' 10"	46' 11"
	T. A. Discoverer	GC	1989	D	28,386	595' 06"	75' 08"	44' 00"
	T. A. Explorer	GC	1987	D	22,500	614' 10"	75' 11"	42' 08"
	T. A. Voyager	GC	1987	D	22,800	614' 10"	75' 11"	44' 04"
IE-3	**ELITE-SHIPPING A/S, COPENHAGEN, DENMARK**							
	Arktis Ace	GC	1993	D	4,111	290' 01"	49' 08"	24' 07"
	Arktis Atlantic	GC	1992	D	4,110	290' 01"	49' 08"	24' 07"
	Arktis Breeze	GC	1987	D	2,671	261' 01"	44' 02"	21' 00"
	Arktis Carrier	GC	1988	D	2,671	261' 01"	44' 02"	21' 00"
	Arktis Crystal	GC	1994	D	5,401	319' 07"	53' 08"	27' 11"
	Arktis Dream	GC	1993	D	4,110	290' 01"	49' 08"	24' 07"
	Arktis Fantasy	GC	1994	D	7,120	331' 08"	63' 00"	30' 06"
	Arktis Fighter	GC	1994	D	7,120	331' 08"	63' 00"	30' 06"
	Arktis Grace	GC	1988	D	2,671	261' 01"	44' 02"	21' 00"
	Arktis Hunter	GC	1995	D	5,401	319' 07"	53' 08"	27' 11"
	Arktis Mariner	GC	1996	D	8,972	330' 09"	67' 01"	36' 01"
	Arktis Mayflower	GC	1996	D	8,972	330' 09"	67' 01"	36' 01"
	Arktis Meadow	GC	1995	D	8,970	330' 09"	66' 03"	36' 01"
	Arktis Meridian	GC	1996	D	8,900	330' 08"	67' 01"	36' 01"
	Arktis Mistral	GC	1999	D	8,950	330' 09"	66' 03"	36' 01"
	Arktis Ocean	GC	1987	D	2,433	249' 07"	38' 03"	21' 00"
	Arktis Pearl	GC	1984	D	2,298	243' 10"	37' 03"	22' 01"
	Arktis Pride	GC	1991	D	4,110	290' 01"	49' 08"	24' 07"
	Arktis Princess	GC	1989	D	2,671	261' 01"	44' 02"	21' 00"
	Arktis Queen	GC	1989	D	2,676	261' 01"	44' 02"	21' 00"
	Arktis River	GC	1986	D	2,433	249' 07"	38' 03"	21' 00"
	Arktis Sea	GC	1984	D	2,298	243' 10"	37' 03"	22' 01"
	Arktis Sirius	GC	1989	D	2,671	261' 01"	44' 02"	21' 00"
	Arktis Sky	GC	1987	D	2,671	261' 01"	44' 02"	21' 00"
	Arktis Spring	GC	1993	D	4,110	290' 01"	49' 08"	24' 07"
	Arktis Star	CO	1993	D	12,200	488' 10"	75' 11"	37' 01"
	Arktis Sun	CO	1993	D	12,216	488' 10"	75' 11"	37' 01"
	Arktis Trader	GC	1987	D	2,433	249' 07"	38' 03"	21' 00"
	Arktis Venture	GC	1992	D	4,110	290' 01"	49' 08"	24' 07"
	CEC Blue	GC	1992	D	4,110	290' 01"	49' 08"	24' 07"
	CEC Dawn	GC	1991	D	4,110	290' 01"	49' 08"	24' 07"
	CEC Faith	GC	1994	D	7,225	331' 08"	63' 00"	30' 06"
	CEC Force	GC	1995	D	7,121	331' 08"	63' 00"	30' 06"
	CEC Future	GC	1994	D	7,120	331' 08"	63' 00"	30' 06"
	CIC Hope	GC	1994	D	5,401	319' 07"	53' 08"	27' 11"
	CIC Light	GC	1993	D	5,401	319' 07"	53' 08"	27' 11"
	CIC Vision	GC	1994	D	5,401	319' 07"	53' 08"	27' 11"
	Industrial Caribe	GC	1992	D	4,117	290' 01"	49' 08"	24' 07"
	Industrial Frontier	GC	1993	D	4,110	290' 01"	49' 08"	24' 07"
IE-4	**ELMIRA SHIPPING & TRADING S.A., ATHENS, GREECE**							
	Aegean Sea	BC	1983	D	31,431	598' 09"	77' 06"	50' 06"
	Mecta Sea	BC	1984	D	28,166	584' 08"	75' 11"	48' 05"
	Tecam Sea	BC	1984	D	28,166	584' 08"	75' 11"	48' 05"
IE-5	**ER DENIZCILIK SANAYI NAKLIYAT VE TICARET A.S., ISTANBUL, TURKEY**							
	Balaban I	BC	1979	D	24,747	562' 06"	75' 00"	46' 00"
IF-1	**FABRICIUS & CO. A/S, MARSTAL, DENMARK**							
	Caroline K	GC	1983	D	2,166	237' 08"	37' 03"	22' 00"
	Emilie K	GC	1982	D	2,150	237' 08"	37' 04"	22' 00"
	Greenland Saga	GC	1989	D	3,200	285' 07"	47' 10"	25' 03"
	Katral 7	GC	1986	D	7,310	350' 06"	54' 07"	31' 03"
	Laola	GC	1980	D	2,920	327' 06"	37' 05"	14' 02"
	Sea Flower	GC	1982	D	1,630	237' 09"	36' 11"	22' 06"
	Sea Lion	GC	1993	D	4,000	290' 00"	49' 03"	24' 07"
	Sea Maid	GC	1984	D/W	1,632	237' 08"	36' 09"	22' 00"

French-flag passenger liner Le Levant cruises the Great Lakes. (Roger LeLievre)

Swallow, registered in the Netherlands, in the Detroit River. (Gene W. Peterson)

Fleet #.	Fleet Name Vessel Name	Type of Vessel	Year Built	Type of Engine	Cargo Cap. or Gross*	Overall Length	Breadth	Depth or Draft*
	Sea Rose	GC	1980	D	1,304	229' 00"	34' 03"	19' 09"
	Susan K	GC	1982	D	2,158	237' 08"	37' 03"	22' 00"
	Vinland Saga	GC	1982	D	932	207' 04"	31' 06"	18' 05"
IF-2	**FAFALIOS SHIPPING S.A., PIRAEUS, GREECE**							
	Irene	BC	1993	D	65,671	738' 02"	72' 02"	59' 01"
	Nea Doxa	BC	1984	D	30,900	617' 03"	76' 00"	47' 07"
	Nea Elpis	BC	1978	D	29,300	593' 03"	76' 00"	47' 07"
	Nea Tyhi	BC	1978	D	29,300	593' 03"	76' 00"	47' 07"
IF-3	**FAIRMONT SHIPPING (H.K.) LTD., HONG KONG, PEOPLE'S REPUBLIC OF CHINA**							
	Gefion	GC	1985	D	12,363	399' 07"	65' 08"	36' 02"
IF-4	**FAR-EASTERN SHIPPING CO., VLADIVOSTOK, RUSSIA**							
	Argut	BC	1990	D	3,600	311' 08"	51' 10"	25' 07"
	Kapitan Milovzorov	BC	1975	D	14,204	497' 10"	69' 01"	38' 00"
IF-5	**FEEDERLINES B.V., GRONINGEN, NETHERLANDS**							
	Marcosul Uruguay	GC	1997	D	7,761	415' 00"	65' 00"	27' 07"
IF-6	**FG-SHIPPING OY AB, HELSINKI, FINLAND**							
	Astrea	RR	1990	D	6,672	423' 07"	70' 01"	43' 06"
	Finnfighter	GC	1978	D	14,931	522' 02"	70' 03"	41' 05"
	Finnmaster	RR	1973	D	5,710	451' 02"	73' 04"	52' 10"
	Finnpine	RR	1984	D	7,669	394' 05"	69' 00"	47' 07"
	Kemira	BK	1981	D	19,323/8,250	369' 09"	57' 05"	34' 06"
IF-7	**FLAGSHIP MANAGEMENT CO. B.V., FARMSUM, NETHERLANDS**							
	Sabinia	TK	2000	D	3,700	292' 04"	44' 00"	23' 06"
IF-8	**FRANCO COMPANIA NAVIERA S.A., ATHENS, GREECE**							
	Rhea	BC	1978	D	29,300	593' 10"	76' 00"	47' 07"
	Stefania I	BC	1985	D	28,269	584' 08"	75' 11"	48' 05"
IF-9	**FREJA TANKERS A/S, COPENHAGEN, DENMARK**							
	Freja Scandic	TK	1981	D	77,442	405' 07"	59' 09"	32' 02"
IG-1	**GALATIA SHIPPING CO. S. A., PIRAEUS, GREECE**							
	Agios Georgios	GC	1970	D	3,062	214' 10"	50' 03"	21' 08"
	Captain Christos	GC	1976	D	11,775	419' 03"	67' 04"	33' 09"
	Dimitra	GC	1973	D	5,792	309' 00"	49' 06"	29' 07"
	Dimitra G	GC	1984	D	9,062	393' 08"	60' 10"	32' 10"
IG-2	**GANYMED (MALTA) LTD., BIRZEBBUGA, MALTA**							
	MSC Boston	CO	1993	D	41,750	794' 00"	105' 09"	75' 06"
	MSC Houston	CO	1994	D	41,570	794' 00"	105' 09"	75' 06"
	Norasia Samantha	CO	1998	D	14,310	708' 08"	87' 06"	62' 02"
	Norasia Savannah	CO	1998	D	14,310	708' 08"	87' 06"	62' 02"
IG-3	**GANYMED SHIPPING GMBH, HAMBURG, GERMANY**							
	Morillo	GC	1971	D	10,800	511' 02"	70' 01"	41' 08"
	MSC New York	CO	1994	D	41,570	794' 00"	106' 00"	75' 06"
	Norasia Malta	CO	1994	D	41,722	773' 04"	106' 00"	63' 04"
	Norasia Scarlett	CO	1999	D	14,310	708' 08"	87' 06"	62' 02"
	Norasia Shamsha	CO	1998	D	14,310	708' 08"	87' 06"	71' 06"
	Norasia Shanghai	CO	1996	D	41,460	794' 02"	106' 00"	75' 06"
	Norasia Sharjah	CO	1994	D	41,570	794' 00"	105' 09"	75' 06"
	Norasia Sheba	CO	1998	D	14,310	708' 08"	87' 06"	62' 02"
	Norasia Singa	CO	1996	D	41,460	794' 02"	106' 00"	75' 06"
IG-4	**GEORGIAN SHIPPING CO. LTD., BATUMI, GEORGIA**							
	Bakradze	TK	1985	D	126,377	496' 05"	73' 07"	40' 00"
	Chavchavadze	TK	1988	D	126,377	496' 05"	73' 07"	40' 00"
	G. Ordzhonikidze	TK	1988	D	126,377	496' 05"	73' 07"	40' 00"
	Gonio	TK	1984	D	126,377	496' 05"	73' 07"	39' 10"
	Kacharava	TK	1984	D	126,377	496' 05"	73' 07"	40' 00"
	Kobuleti	TK	1985	D	126,377	496' 05"	73' 07"	39' 11"
	Makatsarija	TK	1984	D	126,377	496' 05"	73' 07"	40' 00"
	Poti	TK	1981	D	167,174	505' 03"	74' 07"	45' 04"
	Uznadze	TK	1988	D	128,956	496' 05"	73' 07"	39' 10"
	Vachnadze	TK	1985	D	126,377	496' 05"	73' 07"	39' 10"
	Vakhtangov	BC	1984	D	24,105	605' 00"	75' 00"	46' 05"
	Vekua	TK	1987	D	126,377	496' 05"	73' 07"	39' 10"
	Yannis	BC	1984	D	24,105	605' 08"	75' 00"	46' 05"
IG-5	**GODBY SHIPPING A/B, GODBY, FINLAND**							
	Jenolin	GC	1992	D	5,314	345' 04"	55' 11"	27' 01"
	Julia	GC	1993	D	5,314	345' 04"	55' 11"	27' 01"
	Link Star	RR	1989	D	4,453	349' 05"	56' 05"	32' 06"

Fleet #.	Fleet Name Vessel Name	Type of Vessel	Year Built	Type of Engine	Cargo Cap. or Gross*	Overal Length	Breadth	Depth or Draft*
	Mimer	RR	1990	D	4,232	355' 06"	57' 04"	42' 00"
	Mini Star	RR	1988	D	4,452	352' 06"	56' 05"	32' 06"
	Miniforest	GC	1972	D	2,545	290' 04"	42' 01"	26' 02"
	Mistral	RR	1999	D	7,438	503' 05"	68' 05"	46' 05"
IG-6	**GOLDEN SUN CRUISES, PIRAEUS, GREECE**							
	Aegean I	PA	1973	D	11,563*	461' 00"	68' 03"	32' 02"
	Arcadia	PA	1968	D	5,113*	350' 09"	53' 06"	23' 07"
IG-7	**GOLDENPORT SHIPSMANAGEMENT LTD., ATHENS, GREECE**							
	Golden D	BC	1977	D	24,738	565' 02"	75' 02"	44' 08"
IG-8	**GOOD FAITH SHIPPING CO. S.A., PIRAEUS, GREECE**							
	Amitie	AC	1970	D	20,139	485' 07"	74' 10"	44' 03"
	Encouragement	GC	1974	D	19,920	537' 01"	75' 02"	47' 03"
	Enterprise I	GC	1974	D	19,920	537' 01"	75' 02"	47' 03"
	Epos	BC	1975	D	24,482	608' 04"	74' 10"	46' 04"
	Euroreefer	GC	1982	D	3,945	302' 06"	53' 02"	22' 06"
	Krissa	BC	1979	D	20,698	521' 00"	74' 03"	43' 08"
	Mana	GC	1978	D	17,089	505' 03"	72' 11"	41' 03"
	Ocean Grace	GC	1976	D	1,381	212' 01"	31' 06"	16' 01"
	Ocean Lake	GC	1976	D	20,950	521' 08"	75' 06"	44' 03"
IG-9	**GORTHON LINES, HELSINGBORG, SWEDEN**							
	Ada Gorthon	RR	1984	D	9,981	512' 07"	73' 00"	46' 09"
	Alida Gorthon	GC	1977	D	14,299	463' 09"	71' 04"	38' 08"
	Ingrid Gorthon	GC	1977	D	14,298	463' 10"	73' 00"	38' 09"
	Ivan Gorthon	RR	1974	D	3,500	387' 08"	51' 02"	37' 03"
	Joh. Gorthon	RR	1977	D	7,182	512' 07"	69' 07"	47' 01"
	Lovisa Gorthon	RR	1979	D	6,420	440' 07"	69' 01"	37' 09"
	Margit Gorthon	GC	1977	D	14,298	463' 10"	73' 00"	38' 09"
	Maria Gorthon	RR	1984	D	9,995	512' 07"	73' 00"	48' 09"
	Ragna Gorthon	RR	1979	D	7,583	442' 07"	69' 01"	37' 09"
	Viola Gorthon	RR	1987	D	10,917	544' 08"	75' 08"	43' 02"
IG-10	**GOURDOMICHALIS MARITIME S.A., PIRAEUS, GREECE**							
	Kavo Alexandros	BC	1977	D	26,414	567' 09"	74' 10"	48' 05"
	Kavo Sidero	BC	1976	D	26,671	592' 11"	75' 04"	47' 07"
	Kavo Yerakas	BC	1981	D	25,854	585' 00"	75' 08"	45' 11"
IG-11	**GRAIG SHIP MANAGEMENT, CARDIFF, ENGLAND**							
	Clipper Carmarthen	GC	1998	D	8,702	329' 09"	66' 11"	36' 05"
	Clipper Cowbridge	GC	1998	D	8,874	329' 09"	66' 11"	36' 05"
	Industrial Confidence	GC	1998	D	6,714	329' 09"	66' 11"	36' 05"
	Maersk Brooklyn	GC	1998	D	8,702	329' 08"	66' 11"	36' 05"
	Maersk Charleston	GC	1997	D	12,500	329' 08"	67' 00"	36' 05"
	Maersk Savannah	GC	1997	D	8,874	329' 08"	67' 00"	36' 05"
	Maersk Takoradi	GC	1997	D	8,874	329' 08"	67' 00"	36' 05"
	Tracer	GC	1999	D	8,734	330' 05"	67' 07"	36' 05"
IG-12	**GREAT CIRCLE SHIPPING AGENCY LTD., BANGKOK, THAILAND**							
	Chada Naree	BC	1981	D	18,668	479' 03"	75' 01"	41' 04"
	Chalothorn Naree	GC	1977	D	16,953	505' 07"	73' 00"	39' 08"
	Fujisan Maru	BC	1976	D	16,883	481' 03"	75' 02"	40' 00"
	Wana Naree	BC	1980	D	26,977	566' 00"	75' 11"	48' 05"
IG-13	**GREAT LAKES EUROPEAN SHIPPING AS, ORNSKOLDSVIK, SWEDEN**							
	Marinette	GC	1967	D	12,497	503' 03"	66' 07"	36' 09"
	Menominee	GC	1967	D	12,497	503' 03"	66' 07"	36' 09"
	Munksund	GC	1968	D	12,497	503' 03"	66' 07"	36' 09"
IG-14	**GREEN MANAGEMENT AS, MINDE, NORWAY**							
	Nomadic Patria	GC	1978	D	17,160	511' 09"	73' 11"	45' 10"
	Nomadic Pollux	GC	1977	D	17,161	511' 10"	73' 11"	46' 00"
IH-1	**H. C. GRUBE, MARSTAL, DENMARK**							
	Hanne Cartharine	GC	1970	D	2,876	251' 05"	37' 00"	22' 08"
	Jenclipper	GC	1976	D	710	163' 00"	27' 02"	18' 01"
	Jenka	GC	1970	D	710	163' 01"	27' 04"	16' 02"
	Jenlil	GC	1971	D	1,954	242' 10"	35' 07"	19' 09"
	Jentrader	GC	1968	D	710	163' 01"	27' 04"	18' 00"
	Kim	GC	1977	D	1,535	236' 11"	34' 02"	19' 09"
IH-2	**H. H. DANSHIP A/S, SVENDBORG, DENMARK**							
	Kis Sobye	GC	1982	D	1,641	264' 05"	39' 05"	22' 00"
IH-3	**H. S. S. HOLLAND SHIP SERVICE B.V., ROTTERDAM, NETHERLANDS**							
	Carola I	GC	1983	D	9,620	372' 04"	56' 02"	37' 01"

Fleet #.	Fleet Name Vessel Name	Type of Vessel	Year Built	Type of Engine	Cargo Cap. or Gross*	Overall Length	Breadth	Depth or Draft*
	Coral Green	GC	1999	D	15,970	468' 07"	70' 07"	43' 08"
	Maria Green	GC	1998	D	17,539	468' 07"	70' 07"	43' 08"
	Marion Green	GC	1999	D	17,538	468' 07"	70' 07"	43' 08"
	Steel Shuttle	GC	1985	D	1,715	212' 06'	36' 05"	17' 01"
	Steel Sprinter	GC	1985	D	1,715	212' 06'	36' 05"	17' 01"
IH-4	**HALFDAN DITLEV-SIMONSEN & CO. AS, BILLINGSTAD, NORWAY**							
	Viscaya	TK	1982	D	202,026	569' 00"	75' 01"	46' 07"
IH-5	**HANS PETER WEGENER KG, JORK, GERMANY**							
	Atria	GC	1986	D	2,973	288' 08"	42' 09"	24' 05"
	Containerships III	CO	1990	D	6,350	400' 03"	62' 02"	29' 02"
	Containerships IV	CO	1994	D	8,932	495' 10"	64' 06"	30' 06"
	Containerships V	CO	1996	D	8,912	495' 10"	64' 06"	30' 06"
IH-6	**HANSEATIC SHIPPING CO. LTD., LIMASSOL, CYPRUS**							
	Cape Confidence	BC	1982	D	18,649	506' 11"	75' 01"	41' 00"
	Jo Hassel	TK	1986	D	8,139	356' 00"	58' 05"	32' 02"
IH-7	**HAPAG-LLOYD SEETOURISTIK (CRUISES) GMBH, HAMBURG, GERMANY**							
	Bremen	PA	1990	D	6,752*	365' 10"	56' 07"	39' 01"
	c. Columbus	PA	1997	D	14,903*	475' 09"	70' 06"	43' 06"
	Europa	PA	1999	D	28,437*	651' 07"	78' 09"	59' 01"
	Hanseatic	PA	1991	D	8,378*	402' 08"	59' 01"	23' 00"
IH-8	**HARBOR SHIPPING & TRADING CO. S.A., CHIOS, GREECE**							
	Chios Charity	BC	1981	D	29,002	589' 11"	76' 01"	47' 07"
	Chios Charm	BC	1976	D	26,541	600' 06"	74' 11"	47' 01"
	Chios Glory	BC	1972	D	29,197	593' 02"	76' 00"	47' 07"
	Chios Harmony	BC	1977	D	29,337	594' 01"	75' 11"	47' 07"
	Chios Pride	BC	1981	D	28,500	627' 07"	75' 03"	44' 04"
	Chios Spirit	BC	1977	D	17,769	479' 00"	73' 03"	40' 10"
	Galini	BC	1971	D	25,651	591' 06"	75' 02"	45' 00"
	New Venture	BC	1973	D	29,334	593' 02"	75' 10"	47' 06"
IH-9	**HARREN & PARTNER SCHIFFAHRTS GMBH, EMS, GERMANY**							
	Nenufar Atlantico	CO	1996	D	7,200	387' 02"	64' 08"	31' 00"
	Opdr Douro	GC	1994	D	4,766	330' 00"	54' 02"	24' 07"
	Padua	GC	1992	D	3,735	288' 05"	42' 00"	23' 04"
	Pampero	GC	1995	D	5,660	371' 11"	53' 10"	25' 09"
	Pandora	GC	1992	D	3,735	288' 05"	42' 00"	23' 04"
	Paramar	GC	1999	D	4,023	294' 04"	44' 07"	23' 07"
	Rhein Master	GC	1994	D	4,766	330' 00"	54' 02"	24' 07"
	Rheintal	GC	1996	D	4,750	305' 01"	54' 02"	24' 07"
	Scan Pacific	RR	1996	D	5,100	331' 01"	62' 00"	31' 10"
	Scan Partner	RR	1997	D	5,147	331' 01"	62' 04"	23' 02"
	Solymar	GC	1998	D	4,128	294' 04"	44' 07"	23' 07"
	Spirit of Resolution	GC	1997	D	4,766	330' 01"	54' 02"	24' 07"
	Stadt Essen	GC	1997	D	5,125	343' 08"	53' 10"	27' 03"
	Transmar	GC	1998	D	4,023	294' 04'	44' 07"	23' 07"
	Ultramar	GC	1997	D	4,128	294' 04"	44' 07"	23' 07"
IH-10	**HELIKON SHIPPING ENTERPRISES LTD., LONDON, ENGLAND**							
	Elikon	BC	1980	D	16,106	582' 00"	75' 02"	44' 04"
IH-11	**HELLENIC STAR SHIPPING CO. S.A., ATHENS, GREECE**							
	Faith Star	BC	1972	D	16,914	486' 11"	74' 00"	39' 00"
	Glory Star	GC	1977	D	16,543	483' 05"	72' 07"	39' 01"
	Winter Star	BC	1978	D	28,660	655' 06"	75' 09"	45' 11"
	World Star	GC	1980	D	16,640	548' 11"	75' 02"	42' 08"
IH-12	**HERMANN BUSS GMBH & CIE., LEER, GERMANY**							
	Baltic Trader	CO	1995	D	6,928	381' 11"	64' 00"	30' 02"
	Edda	GC	1985	D	2,812	322' 07"	44' 04"	23' 00"
	Industrial Century	GC	1999	D	6,265	328' 00"	56' 05"	30' 04"
	Sun Bird	GC	1999	D	6,265	327' 11"	55' 09"	30' 04"
IH-13	**HERMANN C. BOYE & CO., MARSTAL, DENMARK**							
	Andreas Boye	GC	1979	D	1,304	229' 00"	34' 03"	19' 09"
	Anne Boye	GC	1985	D	1,680	251' 02"	36' 09"	22' 00"
	Birthe Boye	GC	1983	D/W	1,630	237' 08"	36' 11"	22' 00"
	Elisabeth Boye	GC	1990	D	2,650	251' 06"	36' 09"	17' 03"
	Hermann C. Boye	GC	1980	D	1,525	229' 00"	34' 03"	19' 09"
	Industrial Leader	GC	1996	D	4,100	290' 00"	49' 06"	24' 07"
	Lette Lill	GC	1966	D	1,296	217' 00"	35' 00"	21' 00"
IH-14	**HILAL SHIPPING TRADING & INDUSTRY CO., ISTANBUL, TURKEY**							
	Hilal II	BC	1981	D	25,845	585' 00"	75' 09"	45' 11"

Tug South Carolina gets ready to assist Olympic Melody at Indiana Harbor. (Roger LeLievre)

Fleet #.	Fleet Name Vessel Name	Type of Vessel	Year Built	Type of Engine	Cargo Cap. or Gross*	Overall Length	Breadth	Depth or Draft*
II-1	**INTERSCAN SCHIFFAHRTSGESELLSCHAFT MBH, HAMBURG, GERMANY**							
	Christina Star	GC	1997	D	6,366	328' 00"	56' 05"	30' 04"
	Industrial Millennium	GC	1998	D	6,288	328' 00"	55' 09"	30' 04"
	Patriot	GC	1994	D	3,086	270' 06"	41' 03"	21' 08"
	Pamela	GC	1985	D	1,738	273' 07"	37' 01"	17' 09"
	Patria	GC	1995	D	3,519	270' 03"	41' 02"	23' 07"
	Pinta	GC	1993	D	2,795	270' 00"	41' 02"	21' 08"
	Pionier	GC	1989	D	2,801	270' 00"	41' 00"	23' 07"
	Premiere	GC	1985	D	1,631	270' 06"	37' 02"	17' 09"
	Sooneck	GC	1986	D	2,019	270' 07"	37' 01"	17' 09"
IJ-1	**J. BEKKERS CO. B.V., ROTTERDAM, NETHERLANDS**							
	Falcon Carrier	GC	1975	D	21,367	531' 08"	75' 02"	45' 11"
	Falcon Chemist	TK	1977	D	47,546	377' 11"	54' 02"	27' 11"
IJ-2	**J. G. GOUMAS (SHIPPING) CO. S.A., PIRAEUS, GREECE**							
	Alaska Rainbow	BC	1985	D	22,782	515' 11"	75' 07"	44' 08"
	Ghikas	GC	1980	D	17,349	477' 05"	69' 00"	43' 00"
	Washington Rainbow II	BC	1984	D	22,828	515' 11"	75' 07"	44' 08"
IJ-3	**J. G. ROUSSOS SHIPPING S.A., ATHENS, GREECE**							
	Kimolian Earth	BC	1986	D	12,367	399' 07"	65' 08"	36' 02"
	Kimolian Pride	BC	1990	D	20,429	538' 01"	72' 03"	44' 00"
	Pany R	BC	1978	D	22,174	528' 00"	75' 02"	44' 04"
	Semena	BC	1977	D	21,450	529' 06"	75' 00"	44' 07"
	Smaragda	BC	1985	D	17,825	481' 08"	74' 10"	40' 01"
	Vicky Roussos	GC	1985	D	5,011	300' 06"	49' 11"	25' 08"
IJ-4	**J. POULSEN SHIPPING A/S, KORSOR, DENMARK**							
	Ocean Bird	GC	1991	D	4,222	309' 09"	50' 10"	25' 11"
	Sky Bird	GC	1977	D	4,305	298' 11"	47' 08"	27' 11"
IJ-5	**JAISING MARITIME LTD., MUMBAI, INDIA**							
	Jaising Energy	GC	1995	D	2,873	269' 00"	46' 07"	16' 05"
	Jaising Frontier	GC	1995	D	2,873	269' 00"	46' 07"	16' 05"
IJ-6	**JAN WIND SHIPPING, NANSUM, NETHERLANDS**							
	Lida	GC	1974	D	1,448	214' 03"	35' 05"	16' 01"
IJ-7	**JARDINE SHIP MANAGEMENT LTD., HONG KONG, PEOPLE'S REPUBLIC OF CHINA**							
	Golden Laker	BC	1996	D	30,838	607' 01"	77' 05"	48' 11"
IJ-8	**JAYSHIP LTD., LONDON, ENGLAND**							
	Gur Maiden	GC	1976	D	16,251	491' 06"	69' 01"	40' 03"
	Gur Master	GC	1978	D	15,767	492' 00"	69' 00"	40' 03"
	M. Melody	GC	1978	D	15,765	491' 06"	69' 00"	40' 03"
IJ-9	**JO TANKERS B.V., SPIJKENISSE, NETHERLANDS**							
	Jo Adler	TK	1992	D	89,632	456' 00"	69' 09"	34' 03"
	Jo Ask	TK	1997	D	122,075	487' 00"	75' 06"	42' 06"
	Jo Aspen	TK	1991	D	87,839	456' 00"	69' 09"	34' 03"
	Jo Calluna	TK	1986	D	93,865	448' 02"	68' 00"	35' 02"
	Jo Ebony	TK	1986	D	88,443	422' 11"	66' 04"	36' 01"
	Jo Hegg	TK	1985	D	51,200	356' 00"	58' 07"	32' 02"
	Jo Maple	TK	1991	D	60,968	377' 11"	59' 05"	31' 02"
	Jo Palm	TK	1991	D	60,968	377' 11"	59' 05"	31' 02"
	Jo Spirit	TK	1998	D	33,205	352' 02"	52' 02"	30' 02"
IJ-10	**JUGOSLAVENSKA OCEANSKA PLOVIDBA, KOTOR, YUGOSLAVIA**							
	Durmitor	GC	1982	D	17,400	519' 03"	75' 09"	39' 01"
	Grant Carrier	BC	1984	D	30,850	617' 04"	75' 11"	47' 07"
	Lovcen	GC	1982	D	17,386	520' 00"	77' 01"	44' 11"
	Moslavina	GC	1978	D	16,000	517' 03"	75' 00"	43' 00"
IJ-11	**JUHL & EHRHORN, ESBJERG, DENMARK**							
	Elisabeth Clipper	GC	1983	D	1,490	222' 00"	40' 00"	21' 04"
	Karen Clipper	GC	1978	D	1,285	206' 04"	36' 09"	20' 04"
	Mette Clipper	GC	1977	D	1,281	206' 05"	36' 09"	12' 00"
IJ-12	**JUMBO SHIPPING CO. S.A., ROTTERDAM, NETHERLANDS**							
	Daniella	HL	1989	D	7,600	322' 09"	68' 06"	37' 02"
	Fairlane	HL	2000	D	7,300	361' 03"	68' 05"	
	Fairlift	HL	1990	D	7,780	329' 02"	68' 10"	43' 08"
	Fairload	HL	1995	D	7,500	313' 11"	60' 03"	37' 02"
	Fairmast	HL	1983	D	6,833	360' 07"	63' 07"	34' 05"
	Gajah Borneo	HL	1978	D	5,076	327' 05"	59' 02"	32' 00"
	Jumbo Challenger	HL	1983	D	6,375	360' 11"	63' 00"	34' 05"
	Jumbo Spirit	HL	1995	D	5,200	313' 11"	60' 03"	37' 02"
	Jumbo Vision	HL	2000	D	7,300	361' 03"	68' 05"	

Fleet #.	Fleet Name Vessel Name	Type of Vessel	Year Built	Type of Engine	Cargo Cap. or Gross*	Overal Length	Breadth	Depth or Draft*
	Stellamare	HL	1982	D	2,850	289' 04"	51' 02"	24' 00"
	Stellanova	HL	1996	D	5,198	313' 08"	60' 03"	37' 02"
	Stellaprima	HL	1991	D	7,600	329' 02"	68' 10"	43' 08"
IK-1	**KG PAUL HEINRICH GMBH & CO., STEINKIRCHEN, GERMANY**							
	Frauke	GC	1994	D	7,713	352' 06"	64' 06"	34' 09"
IK-2	**K. ARNESEN SHIPPING A/S, KRISTIANSAND, NORWAY**							
	Ana Safi	GC	1975	D	4,106	306' 09"	47' 08'	28' 02"
IK-3	**KIL SHIPPING A/S, GENTOFTE, DENMARK**							
	Celtic Sif	TK	1985	D	48,124	371' 10"	59' 02"	26' 03"
	Chem Baltic	TK	1984	D	47,124	371' 10"	59' 02"	26' 03"
	Kilchem America	TK	1999	D	93,506	393' 08"	68' 11"	40' 04"
	Kilchem Asia	TK	1999	D	93,506	393' 08"	68' 11"	40' 04"
	Malene Sif	TW	1994	D	68,812	382' 06"	62' 04"	33' 02"
IK-4	**KNUTSEN O.A.S. SHIPPING A/S, HAUGESUND, NORWAY**							
	Ellen Knutsen	TK	1992	D	105,193	464' 03"	75' 07"	38' 09"
	Helene Knutsen	TK	1992	D	114,577	464' 08"	75' 07"	39' 10"
	Hilda Knutsen	TK	1989	D	112,275	464' 08"	75' 07"	39' 10"
	Pascale Knutsen	TK	1993	D	112,275	464' 08"	75' 07"	38' 09"
	Sidsel Knutsen	TK	1993	D	163,463	533' 02"	75' 05"	48' 07"
	Synnove Knutsen	TK	1992	D	105,193	464' 03"	75' 07"	38' 09"
	Torill Knutsen	TK	1990	D	112,275	464' 08"	75' 07"	38' 09"
	Turid Knutsen	TK	1993	D	163,463	533' 03"	75' 07"	48' 07"
IK-5	**KRISTIAN GERHARD JEBSEN SKIPSREDERI A/S, BERGEN, NORWAY**							
	Alouette Arrow	GC	1980	D	14,241	522' 04"	70' 03"	36' 10"
	Rathrowan	TK	1991	D	24,046	315' 00"	47' 08"	27' 03'
IL-1	**LATVIAN SHIPPING CO., RIGA, LATVIA**							
	Juris Avots	RR	1983	D	5,500	501' 00"	63' 01"	43' 00"
IL-2	**LATMAR COLUMBIA LTD., LIMASSOL, CYPRUS**							
	Zanis Griva	TK	1985	D	126,377	497' 01"	73' 07"	39' 11"
IL-3	**LEROS MANAGEMENT S.A., ATHENS, GREECE**							
	Tanani	BC	1977	D	27,765	579' 11"	75' 02"	48' 03"
	Titanas	BC	1977	D	28,218	579' 11"	75' 02"	48' 03"
IL-4	**LIBANFRACHT SARL., BEIRUT, LEBANON**							
	Baalbeck	CO	1979	D	7,285	414' 03"	59' 03"	24' 06"
	Carl Metz	GC	1980	D	7,796	417' 05"	58' 11"	32' 00"
	Celine M	GC	1970	D	1,521	257' 05"	38' 11"	20' 05"
	Metz Beirut	GC	1967	D	10,150	492' 07"	66' 05"	38' 05"
	Metz Italia	GC	1967	D	10,080	493' 01"	66' 05"	38' 06"
	Pablo Metz	CO	1970	D	4,250	375' 08"	68' 03"	26' 11"
	Pauline Metz	GC	1970	D	3,030	313' 08"	52' 10"	25' 07"
IL-5	**LINK LINE LTD., PIREAUS, GREECE**							
	Aktis	GC	1976	D	18,627	532' 02"	75' 02"	44' 00"
	Ochimos	GC	1976	D	17,000	521' 11"	75' 00"	43' 04"
	Phaethon	GC	1977	D	24,300	567' 07"	75' 00"	47' 11"
IL-6	**LITHUANIAN SHIPPING CO., KLAIPEDA, LITHUANIA**							
	Akvile	GC	1997	D	5,600	337' 04'	52' 04'	26' 07"
	Algirdas	GC	1991	D	4,168	320' 10"	56' 09"	23' 00"
	Asta	GC	1996	D	5,805	337' 04"	52' 04"	26' 07"
	Audre	GC	1997	D	6,085	337' 04"	52' 04"	26' 07"
	Aukse	GC	1997	D	5,820	337' 04"	52' 04"	26' 07"
	Daina	GC	1998	D	5,836	337' 04"	52' 04"	26' 07"
	Gediminas	GC	1996	D	4,502	324' 10"	54' 02"	25' 03"
	Kapitonas A. Lucka	BC	1980	D	14,550	479' 08"	67' 09"	42' 04"
	Kapitonas Andzejauskas	BC	1978	D	14,550	479' 08"	67' 09"	42' 04"
	Kapitonas Daugela	BC	1975	D	14,631	479' 08"	67' 09"	42' 04"
	Kapitonas Daugirdas	BC	1976	D	14,631	479' 08"	67' 09"	42' 04"
	Kapitonas Domeika	BC	1979	D	14,550	479' 08"	67' 09"	42' 04"
	Kapitonas Kaminskas	BC	1978	D	14,550	479' 08"	67' 09"	42' 04"
	Kapitonas Marcinkus	BC	1977	D	14,550	479' 08"	67' 09"	42' 04"
	Kapitonas Serafinas	BC	1980	D	14,550	479' 08"	67' 09"	42' 04"
	Kapitonas Sevcenko	BC	1977	D	14,550	479' 08"	67' 09"	42' 04"
	Kapitonas Simkus	BC	1976	D	14,550	479' 08"	67' 09"	42' 04"
	Kapitonas Stulpinas	BC	1981	D	14,550	479' 08"	67' 09"	42' 04"
	Kernave	GC	1973	D	4,466	319' 03"	53' 03"	25' 05"
	Kreva	GC	1974	D	4,471	319' 03"	53' 03"	25' 05"
	Medininkai	GC	1974	D	4,471	319' 03"	53' 03"	25' 05"
	Merkine	GC	1973	D	4,464	319' 03"	53' 03"	25' 05"

Fleet #.	Fleet Name Vessel Name	Type of Vessel	Year Built	Type of Engine	Cargo Cap. or Gross*	Overall Length	Breadth	Depth or Draft*
	Mindaugas	GC	1992	D	4,168	320' 10"	56' 09"	23' 00"
	Musa	GC	1993	D	4,485	385' 06"	54' 04"	22' 00"
	Palanga	RR	1979	D	4,788	415' 01"	68' 11"	42' 04"
	Panevezys	RR	1985	D	4,673	413' 01"	53' 03"	36' 04"
	Siauliai	RR	1985	D	4,673	413' 01"	53' 03"	36' 04"
	Voke	GC	1990	D	5,985	458' 08"	54' 04"	22' 00"
	Vytautas	GC	1995	D	4,500	324' 10"	50' 10"	20' 04"
IM-1	**M. ODYSSEOS SHIPMANAGEMENT LTD., NICOSIA, CYPRUS**							
	Bluebill	BC	1977	D	30,242	621' 06"	75' 00"	47' 11"
	Happy Day	BC	1975	D	27,421	597' 01"	74' 11"	48' 03"
	Hellenic Confidence	BC	1977	D	17,616	479' 01"	73' 04"	40' 10"
	Oceanic Confidence	BC	1986	D	17,832	473' 03"	75' 05"	40' 00"
	Tropic Confidence	BC	1986	D	17,832	473' 03"	75' 06"	40' 00"
IM-2	**M. T. M. SHIP MANAGEMENT PTE. LTD., SINGAPORE, SINGAPORE**							
	Chembulk Fortitude	TK	1989	D	104,036	432' 01"	66' 11"	36' 09"
	Chembulk Singapore	TK	1989	D	104,036	433' 01"	66' 11"	36' 09"
	Encounter	TK	1983	D	89,386	413' 05"	65' 09"	36' 09"
	Entity	TK	1985	D	89,474	404' 06"	65' 09"	36' 09"
	Equity	TK	1985	D	89,386	404' 06"	65' 08"	36' 09"
	Espoir	TK	1979	D	105,193	438' 00"	72' 03"	39' 01"
	Grace Pioneer	TK	1983	D	24,531	294' 11"	46' 08"	22' 04"
	Kwan Siu	TK	1976	D	16,203	264' 10"	40' 01"	21' 02"
	Orient Grace	TK	1981	D	42,438	334' 00"	50' 11"	27' 07"
	Pacific Star	TK	1984	D	38,922	351' 01"	52' 07"	26' 11"
	Spring Grace	TK	1980	D	36,777	338' 09"	50' 11"	24' 00"
	Timur Grace	TK	1984	D	34,903	337' 07"	50' 11"	26' 03"
	Timur Queen	TK	1985	D	67,051	399' 04"	56' 06"	31' 10"
IM-3	**MAMMOET SHIPPING (NETHERLAND ANTILLES) B.V., ROOSENDAAL, NETHERLANDS**							
	Enchanter	HL	1998	D	16,069	452' 09"	74' 10"	31' 03"
	Happy Ranger	HL	1998	D	15,065	452' 09"	74' 10"	31' 03"
	Happy River	HL	1998	D	15,700	452' 09"	74' 10"	31' 03"
	Happy Rover	HL	1997	D	15,700	452' 09"	74' 10"	31' 03"
	Project Americas	HL	1979	D	12,811	455' 10"	70' 08"	42' 08"
	Project Arabia	HL	1982	D	12,800	455' 11"	70' 08"	42' 08"
	Project Europa	HL	1983	D	13,493	456' 02"	75' 02"	42' 08"
	Project Orient	HL	1981	D	10,434	454' 07"	70' 08"	42' 08"
	Thor Scan	HL	1982	D	9,800	404' 08"	67' 09"	33' 10"
	Titan Scan	HL	1982	D	9,864	404' 08"	67' 11"	33' 10"
	Tracer	HL	2000	D	8,874	329' 09"	73' 06"	26' 11"
	Tramper	HL	2000	D	8,874	329' 09"	73' 06"	26' 11"
	Transporter	HL	2000	D	8,874	329' 09"	73' 06"	26' 11"
	Traveller	HL	2000	D	8,874	329' 09"	73' 06"	26' 11"
IM-4	**MANSOUR SHIPPING, TARTOUS, SYRIA**							
	Silver River	TK	1999	D	94,079	477' 09"	64' 04"	34' 11"
IM-5	**MARINE MANAGERS LTD., PIRAEUS, GREECE**							
	Trident Mariner	BC	1984	D	28,503	590' 03"	75' 04"	47' 07"
IM-6	**MARINE TRUST LTD., ATHENS, GREECE**							
	Tribels	GC	1974	D	18,029	484' 07"	75' 03"	42' 08"
	Vulcan	BC	1975	D	30,499	625' 06"	75' 00"	47' 10"
IM-7	**MARMARAS NAVIGATION LTD., PIRAEUS, GREECE**							
	Artaki	BC	1977	D	19,077	508' 10"	74' 11"	41' 06"
	Kydonia	BC	1977	D	18,737	479' 03"	75' 00"	41' 04"
	Kyzikos	BC	1978	D	19,374	496' 01"	75' 01"	42' 08"
	Proussa	BC	1979	D	18,750	504' 07"	75' 00"	41' 01"
	Redestos	BC	1977	D	15,180	462' 07"	67' 01"	38' 06"
IM-8	**MARTI SHIPPING & TRADING CO., INC., ISTANBUL, TURKEY**							
	Tevfik Kaptan I	GC	1977	D	1,036	212' 05"	28' 03"	13' 02"
	Zafer Tomba	GC	1970	D	979	189' 01"	31' 00"	13' 05"
IM-9	**MEDITERRANEA DI NAVIGAZIONE S.R.L., RAVENNA, ITALY**							
	Barbarossa	TK	1982	D	163,538	517' 01"	75' 04"	43' 00"
	Fradiavolo	TK	1973	D	31,324	333' 10"	41' 11"	21' 04"
	Metauro	TK	1991	D	29,972	323' 06"	49' 03"	23' 00"
	Normanna	TK	1996	D	69,189	413' 05"	62' 04"	29' 06"
	Sveva	TK	1998	D	108,816	446' 02"	75' 06"	40' 02"
IM-10	**MEDITERRANEAN MARITIME S.A., PIRAEUS, GREECE**							
	Med Glory	BC	1975	D	16,549	465' 09"	71' 07"	40' 00"
	Med Hope	GC	1975	D	11,612	404' 06"	67' 05"	34' 09"
	Med Pride	BC	1984	D	29,651	622' 01"	74' 11"	49' 10"

Fleet #.	Fleet Name Vessel Name	Type of Vessel	Year Built	Type of Engine	Cargo Cap. or Gross*	Overal Length	Breadth	Depth or Draft*
IM-11	**MEDSTAR SHIPMANAGEMENT LTD., LIMASSOL, CYPRUS**							
	Edda	GC	1985	D	2,812	322' 07"	44' 04"	23' 00"
	Gutshof	GC	1997	D	4,477	278' 10"	44' 07"	25' 03"
	Huemmling	GC	1985	D	2,947	322' 06"	44' 07"	22' 00"
	Jonas	GC	1985	D	2,814	322' 07"	44' 04"	23' 00"
	Olivia	GC	1978	D	3,050	264' 08"	47' 00"	20' 09"
IM-12	**METROFIN LTD., ZURICH, SWITZERLAND**							
	Morias	BC	1977	D	21,743	536' 05"	74' 10"	44' 04"
IM-13	**METRON SHIPPING & AGENCIES S.A., PIRAEUS, GREECE**							
	Pontokratis	BC	1981	D	28,738	590' 02"	75' 11"	47' 07"
	Pontoporos	BC	1984	D	29,155	590' 02"	75' 11"	47' 07"
IM-14	**MIKKAL MYKLEBUSTHAUG REDERI, FONNES, NORWAY**							
	Langesund	GC	1979	D	7,906	350' 05"	54' 02"	29' 07"
IM-15	**MIDMAR SHIPPING LTD., DOUGLAS, ISLE OF MAN**							
	Kate	GC	1981	D	7,805	399' 08"	57' 09"	32' 06"
	Kristine	GC	1980	D	7,805	399' 09"	57' 09"	32' 06"
IM-16	**MILLENIUM MARITIME SERVICES LTD., PIRAEUS, GREECE**							
	Clipper Atlantic	GC	1975	D	7,923	399' 05"	57' 09"	32' 06"
	Clipper Pacific	GC	1976	D	7,923	399' 08"	57' 11"	32' 06"
	Millenium Amethyst	GC	1978	D	23,536	539' 02"	75' 00"	46' 05"
	Millenium Condor	BC	1981	D	27,036	627' 07"	75' 03"	44' 03"
	Millenium Eagle	BC	1983	D	28,788	606' 11"	75' 11"	48' 01"
	Millenium Falcon	BC	1981	D	27,048	627' 07"	75' 03"	44' 03"
	Millenium Golden Hind	BC	1978	D	16,560	537' 11"	75' 03"	38' 09"
	Millenium Harmony	GC	1978	D	16,711	537' 11"	75' 03"	38' 09"
	Millenium Hawk	BC	1984	D	28,791	606' 11"	75' 11"	48' 01"
	Millenium Leader	BC	1984	D	37,489	599' 09"	93' 03"	49' 11"
	Millenium Majestic	GC	1979	D	17,154	477' 05"	69' 00"	43' 00"
	Millenium Osprey	BC	1984	D	28,786	606' 11"	75' 11"	48' 01"
	Millenium Raptor	BC	1982	D	30,670	617' 04"	76' 00"	47' 07"
	Millenium Yama	GC	1979	D	23,169	539' 02"	75' 00"	46' 04"
IM-17	**MONTE CARLO SHIPPING S.A.M., MONTE CARLO, MONACO**							
	Black Swan	BC	1978	D	23,573	539' 02"	75' 00"	46' 06"
IM-18	**MONTEVERDE DI NAVIGAZIONE S.R.L., NAPLES, ITALY**							
	Chica	GC	1985	D	7,250	365' 02"	55' 10"	29' 07"
	Serenade	BC	1972	D	6,341	332' 07"	52' 07"	30' 03"
	Vela	GC	1977	D	5,166	294' 00"	49' 00"	29' 07"
IM-19	**MURMANSK SHIPPING CO., MURMANSK, RUSSIA**							
	Admiral Ushakov	BC	1979	D	19,885	531' 07"	75' 01"	44' 05"
	Aleksandr Nevskiy	BC	1978	D	19,590	532' 02"	75' 02"	44' 05"
	Aleksandr Suvorov	BC	1979	D	19,590	532' 02"	75' 02"	44' 05"
	Dmitriy Donskoi	BC	1977	D	19,885	531' 10"	75' 02"	44' 05"
	Dmitriy Pozharskiy	BC	1977	D	19,885	531' 10"	75' 02"	44' 05"
	Ivan Bogun	BC	1981	D	19,885	531' 10"	75' 02"	44' 05"
	Ivan Susanin	BC	1981	D	19,885	531' 10"	75' 02"	44' 05"
	Kapitan Bochek	BC	1982	D	19,253	531' 10"	75' 02"	44' 05"
	Kapitan Chukhchin	BC	1981	D	19,240	531' 10"	75' 02"	44' 05"
	Kapitan Kudley	BC	1983	D	19,252	531' 10"	75' 02"	44' 05"
	Kuzma Minin	BC	1980	D	19,885	531' 10"	75' 02"	44' 05"
	Mikhail Kutuzov	BC	1979	D	19,590	531' 10"	75' 01"	44' 05"
	Mikhail Strekalovskiy	BC	1981	D	19,252	531' 10"	75' 02"	44' 05"
	Pyotr Velikiy	BC	1978	D	19,885	531' 10"	75' 02"	44' 05"
	Stepan Razin	BC	1980	D	19,590	531' 09"	75' 01"	44' 05"
	Tonya Bondarchuk	GC	1972	D	4,687	346' 07"	51' 04"	26' 03"
	Yuriy Dolgorukiy	BC	1980	D	19,885	532' 02"	75' 02"	44' 05"
IN-1	**NARVAL SHIPPING CORP., PIRAEUS, GREECE**							
	Cay	BC	1976	D	18,726	507' 09"	73' 11"	41' 01"
	Lyra	BC	1976	D	27,140	579' 10"	75' 00"	46' 04"
	Paragon	BC	1977	D	29,039	593' 03"	75' 11"	47' 07"
	Rays	BC	1977	D	29,321	594' 00"	76' 00"	47' 07"
IN-2	**NAUTILUS CHARTERING N.V., KALMTHOUT, BELGIUM**							
	Dennis Danielsen	GC	1978	D	2,537	261' 10"	43' 00"	24' 08"
IN-3	**NAVARONE S.A., PIRAEUS, GREECE**							
	Mallard	GC	1977	D	18,791	479' 03"	75' 01"	41' 05"
IN-4	**NAVIERA PENINSULAR S.A., BILBAO, SPAIN**							
	Biga	GC	1984	D	4,130	299' 07"	47' 03"	28' 07"

Sjard, of Germany, passes Mission Point at the Soo, headed for the St. Lawrence Seaway and back home.
(David Swain)

Greek-flag passenger liner Arcadia offers a variety of Great Lakes adventures this summer. *(To find out more, call (877) 777-4524)*

Fleet #.	Fleet Name / Vessel Name	Type of Vessel	Year Built	Type of Engine	Cargo Cap. or Gross*	Overall Length	Breadth	Depth or Draft*
	Calabria	GC	1977	D	6,280	338' 04"	54' 07"	27' 03"
	Crimea	GC	1978	D	6,280	338' 04"	54' 07"	27' 03"
	Guajira	GC	1981	D	3,054	276' 11"	45' 06"	20' 11"
	Iberica	GC	1973	D	5,625	327' 04"	50' 01"	27' 01"
	Misty	GC	1983	D	8,150	392' 01"	60' 10"	31' 03"
	Kenai	GC	1979	D	6,202	350' 06"	51' 10"	28' 06"
	Zapata	GC	1985	D	9,611	401' 11"	60' 09"	32' 10"
IN-5	**NAVIERA POSEIDON, HAVANA, CUBA**							
	Agate Islands	GC	1977	D	13,021	489' 02"	68' 06"	37' 11"
	Aiana	GC	1985	D	24,232	579' 05'	75' 02"	45' 11"
	East Islands	GC	1986	D	15,120	472' 06'	67' 02"	38' 07"
	Gabyama	GC	1985	D	24,232	579' 05'	75' 02"	45' 11"
	Irina	GC	1977	D	15,088	462' 07"	67' 02"	38' 06"
	Lilac Islands	GC	1983	D	15,175	472' 05"	67' 02"	38' 07"
	Lotus Islands	GC	1983	D	15,175	472' 05"	67' 02"	38' 07"
	South Islands	GC	1986	D	15,147	472' 05"	67' 02"	38' 07"
	Tephys	GC	1975	D	15,123	462' 07"	67' 02"	38' 06"
	West Islands	GC	1986	D	15,136	472' 06"	67' 01"	38' 07"
IN-6	**NAVIGATION MARITIME BULGARE LTD., VARNA, BULGARIA**							
	Balkan	BC	1975	D	25,714	607' 08"	74' 10"	46' 05"
	Kamenitza	BC	1980	D	24,150	605' 08"	75' 00"	46' 05"
	Kapitan Georgi Georgiev	BC	1980	D	24,150	605' 08"	75' 00"	46' 05"
	Malyovitza	BC	1983	D	24,456	605' 00"	75' 05"	46' 06"
	Milin Kamak	BC	1979	D	24,285	607' 07"	75' 00"	46' 05"
	Okoltchitza	BC	1982	D	24,148	605' 08"	75' 05"	46' 06"

Fleet #.	Fleet Name Vessel Name	Type of Vessel	Year Built	Type of Engine	Cargo Cap. or Gross*	Overall Length	Breadth	Depth or Draft*
	Perelik	BC	1998	D	13,887	437' 10"	72' 11"	36' 07"
	Persensk	BC	1998	D	13,902	466' 04"	73' 09"	36' 07"
	Shipka	BC	1979	D	24,285	607' 07"	75' 00"	46' 05"
IN-7	**NEPTUNE TRADING, INC., BASSETERRE, ST. KITTS-NEVIS**							
	Altair	GC	1979	D	2,534	261' 10"	42' 10"	24' 08"
IN-8	**NESTE OYJ, ESPOO, FINLAND**							
	Kihu	TK	1984	D	160,507	527' 11"	76' 00"	46' 08"
	Lunni	TK	1976	D	108,231	539' 06"	72' 09"	39' 04"
	Melkki	TK	1982	D	82,417	461' 11"	69' 08"	32' 04"
	Rankki	TK	1982	D	82,417	461' 11"	69' 08"	32' 04"
	Sirri	TK	1981	D	47,502	351' 01"	59' 00"	30' 01"
	Sotka	TK	1976	D	101,991	539' 07"	73' 00"	39' 05"
	Tavi	TK	1985	D	160,507	527' 11"	76' 00"	58' 05"
	Tiira	TK	1977	D	108,231	539' 07"	72' 10"	39' 05"
	Uikku	TK	1977	D	108,231	539' 07"	73' 00"	39' 05"
	Vikla	TK	1982	D	53,490	437' 04"	63' 02"	31' 03"
IN-9	**NISSEN KAIUN K.K., HAKATA, JAPAN**							
	Rubin Eagle	BC	1995	D	18,315	447' 10"	74' 10"	40' 00"
	Rubin Falcon	BC	1996	D	18,000	486' 01"	74' 10"	40' 00"
	Rubin Halcyon	BC	1997	D	18,315	486' 01"	74' 10"	40' 00"
	Rubin Hawk	BC	1995	D	18,233	486' 01"	74' 10"	40' 00"
	Rubin Lark	BC	1997	D	18,315	486' 01"	74' 10"	40' 00"
	Rubin Stork	BC	1996	D	18,315	446' 00"	74' 10"	40' 00"
IN-10	**NORDANE SHIPPING A/S, SVENDBORG, DENMARK**							
	Gerda Vesta	GC	1983	D	2,610	243' 03"	36' 10"	22' 00"
	Helle Stevns	GC	1980	D	7,909	349' 08"	54' 03"	29' 06"
	Nadia J	GC	1984	D	1,040	215' 09"	32' 10"	26' 07"
	Stevnsland	GC	1972	D	2,510	290' 04"	45' 05"	26' 03"
	Stevns Bulk	GC	1975	D	3,320	246' 01"	43' 08"	25' 04"
	Stevns Pearl	GC	1984	D	5,900	327' 09"	58' 06"	29' 07"
	Stevns Sea	GC	1972	D	3,610	290' 04"	45' 04"	26' 03"
	Stevns Trader	GC	1970	D	2,245	290' 04"	45' 05"	26' 03"
IN-11	**NORDSCHWEDEN FRACHTDIENST GMBH VERWALTUNGSGESELLSCHAFT, EMS, GERMANY**							
	Anja	GC	2000	D	8,700	419' 06"	52' 00"	32' 00"
IN-12	**NORTHERN SHIPPING CO., ARKHANGELSK, RUSSIA**							
	Fyodor Varaksin	BC	1977	D	14,220	497' 10"	69' 01"	38' 00"
	Kapitan Alekseyev	GC	1971	D	16,618	556' 05"	71' 07"	43' 05"
	Kapitan Glazachev	BC	1976	D	14,200	497' 10"	69' 01"	38' 00"
	Kapitan Zamyatin	BC	1976	D	14,200	497' 10"	69' 01"	38' 00"
	Nikolay Novikov	BC	1973	D	13,955	492' 11"	69' 01"	38' 00"
	Petr Strelkov	BC	1977	D	14,200	497' 10"	69' 01"	38' 00"
	Vasiliy Musinskiy	BC	1974	D	14,200	497' 10"	69' 01"	38' 00"
	Vladimir Timofeyev	BC	1973	D	14,204	493' 00"	69' 01"	38' 00"
IN-13	**NOVOROSSIYSK SHIPPING CO., NOVOROSSIYSK, RUSSIA**							
	Boris Livanov	BC	1986	D	23,920	605' 09"	75' 00"	46' 05"
	Khirurg Vishnevskiy	TK	1988	D	126,377	497' 01"	73' 07"	39' 10"
	Sergey Lemeshev	BC	1983	D	24,110	605' 08"	74' 10"	46' 05"
	Vladimir Vysotskiy	TK	1988	D	128,315	497' 01"	73' 07"	39' 10"
IO-1	**O. T. TONNEVOLD AS, GRIMSTAD, NORWAY**							
	Thordis	GC	1982	D	6,348	477' 06"	58' 05"	34' 06"
	Thorfrid	GC	1982	D	6,434	390' 02"	56' 06"	32' 10"
	Thorgull	GC	1983	D	6,325	477' 07"	58' 05"	34' 06"
	Thorhild	GC	1983	D	6,666	452' 02"	61' 02"	33' 08"
	Thornburg	GC	1981	D	4,447	332' 04"	56' 02"	29' 07"
	Thorndale	GC	1981	D	4,380	332' 04"	55' 11"	29' 06"
	Thorunn	GC	1982	D	6,370	477' 06"	58' 06"	34' 05"
IO-2	**OCEANBULK MARITIME S.A., ATHENS, GREECE**							
	Aurora	GC	1976	D	15,513	491' 05"	69' 00"	40' 03"
	Corrin	BC	1979	D	24,326	565' 03"	75' 03"	44' 08"
	Etoile	GC	1990	D	17,430	520' 10"	75' 00"	44' 00"
	Strange Attractor	BC	1978	D	28,873	593' 02"	76' 00"	47' 07"
IO-3	**ODYSSEY INVESTMENTS CO. LTD., PIRAEUS, GREECE**							
	Floria I	GC	1981	D	12,720	492' 09"	69' 01"	37' 01"
	Minthi	GC	1983	D	13,124	492' 08"	69' 04"	37' 01"
	Ziria	GC	1983	D	16,208	532' 06"	73' 00"	44' 00"
IO-4	**OLYMPIC SHIPPING AND MANAGEMENT S.A., ATHENS, GREECE**							
	Calliroe Patronicola	BC	1985	D	29,608	599' 09"	75' 11"	48' 07"

Fleet #.	Fleet Name Vessel Name	Type of Vessel	Year Built	Type of Engine	Cargo Cap. or Gross*	Overall Length	Breadth	Depth or Draft*
	Olympic Melody	BC	1984	D	29,640	599' 09"	75' 11"	48' 07"
	Olympic Mentor	BC	1984	D	29,693	599' 09"	75' 11"	48' 07"
	Olympic Merit	BC	1985	D	29,611	599' 09"	75' 11"	48' 07"
	Olympic Miracle	BC	1984	D	29,670	599' 09"	75' 11"	48' 07"
IO-5	ORIENT OVERSEAS CONTAINER LINE LTD., HONG KONG, PEOPLE'S REPUBLIC OF CHINA							
	OOCL Alliance	CO	1977	D	17,607	554' 06"	82' 08"	51' 06"
	OOCL America	CO	1995	D	67,741	905' 06"	131' 03"	69' 11"
	OOCL Applause	CO	1977	D	16,955	554' 00"	82' 08"	51' 07"
	OOCL Belgium	CO	1998	D	40,972	803' 10"	105' 10"	62' 05"
	OOCL Britain	CO	1996	D	67,958	905' 06"	131' 03"	79' 09"
	OOCL California	CO	1995	D	67,765	905' 06"	127' 11"	79' 09"
	OOCL Canada	CO	1996	D	33,659	708' 08"	105' 09"	62' 04"
	OOCL China	CO	1996	D	67,625	905' 06"	134' 02"	79' 09"
	OOCL Envoy	CO	1979	D	40,379	823' 06"	105' 10"	61' 05"
	OOCL Exporter	CO	1976	D	41,587	902' 03"	100' 05"	62' 01"
	OOCL Fair	CO	1987	D	40,560	790' 08"	105' 08"	69' 07"
	OOCL Faith	CO	1985	D	40,560	790' 08"	105' 08"	69' 03"
	OOCL Fidelity	CO	1987	D	40,560	790' 08"	106' 00"	69' 03"
	OOCL Fortune	CO	1985	D	40,560	790' 08"	105' 08"	69' 03"
	OOCL Freedom	CO	1985	D	44,452	790' 08"	105' 08"	69' 03"
	OOCL Friendship	CO	1987	D	45,763	816' 11"	105' 10"	69' 03"
	OOCL Hong Kong	CO	1995	D	67,637	905' 06"	131' 03"	79' 09"
	OOCL Japan	CO	1996	D	67,765	905' 06"	131' 03"	79' 09"
	OOCL Netherlands	CO	1997	D	67,473	905' 06"	131' 03"	79' 09"
	OOCL Singapore	CO	1997	D	67,473	905' 07"	134' 02"	79' 09"
IO-6	"ORION" SCHIFFAHRTS-GESELLSCHAFT REITH & CO., HAMBURG, GERMANY							
	Baltia	BC	1986	D	12,337	399' 07"	65' 07"	36' 01"
	Caro	BC	1984	D	19,429	485' 07"	75' 09"	41' 08"
	Concordia	GC	1985	D	8,881	378' 00"	61' 01"	32' 02"
	Crio	BC	1984	D	19,483	485' 07"	75' 09"	41' 08"
	Fortuna	GC	1984	D	8,875	378' 00"	61' 01"	32' 02"
	Gotia	GC	1985	D	12,349	399' 07"	65' 07"	36' 01"
	Hero	BC	1984	D	19,505	485' 11"	75' 10"	41' 08"
	Ida	BC	1995	D	18,172	486' 01"	74' 10"	40' 00"
	Lita	BC	1995	D	18,173	486' 01"	74' 10"	40' 00"
	Meta	BC	1987	D	18,612	477' 04"	75' 11"	40' 08"
	Patria	GC	1985	D	8,880	377' 11"	61' 01"	32' 02"
	Rugia	BC	1986	D	12,342	399' 07"	65' 08"	36' 02"
IP-1	P&O NEDLLOYD B.V., ROTTERDAM, NETHERLANDS							
	Nedlloyd Africa	CO	1992	D	47,157	873' 08"	106' 00"	76' 03"
	Nedlloyd America	CO	1992	D	47,042	872' 08"	105' 10"	76' 03"
	Nedlloyd Asia	CO	1991	D	46,985	872' 08"	105' 10"	76' 03"
	Nedlloyd Clarence	CO	1983	D	35,890	689' 00"	106' 00"	61' 08"
	Nedlloyd Clement	CO	1983	D	35,890	689' 00"	106' 00"	61' 08"
	Nedlloyd Colombo	CO	1982	D	32,841	692' 10"	105' 10"	62' 05"
	Nedlloyd Europa	CO	1991	D	47,157	872' 08"	106' 00"	76' 03"
	Nedlloyd Hongkong	CO	1994	D	51,151	915' 09"	124' 02"	76' 03"
	Nedlloyd Honshu	CO	1995	D	55,242	915' 09"	124' 02"	76' 03"
	Nedlloyd Hoorn	CO	1979	D	48,439	848' 01"	106' 00"	79' 03"
	Nedlloyd Marne	CO	1989	D	14,101	514' 08"	75' 00"	36' 09"
	Nedlloyd Musi	CO	1989	D	14,170	514' 07"	75' 00"	36' 09"
	Nedlloyd Oceania	CO	1992	D	46,985	872' 08"	105' 10"	76' 03"
	P&O Nedlloyd Auckland	CO	1998	D	37,842	689' 04"	105' 08"	63' 08"
	P&O Nedlloyd Brisbane	CO	1985	D	53,726	798' 09"	105' 10"	61' 09"
	P&O Nedlloyd Buenos Aires	CO	1984	D	29,930	598' 09"	100' 03"	53' 02"
	P&O Nedlloyd Houston	CO	1983	D	29,730	599' 07"	100' 03"	53' 02"
	P&O Nedlloyd Jakarta	CO	1998	D	37,842	690' 04"	105' 10"	63' 08"
	P&O Nedlloyd Los Angeles	CO	1980	D	23,678	675' 09"	101' 08"	61' 07"
	P&O Nedlloyd Rotterdam	CO	1998	D	88,669	983' 11"	140' 06"	80' 01"
	P&O Nedlloyd Southhampton	CO	1998	D	88,669	983' 11"	140' 06"	80' 01"
	P&O Nedlloyd Sydney	CO	1998	D	38,170	689' 04"	105' 08"	63' 08"
	P&O Vera Cruz	CO	1984	D	29,730	599' 07"	100' 01"	53' 02"
IP-2	PACC SHIP MANAGERS PTE. LTD., SINGAPORE, SINGAPORE							
	Alam Jaya	GC	1996	D	2,500	226' 04"	59' 00"	15' 08"
	Alam Karang	TK	1985	D	51,621	377' 04"	58' 05"	28' 11"
	Alam Kembong	TK	1985	D	63,736	383' 06"	59' 09"	32' 02"
	Alam Kerisi	TK	1982	D	57,867	372' 08"	57' 05"	31' 06"
	Alam Pari	TK	1981	D	27,191	308' 06"	47' 04"	24' 08"
	Alam Sejahtera	BC	1985	D	29,692	599' 09"	75' 10"	48' 07"
	Alam Sempurna	BC	1984	D	28,094	584' 08"	75' 11"	48' 05"

Fleet #.	Fleet Name Vessel Name	Type of Vessel	Year Built	Type of Engine	Cargo Cap. or Gross*	Overal Length	Breadth	Depth or Draft*
	Alam Senang	BC	1984	D	28,098	584' 08"	75' 11"	48' 05"
	Alam Tabah	GC	1977	D	15,098	470' 06"	65' 02"	40' 06"
	Alam Talang	GC	1985	D	17,322	477' 05"	69' 00"	43' 01"
	Alam Tangkas	GC	1979	D	15,097	470' 06"	65' 01"	40' 06"
	Alam Tegas	GC	1979	D	17,187	477' 05"	69' 00"	43' 00"
	Alam Teguh	GC	1980	D	17,169	477' 06"	69' 00"	43' 00"
	Alam Teladan	GC	1979	D	17,168	477' 04"	69' 01"	43' 00"
	Alam Tenega	GC	1977	D	15,097	470' 06"	65' 01"	40' 06"
	Alam Tenggiri	GC	1985	D	17,322	477' 05"	69' 00"	43' 01"
	Alam Tenteram	BC	1979	D	16,902	477' 04"	69' 00"	43' 00"
	Ikan Selar	BC	1978	D	21,652	539' 02"	75' 02"	44' 06"
	Ikan Sepat	BC	1984	D	28,503	590' 03"	75' 04"	47' 07"
	Ikan Tamban	GC	1980	D	17,159	477' 05"	69' 00"	43' 00"
	Ikan Tanda	GC	1979	D	16,916	477' 05"	69' 00"	43' 00"
	Union	BC	1984	D	28,166	584' 08"	75' 11"	48' 05"
	United	BC	1984	D	27,223	584' 08"	75' 11"	48' 05"
IP-3	**PAN NAUTIC S.A., LUGANO, SWITZERLAND**							
	Alsyta	GC	1979	D	6,110	274' 07"	56' 01"	33' 03"
	Andrea	GC	1978	D	6,110	274' 07"	56' 01"	33' 03"
	Anita G.	GC	1979	D	7,800	321' 10"	56' 01"	33' 03"
IP-4	**PAN OCEAN SHIPPING CO. LTD., SEOUL, SOUTH KOREA**							
	Pan Hope	BC	1977	D	22,289	539' 02"	75' 03"	44' 06"
	Pan Noble	BC	1977	D	27,307	580' 10"	75' 02"	46' 03"
	Pan Voyager	BC	1985	D	29,432	589' 11"	75' 09"	47' 07"
IP-5	**PEGASUS DENIZEILIK, ISTANBUL, TURKEY**							
	Mina Cebi	BC	1980	D	27,311	627' 07"	75' 03"	44' 03"
IP-6	**PERGAMOS SHIPPING CO. S.A., PIRAEUS, GREECE**							
	Adventure	GC	1971	D	15,178	466' 09"	65' 00"	40' 06"
	Astron	GC	1976	D	14,800	462' 06"	67' 04"	38' 06"
IP-7	**PETER DOHLE SCHIFFAHRTS-KG (GMBH & CO.), HAMBURG, GERMANY**							
	Alexandria	GC	1994	D	6,918	351' 04"	59' 11"	26' 03"
	Skagen	GC	1999	D	3,440	283' 06"	42' 00"	23' 04"
IP-8	**PHOENOCEAN LTD., SURREY, ENGLAND**							
	Demi Green	BC	1983	D	12,296	423' 04"	65' 08"	36' 09"
	Nornes	BC	1976	D	6,258	339' 09"	52' 06"	28' 11"
IP-9	**PINAT GIDA SANAYI VE TICARET A.S., ISTANBUL, TURKEY**							
	Ihsan	GC	1993	D	10,560	420' 05"	59' 01"	34' 05"
	Kevser Gunes	GC	1994	D	11,307	441' 01"	59' 01"	34' 09"
	Maersk Manila	CO	1996	D	12,630	460' 11"	68' 03"	38' 05"
	Suat Ulusoy	GC	1995	D	11,366	441' 01"	59' 01"	34' 09"
IP-10	**POLCLIP (LUXEMBOURG) S.A., LUXEMBOURG, LUXEMBOURG**							
	Clipper Eagle	BC	1994	D	16,900	490' 04"	76' 00"	39' 08"
	Clipper Falcon	BC	1994	D	16,900	490' 04"	76' 00"	39' 08"
IP-11	**POLISH STEAMSHIP CO., SZCZECIN, POLAND**							
	Irma	BC	2000	D	34,948	655' 10"	77' 05"	50' 02"
	Iryda	BC	1999	D	34,946	655' 10"	77' 07"	50' 02"
	Isa	BC	1999	D	34,939	655' 10"	77' 07"	50' 02"
	Isadora	BC	1999	D	34,948	655' 10"	77' 05"	50' 02"
	Isolda	BC	1999	D	34,949	655' 10"	77' 07"	50' 02"
	Kopalnia Borynia	BC	1989	D	11,898	471' 08"	63' 08"	36' 05"
	Kopalnia Halemba	BC	1990	D	11,715	471' 01"	63' 08"	36' 05"
	Kopalnia Jeziorko	BC	1971	D	13,665	481' 06"	65' 09"	37' 01"
	Kopalnia Machow	BC	1972	D	14,036	475' 05"	67' 11"	37' 05"
	Kopalnia Piaseczno	BC	1971	D	13,665	481' 04"	65' 09"	37' 01"
	Kopalnia Rydultowy	BC	1990	D	11,702	471' 01"	63' 08"	36' 05"
	Kopalnia Sosnowiec	BC	1974	D	14,179	477' 09"	67' 09"	37' 03"
	Kopalnia Szczyglowice	BC	1969	D	12,480	465' 04"	63' 01"	37' 05"
	Kopalnia Walbrzych	BC	1975	D	14,176	477' 05"	67' 09"	37' 03"
	Kopalnia Ziemowit	BC	1991	D	11,722	471' 05"	63' 08"	36' 05"
	Kopalnia Zofiowka	BC	1975	D	14,176	477' 09"	67' 09"	37' 03"
	Odranes	BC	1992	D	13,790	471' 05"	68' 08"	37' 02"
	Orla	BC	1999	D	17,064	490' 02"	76' 00"	39' 08"
	Pilica	BC	1999	D	17,064	490' 02"	76' 00"	39' 08"
	Pomorze Zachodnie	BC	1985	D	26,696	591' 04"	75' 11"	45' 08"
	Warta	BC	1992	D	13,790	471' 05"	68' 08"	37' 02"
	Wisla	BC	1992	D	13,770	471' 05"	68' 08"	37' 02"
	Ziemia Chelminska	BC	1984	D	26,700	591' 04"	75' 11"	45' 08"
	Ziemia Gnieznienska	BC	1985	D	26,696	591' 04"	75' 11"	45' 08"

Fleet #.	Fleet Name Vessel Name	Type of Vessel	Year Built	Type of Engine	Cargo Cap. or Gross*	Overall Length	Breadth	Depth or Draft*
	Ziemia Suwalska	BC	1984	D	26,706	591' 04"	75' 11"	45' 08"
	Ziemia Tarnowska	BC	1985	D	26,700	591' 04"	75' 11"	45' 08"
	Ziemia Zamojska	BC	1984	D	26,600	591' 04"	75' 11"	45' 08"
IP-12	**PREKOOKEANSKA PLOVIDBA, BAR, YUGOSLAVIA**							
	Obod	GC	1988	D	18,235	543' 00"	75' 07"	44' 00"
IP-13	**PRIMAL SHIPMANAGEMENT, INC., ATHENS, GREECE**							
	Blade Runner	BC	1977	D	26,874	580' 09"	75' 04"	47' 07"
IP-14	**PRIME ORIENT SHIPPING S.A., PANAMA, PANAMA**							
	Luna Verde	BC	1986	D	26,706	591' 06"	75' 10"	48' 07"
IP-15	**PRISCO (UK) LTD., LONDON, ENGLAND**							
	Jakov Sverdlov	TK	1989	D	128,956	496' 01"	73' 05"	39' 10"
	Kapitan Korotaev	TK	1988	D	128,956	496' 06"	73' 08"	40' 00"
	Kapitan Rudnev	TK	1988	D	128,956	496' 01"	73' 05"	41' 01"
IP-16	**PYRSOS MANAGING CO., PIRAEUS, GREECE**							
	Amaryllis	GC	1983	D	23,000	539' 02"	75' 02"	46' 05"
	Anax	BC	1979	D	30,084	622' 00"	74' 10"	49' 10"
	Anemone	GC	1979	D	17,179	477' 04"	68' 11"	43' 00"
	Audacious	BC	1977	D	27,560	600' 06"	74' 08"	43' 09"
	Clipper Antares	BC	1986	D	17,777	481' 05"	74' 10"	40' 01"
	Eagle Quick	GC	1990	D	3,168	299' 03"	49' 05'	24' 11"
	Industrial Hope	GC	1990	D	3,194	299' 04"	49' 03"	25' 00"
IR-1	**RASSEM SHIPPING AGENCY, BEIRUT, LEBANON**							
	Seba M.	GC	1976	D	11,680	424' 01"	64' 05"	34' 06"
IR-2	**REDERI DONSOTANK A/B, DONSO, SWEDEN**							
	Navigo	TK	1992	D	123,471	466' 10"	72' 06"	42' 00"
IR-3	**REEDEREI "NORD" KLAUS E. OLDENDORFF LTD., LIMASSOL, CYPRUS**							
	San Marino	TK	1988	D	71,189	414' 10"	68' 07"	32' 04"
IR-4	**REEDEREI HANS-PETER ECKHOFF GMBH CO. HG, HOLLENSTEDT, GERMANY**							
	Kamilla	GC	1985	D	2,785	322' 06"	44' 07"	23' 00"
IR-5	**REEDEREI WESER-SCHIFFAHRTS-AGENTUR GMBH & CO. KG, BRAKE, GERMANY**							
	Abitibi Claiborne	GC	1986	D	7,879	403' 07"	65' 08"	34' 06"
	Abitibi Orinoco	GC	1986	D	7,875	404' 11"	65' 09"	34' 06"
IR-6	**REGAL AGENCIES CORP., PIRAEUS, GREECE**							
	Dali	GC	1977	D	18,784	479' 03"	75' 00"	41' 04"
	Kent Forest	BC	1978	D	14,931	522' 02"	69' 02"	41' 04"
IR-7	**REX SHIPPING CORP., ATHENS, GREECE**							
	Atticos	BC	1976	D	29,165	593' 03"	75' 11"	47' 07"
IR-8	**RIGEL SCHIFFAHRTS GMBH, BREMEN, GERMANY**							
	Alsterstern	TK	1994	D	125,327	529' 05"	75' 05"	38' 05"
	Donaustern	TK	1995	D	123,371	529' 05"	75' 05"	38' 05"
	Havelstern	TK	1994	D	126,264	529' 05"	75' 05"	38' 05"
	Isarstern	TK	1995	D	123,830	529' 05"	75' 05"	38' 05"
	Ledastern	TK	1993	D	76,737	405' 11"	58' 01"	34' 09"
	Oderstern	TK	1992	D	65,415	360' 00"	58' 02"	34' 09"
	Rheinstern	TK	1993	D	127,937	529' 05"	75' 05"	38' 05"
	Travestern	TK	1993	D	123,346	529' 05"	75' 05"	38' 05"
	Weserstern	TK	1992	D	65,415	360' 00"	58' 02"	34' 09"
IS-1	**S. FRANGOULIS (SHIP MANAGEMENT) LTD., PIRAEUS, GREECE**							
	Stamon	GC	1977	D	17,509	485' 11"	71' 04"	40' 00"
IS-2	**SAMIN SHIPPING CO. LTD., CONSTANTZA, ROMANIA**							
	Abdul S	GC	1971	D	16,829	508' 01"	75' 03"	42' 08"
	Abeer S	GC	1974	D	8,001	399' 08"	57' 09"	32' 06"
	Rabee S	BC	1976	D	8,186	385' 10"	59' 02"	29' 07"
	Zenobia S	BC	1976	D	8,197	385' 10"	59' 02"	29' 07"
IS-3	**SANDFORD SHIP MANAGEMENT LTD., VENTNOR, ISLE OF WIGHT**							
	Clipper Fidelity	GC	1978	D	15,078	470' 06"	65' 02"	40' 06"
	Rothnie	GC	1978	D	17,199	477' 05"	69' 00"	43' 00"
IS-4	**SCANDIA SHIPPING HELLAS, INC., ATHENS, GREECE**							
	Armonikos	BC	1979	D	30,689	674' 03"	75' 08"	47' 07"
IS-5	**SCANSCOT SHIPPING SERVICES (DEUTSCHLAND) GMBH, HAMBURG, GERMANY**							
	Scan Arctic	RR	1998	D	7,331	415' 01"	66' 07"	33' 02"
	Scan Atlantic	RR	1999	D	7,100	416' 02"	67' 07"	37' 09"
	Scan Bothnia	RR	1998	D	7,493	415' 01"	65' 07"	37' 09"
	Scan Finlandia	RR	2000	D	7,172	415' 01"	65' 07"	37' 09"

Strange Attractor in the St. Marys River. (Glenn Blaszkiewicz)

STRANGE ATTRACTOR

Fleet #.	Fleet Name / Vessel Name	Type of Vessel	Year Built	Type of Engine	Cargo Cap. or Gross*	Overall Length	Breadth	Depth or Draft*
	Scan Germania	RR	2000	D	7,172	415' 01"	65' 07"	37' 09"
	Scan Hansa	RR	1999	D	7,228	416' 02"	67' 07"	37' 09"
	Scan Oceanic	RR	1997	D	5,085	331' 00"	61' 00"	31' 10"
	Scan Polaris	RR	1996	D	5,100	331' 00"	61' 00"	31' 10"
IS-6	SEAARLAND SHIPPING MANAGEMENT GMBH, VILLACH, AUSTRIA							
	Allegra	TK	1986	D	179,112	536' 07"	75' 06"	37' 09"
	Conny	TK	1984	D	176,879	536' 07"	75' 06"	37' 09"
	Giacinta	TK	1984	D	176,879	536' 07"	75' 06"	37' 09"
	Grazia	TK	1987	D	176,879	536' 07"	75' 06"	37' 09"
	Peonia	BC	1983	D	27,995	647' 08"	75' 10"	46' 11"
IS-7	SEAGER CORP., ATHENS, GREECE							
	Ithaki	BC	1977	D	27,540	600' 06"	74' 08"	47' 01"
IS-8	SEALINK MARINE, INC., PIRAEUS, GREECE							
	Finikas	BC	1979	D	26,796	599' 05"	73' 09"	46' 08"
IS-9	SEA-PRAXIS MARITIME CO. LTD., NICOSIA, CYPRUS							
	Apollo C	GC	1983	D	12,665	492' 08"	69' 01"	33' 00"
IS-10	SEASCOT SHIPTRADING LTD., GLASGOW, SCOTLAND							
	Nyanza	GC	1978	D	16,923	497' 10"	71' 08"	40' 09"
IS-11	SEASTAR NAVIGATION CO. LTD., ATHENS, GREECE							
	Periandros	BC	1974	D	26,784	579' 10"	75' 01"	46' 03"
	Polydefkis	BC	1976	D	30,244	621' 06"	75' 00"	47' 11"
	Pytheas	BC	1981	D	29,514	590' 01"	76' 00"	47' 07"
IS-12	SEA SUPERIORITY SA, ATHENS, GREECE							
	Gulfbreeze	TK	1982	D	85,191	416' 08"	65' 09"	36' 09"
	Gulfstream	TK	1975	D	167,231	561' 04"	73' 08"	42' 06"
IS-13	SEAWAYS SHIPPING ENTERPRISES LTD., PIRAEUS, GREECE							
	Triena	BC	1991	D	16,979	520' 10"	75' 00"	44' 00"
IS-14	SEVEN SEAS MARITIME LTD., LONDON, ENGLAND							
	Alma	GC	1980	D	17,520	502' 10"	70' 07"	42' 04"
	Alycia	GC	1975	D	20,950	521' 08"	75' 06"	44' 03"
	Amazonia	BC	1977	D	15,661	479' 00"	69' 08"	38' C9"
	Arethusa	BC	1973	D	22,593	539' 02"	75' 02"	44' 06"
	Arosa	BC	1975	D	30,499	625' 06"	75' 00"	47' 10"
IS-15	SHERIMAR MANAGEMENT CO. LTD., ATHENS, GREECE							
	A. M. Spiridon	GC	1968	D	3,780	309' 02"	47' 11"	26' 00"
	Blue Bay	BC	1972	D	22,302	522' 04"	75' 02"	42' 11"
	Blue Lagoon	GC	1979	D	5,500	417' 11"	59' 00"	33' 09"
	Blue Marine	GC	1974	D	15,107	454' 02"	70' 04"	39' 05"
	Noor	GC	1967	D	5,912	353' 05"	50' 09"	27' 07"
	S. M. Spiridon	GC	1967	D	2,730	287' 05"	42' 10"	23' 00"
IS-16	SHIH WEI NAVIGATION CO. LTD., TAIPEI, TAIWAN							
	Royal Pescadores	BC	1997	D	18,369	486' 01"	74' 10"	40' 00"
IS-17	SHUNZAN KAIUN CO. LTD., EHIME, JAPAN							
	Spring Laker	BC	1996	D	30,855	577' 05"	77' 05"	48' 11"
	Spring Ocean	BC	1986	D	11,769	382' 00"	75' 05"	44' 00"
	Spring Trader	RR	1989	D	8,242	377' 04"	63' 00"	26' 03"
IS-18	SIDEMAR SERVIZI ACCESSORI S.P.A., GENOA, ITALY							
	Cygnus	BC	1987	D	28,500	610' 03"	75' 11"	46' 11"
	Galassia	BC	1987	D	29,369	610' 03"	75' 11"	46' 11"
	Gemini	BC	1986	D	28,500	610' 03"	75' 11"	46' 11"
	Sagittarius	BC	1987	D	29,365	610' 03"	75' 10"	46' 11"
	Sideracrux	GC	1983	D	7,988	328' 09"	57' 10"	29' 07"
	Sidercastor	GC	1982	D	7,988	328' 09"	57' 10"	29' 07"
	Siderpollux	GC	1982	D	8,010	328' 09"	57' 10"	29' 07"
IS-19	SILVER SHIPPING LTD., KINGSTOWN, ST. VINCENT & THE GRENADINES							
	Concorde	TK	1975	D	24,518	319' 11"	52' 06"	24' 11"
IS-20	SINGA STAR PTE. LTD., SINGAPORE, SINGAPORE							
	Changi Hope	BC	2000	D	18,320	486' 01"	74' 10"	40' 00"
IS-21	SLOBODNA PLOVIDBA, SIBENIK, CROATIA							
	Bilice	BC	1976	D	19,056	319' 11"	74' 11"	41' 01"
	Biograd	GC	1988	D	8,490	392' 01"	60' 10"	31' 03"
	Dinara	BC	1974	D	26,962	599' 04"	73' 09"	46' 07"
	Primosten	BC	1972	D	7,580	404' 05"	56' 00"	29' 07"
	Prvic	GC	1973	D	6,450	370' 02"	54' 00"	27' 07"
	Skradin	BC	1976	D	19,055	506' 03"	74' 10"	41' 01"

Fleet #.	Fleet Name Vessel Name	Type of Vessel	Year Built	Type of Engine	Cargo Cap. or Gross*	Overal Length	Breadth	Depth or Draft*
IS-22	**SOCIETE ANONYME MONEGASQUE D' ADMINISTRATION MARITIME ET AERIENNE, MONTE CARLO, MONACO**							
	Beta I	BC	1977	D	40,754	602' 07"	90' 07"	55' 10"
	Emerald Park	TK	1992	D	61,560	341' 02"	61' 08"	31' 04"
	Gemini	BC	1977	D	27,106	585' 11"	75' 00"	47' 04"
	Holland Park	TK	1983	D	59,440	387' 00"	57' 06"	32' 08"
	Hydra	BC	1977	D	26,715	567' 08"	74' 10"	48' 05"
	Sunniva	TK	1990	D	5,006*	367' 05"	61' 08"	31' 02"
IS-23	**SOCIETE NATIONALE DE TRANSPORT MARITIME & COMPAGNIE NATIONALE ALGERIENNE DE NAVIGATION MARITIME, ALGIERS, ALGERIA**							
	Batna	BC	1978	D	20,586	512' 05"	74' 10"	44' 04"
	Nememcha	BC	1978	D	26,145	565' 02"	75' 11"	47' 01"
IS-24	**SOENDERBORG REDERIAKTIESELSKAB, EGERNSUND, DENMARK**							
	Bison	GC	1977	D	1,370	238' 02"	43' 00"	22' 02"
IS-25	**SOHTORIK DENIZCILIK SANAYI VE TICARET A.S., ISTANBUL, TURKEY**							
	Duden	BC	1981	D	26,975	567' 07"	74' 11"	48' 05"
	Eber	BC	1978	D	18,739	504' 07"	75' 01"	41' 00"
	Med Transporter	BC	1973	D	21,570	510' 03"	75' 02"	44' 00"
	Sapanca	BC	1975	D	19,030	506' 04"	75' 00"	41' 00"
IS-26	**SOLAR SCHIFFAHRTSGES MBH & CO. KG, BREMEN, GERMANY**							
	Argonaut	GC	1978	D	2,384	283' 10"	42' 09"	24' 11"
IS-27	**SPAR SHIPPING A.S., BERGEN, NORWAY**							
	Spar Garnet	BC	1984	D	30,686	589' 11"	75' 10"	50' 11"
	Spar Jade	BC	1984	D	30,674	589' 11"	75' 10"	50' 11"
	Spar Opal	BC	1984	D	28,214	585' 00"	75' 10"	48' 05"
	Spar Ruby	BC	1985	D	28,259	584' 08"	75' 11"	48' 05"
IS-28	**SPLIETHOFF'S BEVRACHTINGSKANTOOR LTD., AMSTERDAM, NETHERLANDS**							
	Achtergracht	GC	1990	D	12,150	425' 10"	62' 05"	38' 03"
	Admiralengracht	GC	1990	D	12,150	425' 10"	62' 05"	38' 03"
	Alexandergracht	GC	1991	D	12,150	425' 10"	62' 05"	38' 03"
	Amstelgracht	GC	1990	D	12,150	425' 10"	62' 05"	38' 03"
	Anjeliersgracht	GC	1990	D	12,150	425' 10"	62' 05"	38' 03"
	Ankergracht	GC	1991	D	12,150	425' 10"	62' 05"	38' 03"
	Apollogracht	GC	1991	D	12,150	425' 10"	62' 05"	38' 03"
	Archangelgracht	GC	1990	D	12,150	425' 10"	62' 05"	38' 03"
	Artisgracht	GC	1990	D	12,150	425' 10"	62' 05"	38' 03"
	Atlasgracht	GC	1991	D	12,150	425' 10"	62' 05"	38' 03"
	Bakengracht	GC	1981	D	3,489	263' 02"	52' 10"	34' 06"
	Barentzgracht	GC	1981	D	3,444	263' 02"	52' 10"	34' 06"
	Bataafgracht	GC	1981	D	3,444	263' 02"	52' 10"	34' 06"
	Beursgracht	GC	1981	D	3,448	263' 02"	52' 10"	34' 06"
	Bickersgracht	GC	1981	D	3,488	263' 02"	52' 10"	34' 06"
	Edisongracht	GC	1994	D	12,760	447' 04"	62' 05"	38' 03"
	Eemsgracht	GC	1995	D	12,754	447' 04"	62' 05"	38' 03"
	Egmondgracht	GC	1994	D	12,760	447' 04"	62' 05"	38' 03"
	Elandsgracht	GC	1995	D	12,754	447' 04"	62' 05"	38' 03"
	Emmagracht	GC	1995	D	12,760	447' 04"	62' 05"	38' 03"
	Erasmusgracht	GC	1994	D	13,000	447' 04"	62' 05"	38' 03"
	Eurogracht	GC	1995	D	12,754	447' 04"	62' 05"	38' 03"
	Heerengracht	GC	1981	D	4,550	312' 11"	52' 11"	34' 05"
	Hudsongracht	GC	1982	D	4,510	312' 11"	52' 10"	34' 06"
	Humbergracht	GC	1982	D	4,517	312' 11"	52' 10"	34' 06"
	Kaapgracht	GC	1984	D	8,038	348' 09"	52' 11"	34' 05"
	Keizersgracht	GC	1983	D	4,990	348' 07"	52' 11"	34' 06"
	Kielgracht	GC	1984	D	5,022	348' 09"	52' 11"	34' 05"
	Klippergracht	GC	1984	D	5,022	348' 09"	52' 11"	34' 05"
	Koggegracht	GC	1983	D	5,022	348' 09"	54' 06"	34' 05"
	Koningsgracht	GC	1983	D	5,022	348' 09"	54' 06"	34' 05"
	Lauriergracht	GC	1988	D	9,656	371' 02"	63' 07"	37' 01"
	Leliegracht	GC	1987	D	9,601	371' 02"	63' 01"	37' 01"
	Lemmergracht	GC	1988	D	9,682	371' 02"	63' 01"	37' 00"
	Levantgracht	GC	1988	D	9,595	371' 03"	63' 01"	37' 00"
	Lijnbaansgracht	GC	1988	D	9,606	371' 02"	63' 07"	37' 01"
	Looiersgracht	GC	1987	D	9,606	371' 02"	63' 07"	37' 01"
	Lootsgracht	GC	1989	D	9,682	371' 03"	63' 01"	37' 00"
	Palmgracht	GC	1985	D	9,536	370' 09"	62' 05"	36' 05"
	Parkgracht	GC	1986	D	9,656	371' 02"	62' 03"	37' 01"
	Pauwgracht	GC	1986	D	9,340	370' 09"	62' 05"	36' 05"
	Pietersgracht	GC	1986	D	9,340	370' 09"	62' 05"	37' 01"

Fleet #.	Fleet Name Vessel Name	Type of Vessel	Year Built	Type of Engine	Cargo Cap. or Gross*	Overall Length	Breadth	Depth or Draft*
	Pijlgracht	GC	1985	D	9,650	370' 09"	62' 05"	36' 05"
	Poolgracht	GC	1986	D	9,672	371' 02"	62' 03"	37' 01"
	Prinsengracht	GC	1985	D	9,498	370' 09"	62' 05"	36' 05"
IS-29	SPLIT SHIP MANAGEMENT LTD., SPLIT, CROATIA							
	Alka	GC	1979	D	14,930	532' 07"	73' 00"	43' 11"
	Bol	GC	1980	D	14,930	532' 07"	73' 00"	43' 11"
	Hope I	BC	1982	D	30,900	617' 03"	76' 00"	47' 07"
	Jelsa	GC	1977	D	13,450	532' 07"	73' 00"	43' 11"
	Kairos	GC	1977	D	8,538	424' 03"	63' 02"	33' 08"
	Kraljica Mira	RR	1965	D	752	283' 04"	53' 10"	17' 05"
	Marjan I	GC	1978	D	13,450	532' 07"	73' 00"	43' 11"
	Solin	GC	1985	D	23,240	579' 05"	75' 00"	45' 11"
	Solta	BC	1984	D	29,785	622' 00"	74' 11"	49' 10"
	Split	GC	1981	D	22,042	585' 08"	75' 02"	46' 00"
	Topaz	GC	1975	D	4,798	288' 09"	42' 08"	25' 07"
IS-30	STFA MARITIME INDUSTRY & TRADING CO., ISTANBUL, TURKEY							
	Danis Koper	BC	1978	D	22,174	528' 00"	75' 02"	44' 04"
	R. Dedeoglu	BC	1986	D	23,930	579' 05"	75' 00"	45' 11"
IS-31	SURRENDRA OVERSEAS LTD., CALCUTTA, INDIA							
	APJ Anand	BC	1977	D	16,882	459' 04"	73' 04"	41' 00"
	APJ Angad	BC	1977	D	27,305	581' 08"	75' 02"	47' 11"
	APJ Anjli	BC	1982	D	27,192	577' 05"	75' 11"	47' 11"
	APJ Karan	BC	1977	D	27,305	581' 08"	75' 02"	47' 11"
	APJ Sushma	BC	1983	D	27,213	577' 05"	75' 11"	47' 11"
IT-1	T. S. SHIPPING, INC., PANAMA, PANAMA							
	Sun Glory	GC	1989	D	6,836	318' 08"	59' 01"	42' 08"
IT-2	TARGET MARINE S.A., PIRAEUS, GREECE							
	Corithian Trader	BC	1973	D	27,398	599' 10"	73' 06"	46' 07"
IT-3	TEAM SHIP MANAGEMENT AS, BERGEN, NORWAY							
	Daviken	BC	1987	D	34,752	729' 00"	75' 11"	48' 05"
	Goviken	BC	1987	D	34,752	729' 00"	75' 11"	48' 05"
	Inviken	BC	1984	D	30,052	621' 05"	75' 01"	47' 11"
	Sandviken	BC	1986	D	34,685	728' 09"	75' 11"	48' 05"
	Utviken	BC	1985	D	30,052	621' 05"	75' 01"	47' 11"
IT-4	TECHNOMAR SHIPPING, INC., ATHENS, GREECE							
	CMBT Esprit	GC	1982	D	21,894	549' 03"	75' 02"	46' 00"
	Dimitris Y	BC	1983	D	28,192	584' 08"	75' 11"	48' 05"
IT-5	TEO SHIPPING CORP., PIRAEUS, GREECE							
	Antalina	BC	1984	D	28,082	584' 08"	75' 11"	48' 05"
	Erikousa Wave	BC	1986	D	26,858	600' 08"	73' 08"	46' 08"
	Marilis T.	BC	1984	D	28,097	584' 08"	75' 11"	47' 10"
	Sevilla Wave	BC	1986	D	26,858	600' 08"	73' 08"	46' 08"
	Vamand Wave	BC	1985	D	28,303	580' 08"	75' 11"	47' 07"
IT-6	THAMES SHIPBROKERS LTD., LONDON, ENGLAND							
	Daniella	GC	1988	D	17,506	520' 11"	74' 11"	44' 00"
IT-7	THE EGYPTIAN NAVIGATION CO., ALEXANDRIA, EGYPT							
	Abu Egila	GC	1984	D	12,600	436' 00"	67' 05"	40' 00"
	Alexandria	GC	1991	D	12,802	436' 00"	67' 04"	40' 00"
IT-8	THE SHIPPING CORP. OF INDIA LTD., BOMBAY, INDIA							
	Lok Maheshwari	BC	1986	D	26,728	605' 03"	75' 03"	47' 03"
	Lok Pragati	BC	1984	D	26,928	564' 11"	75' 00"	48' 03"
	Lok Prakash	BC	1989	D	26,790	606' 11"	75' 04"	47' 03"
	Lok Pratap	BC	1993	D	26,718	605' 09"	75' 04"	47' 04"
	Lok Pratima	BC	1989	D	26,925	565' 09"	74' 11"	48' 03"
	Lok Prem	BC	1990	D	26,714	605' 08"	75' 04"	47' 03"
	Lok Rajeshwari	BC	1988	D	26,639	605' 08"	75' 04"	47' 03"
	State of Haryana	GC	1983	D	16,799	465' 07"	75' 02"	47' 04"
IT-9	THENAMARIS (SHIPS MANAGEMENT), INC., ATHENS, GREECE							
	Sealink	BC	1983	D	28,234	639' 09"	75' 10"	46' 11"
	Seaharmony II	BC	1984	D	28,251	639' 09"	75' 10"	46' 11"
	Searanger II	BC	1976	D	29,300	594' 01"	76' 00"	47' 07"
IT-10	TOKUMARU KAIUN K.K., TOKYO, JAPAN							
	Golden Shield	TK	1982	D	88,594	416' 08"	65' 08"	36' 09"
IT-11	TOMASOS BROTHERS, INC., PIRAEUS, GREECE							
	Alexis	BC	1984	D	27,048	599' 10"	75' 04"	42' 04"

Fleet #.	Fleet Name / Vessel Name	Type of Vessel	Year Built	Type of Engine	Cargo Cap. or Gross*	Overal Length	Breadth	Depth or Draft*
IT-12	**TOMAZOS SHIPPING CO. LTD., PIRAEUS, GREECE**							
	Jeannie	BC	1977	D	27,541	600' 06"	74' 08"	47' 01"
	Kalisti	BC	1981	D	30,900	617' 06"	76' 00"	47' 07"
IT-13	**TRANSMAN SHIPPING ENTERPRISES S.A., ATHENS, GREECE**							
	Luckyman	BC	1980	D	27,000	584' 08"	75' 10"	48' 05"
IT-14	**TRITON BEREEDERUNGS GMBH & CO. KG, LEER, GERMANY**							
	Lebasse	GC	1996	D	3,526	290' 08"	42' 04"	23' 04"
IU-1	**UNION MARINE ENTERPRISES S.A. OF PANAMA, PIRAEUS, GREECE**							
	Capetan Michalis	BC	1981	D	28,600	593' 03"	75' 11"	47' 07"
IU-2	**UNIVAN SHIP MANAGEMENT LTD., HONG KONG, PEOPLE'S REPUBLIC OF CHINA**							
	Pathum Navee	GC	1972	D	20,814	515' 00"	75' 00"	44' 03"
IV-1	**V. SHIPS (CYPRUS) LTD., LIMASSOL, CYPRUS**							
	Cheetah	BC	1977	D	27,535	584' 08"	75' 02"	48' 03"
	Chelsea Bridge	GC	1978	D	22,356	549' 07"	75' 03"	45' 11"
	Lynx	BC	1978	D	29,536	584' 07"	75' 00"	48' 03"
IV-2	**VANGUARD ENTERPRISE CO. LTD., HIROSHIMA, JAPAN**							
	Moor Laker	BC	1984	D	27,915	584' 08"	69' 03"	48' 05"
IV-3	**VENUS SHIPPING CORP., MANILA, PHILIPPINES**							
	Baltic Confidence	BC	1979	D	17,686	481' 03"	75' 01"	40' 01"
	Euorpean Confidence	BC	1980	D	16,533	465' 11"	71' 07"	40' 01"
IV-4	**VERGOS MARINE MANAGEMENT, PIRAEUS, GREECE**							
	Verdon	BC	1981	D	26,350	594' 09"	75' 00"	47' 01"
	Verily	BC	1982	D	26,450	594' 09"	75' 00"	47' 01"
IW-1	**W. BOCKSTIEGEL REEDEREI KG, EMDEN, GERMANY**							
	Malte B	GC	1998	D	3,440	283' 06"	42' 00"	23' 04"
	Nils B	GC	1998	D	3,440	283' 06"	42' 00"	23' 04"
IW-2	**WAGENBORG SHIPPING B.V., DELFZIJL, NETHERLANDS**							
	Arion	GC	1997	D	9,100	441' 04"	54' 02"	32' 02"
	Dintelborg	GC	1999	D	8,865	437' 08"	52' 02"	32' 02"
	Dongeborg	GC	1999	D	9,000	437' 08"	52' 02"	32' 02"
	Egbert Wagenborg	GC	1998	D	9,100	441' 04"	54' 02"	32' 02"
	Flinterborg	GC	1990	D	3,015	269' 02"	41' 04"	21' 08"
	Flinterdam	GC	1995	D	4,506	327' 07"	44' 09"	23' 07"
	Flinterdijk	GC	1978	D	2,955	263' 02"	41' 00"	21' 08"
	Flinterland	GC	1994	D	4,216	300' 01"	44' 08"	23' 07"
	Flintermar	GC	1994	D	4,170	300' 01"	44' 09"	23' 07"
	Flinterzijl	GC	1996	D	4,540	325' 09"	44' 09"	23' 07"
	Kasteelborg	GC	1998	D	9,025	428' 08"	52' 01"	33' 06"
	Keizersborg	GC	1996	D	9,025	428' 08"	52' 01"	33' 06"
	Koningsborg	GC	1999	D	9,067	428' 08"	52' 01"	33' 06"
	Kroonborg	GC	1995	D	9,025	428' 08"	52' 01"	33' 06"
	Markborg	GC	1997	D	9,100	441' 04"	54' 02"	32' 02"
	Merweborg	GC	1998	D	9,100	441' 04"	54' 02"	32' 02"
	Michiganborg	GC	1999	D	9,200	441' 03"	54' 02"	32' 02"
	Moezelborg	GC	1999	D	9,100	441' 04"	54' 02"	32' 02"
	Morraborg	GC	1999	D	8,800	441' 05"	54' 06"	32' 02"
	MSC Baltic	GC	1998	D	9,100	441' 04"	54' 02"	32' 02"
	Musselborg	GC	1999	D	9,100	441' 04"	54' 02"	32' 02"
	Vaasaborg	GC	1999	D	8,300	434' 00"	52' 01"	31' 07"
	Vechtborg	GC	1998	D	8,300	434' 00"	52' 01"	31' 07"
	Veerseborg	GC	1998	D	8,300	433' 09"	52' 01"	31' 07"
	Vlieborg	GC	1999	D	8,300	434' 00"	52' 01"	31' 07"
	Vlistborg	GC	1999	D	8,300	434' 00"	52' 01"	31' 07"
	Voorneborg	GC	1999	D	8,300	434' 00"	52' 01"	31' 07"
	Zeus	GC	2000	D	9,100	428' 08"	52' 01"	33' 06"
IW-3	**WILSON SHIP MANAGEMENT (BERGEN) AS, BERGEN, NORWAY**							
	Brunto	BC	1977	D	12,100	478' 07"	64' 04"	35' 00"
	Fossnes	BC	1995	D	16,880	490' 03"	76' 00"	39' 08"
	General Cabal	BC	1976	D	12,100	477' 04"	64' 03"	34' 11"
IZ-1	**Z. & G. HALCOUSSIS CO. LTD., PIRAEUS, GREECE**							
	Agiodektini	BC	1977	D	18,611	500' 05"	75' 01"	41' 00"
	Akti	BC	1977	D	28,935	593' 10"	76' 00"	47' 07"
	Alexandria	BC	1981	D	29,372	589' 11"	76' 00"	47' 00"

Vessel
Museums

City of Milwaukee docked at
Manistee, MI. *(Roger LeLievre)*

Fleet #.	Fleet Name / Vessel Name	Type of Vessel	Year Built	Type of Engine	Cargo Cap. or Gross*	Overal Length	Breadth	Depth or Draft*

MU-1 — BERNIER MARITIME MUSEUM, 55 DES PIONNIERS RUE, L' ISLET, QC — (418)-247-5001

Daniel McAllister		TB	1907	D	268*	115' 00"	23' 02"	12' 00"

(Helena '07 - '57, Helen M. B. '57 - '66)

(Former McAllister Towing & Salvage, Inc. vessel — Currently laid up in Montreal, QC.)

| Ernest Lapointe | | IB | 1941 | R | 1,179* | 185' 00" | 36' 00' | 22' 06" |

(Former Canadian Coast Guard ice breaker.) In use as a museum in L'Islet, QC. Open all year.

MU-2 — BUFFALO AND ERIE COUNTY NAVAL & MILITARY PARK, 1 NAVAL PARK COVE, BUFFALO, NY — (716)-847-1773

| Croaker | [IXSS-246] | SS | 1944 | D/V | 1,526* | 311' 07" | 27' 02" | 33' 09" |

(Former U. S. Navy "Emergency Program (Gato)" class submarine [SS/SSK/AGSS/IXSS-246] which was stricken 20 December, 1971.)

(The USS Croaker is credited with sinking 11 enemy vessels totaling 19,710 tons during WW II.)

| Little Rock | [CLG-4] | CLG | 1945 | T | 10,670* | 610' 01" | 66' 04" | 25' 00"* |

(Former U. S. Navy "Cleveland/Little Rock" class guided missle cruiser [CL-92/CLG-4] which was stricken 22 November, 1976.)

| PTF-17 | [PTF-17] | PT | 1968 | D | 69* | 80' 04" | 24' 07" | 6' 10"* |

(Former U. S. Navy "Trumpy" class fast patrol boat [PTF-17] which was stricken in 1979.)

| The Sullivans | | DD | 1943 | T | 2,500* | 376' 06" | 39' 08" | 22' 08" |

(Launched as USS Putnam [DD-537])

(Former U. S. Navy "Fletcher" class destroyer [DD-537] which was stricken 1 December, 1974.)

(The USS The Sullivans earned 9 Battle Stars during World War II and 2 Battle Stars during the Korean Conflict.) Above four in use as museum vessels in Buffalo, NY. Open seasonally, April to November.

MU-3 — CANAL PARK MARINE MUSEUM, 600 SOUTH LAKE AVE., DULUTH, MN — (218)-727-2497

| Bayfield | | TB | 1953 | D | 23* | 45' 00" | 13' 00" | 7' 00"* |

(Former U. S. Army Corps of Engineers vessel.) In use as a museum in Duluth, MN. Open all year.

MU-4 — GREAT LAKES CENTER FOR MARINE HISTORY, 2911 LEON AVE., LANSING, MI — (906) 643-0392

| Maple | [WAGL-234] | LT | 1939 | D | 350* | 122' 03" | 27' 00" | 7' 06"* |

(USCGC Maple [WLI/WAGL-234] '39 - '73, Roger R. Simons '73 - '94)

(Former U. S. Coast Guard "122-Foot" class lighthouse tender [WLI/WAGL-234] / EPA vessel which last operated in 1991.) In use as a museum in St. Ignace, MI. Open 15 May-15 October and by appointment.

MU-5 — GREAT LAKES CLIPPER PRESERVATION ASSOCIATION, P.O. BOX 1370, MUSKEGON, MI — (231)-755-0990

| Milwaukee Clipper | | PA | 1904 | Q | 4,272 | 361' 00" | 45' 00" | 28' 00" |

(Juniata '04 - '41)

(Former Wisconsin & Michigan Steamship Company vessel which last operated in 1970.) Currently undergoing conversion to a museum at Muskegon, MI. Open seasonally, call for schedule.

MU-6 — GREAT LAKES HISTORICAL SOCIETY, 1089 EAST 9TH ST., CLEVELAND, OH — (216)-566-8770

| Cod | [IXSS-224] | SS | 1943 | D/V | 1,525* | 311' 08" | 27' 02" | 33' 09" |

(Former U.S. Navy "Albacore (Gato)" class submarine [SS/AGSS/IXSS-224] which was stricken 15 December, 1971.)

(The USS Cod earned 7 Battle Stars and sank 26,985 tons during World War II.) In use as a museum in Cleveland, OH. Open seasonally, 1 May to the end of September.

MU-7 — H. LEE WHITE MARINE MUSEUM, P.O. BOX 101, WEST FIRST ST. PIER. OSWEGO, NY — (315)-342-0480

| Major Elish K. Henson | | TB | 1943 | D | 305* | 115' 00" | 28' 00" | 14' 00" |

(Major Elish K. Henson '43 - '47, U. S. Army LT-5 '47 - '47, Nash '47 - '95)

(Former U. S. Army Corps of Engineers vessel which last operated in 1989.) In use as a museum vessel in Oswego, NY. Open seasonally, May to September.

MU-8 — HARBOR HERITAGE SOCIETY, 1001 EAST 9TH ST., CLEVELAND, OH — (216)-574-6262

| William G. Mather {2} | | BC | 1925 | T | 13,950 | 618' 00" | 62' 00" | 32' 00" |

(Former Cleveland-Cliffs Steamship Co. vessel which last operated 21 December, 1980.) In use as a museum in Cleveland, OH. Open seasonally, May to October.

MU-9 — HMCS FRASER, P.O. BOX 233 UNIT 17, 450 LaHAVE ST., BRIDGEWATER, NS — (902)-624-1557

| Fraser | [DDH-233] | FF | 1957 | T | 2,858* | 366' 00" | 42' 00" | 19' 08"* |

(Former Royal Canadian Navy "St. Laurent (River)" class helicopter-carrying frigate [DDE/DDH-233] which was stricken in 1994.) In use as a museum in Bridgewater, NS.

MU-10 — HMCS HAIDA NAVAL MUSEUM, 955 LAKESHORE BLVD. WEST, TORONTO, ON. — (416)-314-9870

| Haida | [G-63] | DD | 1943 | T | 2,744* | 377' 00" | 37' 06" | 15' 02" |

(Former Royal Canadian Navy "Tribal" class destroyer [G-63 / DDE-215] which was stricken 11 October 1963.) In use as a museum in Toronto, ON. Open seasonally, mid May to Labor Day.

MU-11 — IRVIN ORE BOAT TOURS, 350 HARBOR DR.. DULUTH, MN — (218)-722-7876

| Lake Superior | | TB | 1943 | D | 248* | 114' 00" | 26' 00" | 13' 08" |

(Major Emil H. Block '43 - '47, U. S. Army LT-18 '47 - '50)

(Former U. S. Army Corps of Engineers vessel which last operated in 1995.)

| William A. Irvin | | BC | 1938 | T | 14,050 | 610' 09" | 60' 00" | 32' 06" |

(Former United States Steel Corp. vessel which last operated 16 December, 1978.) Above two in use as museum in Duluth, MN. Open seasonally, late spring to autumn.

Fleet #.	Fleet Name / Vessel Name	Type of Vessel	Year Built	Type of Engine	Cargo Cap. or Gross*	Overall Length	Breadth	Depth or Draft*
MU-12	**LAKE COUNTY HISTORICAL SOCIETY, 520 SOUTH AVE., TWO HARBORS, MN — (218)-834-4898**							
	Edna G.	TB	1896	R	154*	102' 00"	23' 00"	14' 06"

(Former Duluth, Missabe & Iron Range Railroad tug which last operated in 1981.)
In use as a museum in Two Harbors, MN. Open seasonally, call for schedule.

MU-13	**LE SAULT DE SAINTE MARIE HISTORIC SITES, INC., 501 EAST WATER ST., SAULT STE. MARIE, MI — (906)-632-3658**							
	Valley Camp {2}	BC	1917	R	12,000	550' 00"	58' 00"	31' 00"

(Louis W. Hill '17 - '55)
(Former Republic Steel Corp. vessel which last operated in 1967.)
In use as a museum in Sault Ste. Marie, MI. Open seasonally, 15 May to 15 October.

MU-14	**MARINE MUSEUM OF THE GREAT LAKES AT KINGSTON, 55 ONTARIO ST., KINGSTON, ON — (613)-542-2261**							
	Alexander Henry	IB	1959	D	1,674*	210' 00"	44' 00"	17' 09"

(Former Canadian Coast Guard vessel which was stricken in 1985.)
In use as a museum in Kingston, ON. Museum open all year, vessel open seasonally, May to Sept.

MU-15	**MARINE MUSEUM OF UPPER CANADA, EXHIBITION PLACE, TORONTO, ON — (416)-392-1765**							
	Ned Hanlan	TB	1932	R	105*	79' 06"	19' 00"	9' 09"

(Former Municipality of Toronto vessel which last operated in 1965.)
In use as a museum in Toronto, ON. Museum open all year, vessel open seasonally, call for schedule.

MU-16	**MUSEUM OF SCIENCE AND INDUSTRY, 5700 SOUTH LAKE SHORE DR., CHICAGO, IL — (773)-684-1414**							
	U-505	SS	1941	D/V	1,178*	252' 00"	22' 04"	15' 05"*

(Former German Type IX-C submarine, captured in the Atlantic Ocean off Africa on 4 June, 1944.)
(When captured in 1944, the U-505 was the first enemy man-of-war captured by the U. S. Navy in battle on the high seas since 1815. The U-505 is credited with sinking 47,000 tons during WW II.)
In use as a museum in Chicago, IL. Open all year.

MU-17	**MUSEUM SHIP WILLIS B. BOYER, P.O. BOX 50406, TOLEDO, OH — (419)-936-3070**							
	Willis B. Boyer	BC	1911	T	15,000	617' 00"	64' 00"	33' 01"

(Col. James M. Schoonmaker '11 - '69)
(Former Cleveland-Cliffs Steamship Co. vessel which last operated 17 December, 1980.)
In use as a museum in Toledo, OH at International Park. Open all year.

MU-18	**NORGOMA MUSEUM SHIP, 851 GREAT NORTHERN BLVD., SAULT STE. MARIE, ON — (705)-256-7447**							
	Norgoma	PA	1950	D	1,477*	188' 00"	37' 06"	22' 06"

(Former Ontario Northland Transportation Commision vessel which last operated in 1974.)
In use as a museum in Sault Ste. Marie, ON. Open seasonally, mid April to October.

MU-19	**NORISLE BISTRO, 3080 LOUIS ST., VAL CARON, ON — (705)-859-2434**							
	Norisle	PA	1946	R	1,668*	215' 09"	36' 03"	16' 00"

(Former Ontario Northland Transportation Commission vessel which last operated in 1957.)
In use as a museum/restaurant in Manitowaning, ON. Open seasonally, 1 June to Labor Day.

MU-20	**PENNSYLVANIA HISTORICAL & MUSEUM COMMISSION, 150 FRONT ST. SUITE 1, ERIE, PA — (814)-871-4596**							
	Niagara	2B	1813	W	295*	198' 00"	32' 00"	10' 06"

(Former U. S. Navy Brigantine from the War of 1812.) In use as an operational museum in Erie, PA.

MU-21	**PETERSEN STEAMSHIP CO., 219 UNION, DOUGLAS, MI — (616)-857-2464**							
	Keewatin	PA	1907	Q	3,856*	346' 00"	43' 08"	26' 06"

(Former Canadian Pacific Railway Company vessel which last operated in October, 1965.)

	Reiss	TB	1913	R	99*	80' 00"	20' 00"	12' 06"

(Q. A. Gillmore '13 - '32)
(Former Reiss Steamship Company vessel which last operated in 1969.)
Above two in use as museum vessels in Douglas, MI. Open seasonally, Memorial Day to Labor Day.

MU-22	**PORT HURON MUSEUM OF ARTS & HISTORY, 920 PINE GROVE AVE., PORT HURON, MI — (810)-985-7101**							
	WLV 526 **[HURON]**	LS	1920	D	392*	96' 05"	24' 00"	10' 00"*

(Former U. S. Coast Guard "96 Foot" class lightship [LS-103, WAL/WLV-526] which was stricken 25 August, 1970.)
(The "Huron" lightship was the only lightship ever painted black in U. S. Coast Guard service and as such was always passed to port.) In use as a museum in Port Huron, MI.

MU-23	**S. S. CANADIANA PRESERVATION SOCIETY, 17 DELRAY DR., CHEEKTOWAGA, NY — (716)-833-2998**							
	Canadiana	PA	1910	R	974*	216' 00"	45' 00"	18' 10"

(Former Lake Erie Excursion Co. vessel last operated in 1958.) Remains at Humberstone, ON.

MU-24	**S. S. METEOR MARITIME MUSEUM, P.O. BOX 775, SUPERIOR, WI — (715)-392-5742**							
	Col. D. D. Gaillard	DR	1916	B	712*	116' 00"	41' 00"	13' 09"*

(Former U. S. Army Corps of Engineers vessel.)

	Meteor	TK	1896	R	40,100	380' 00"	45' 00"	26' 00"

(Frank Rockefeller 1896 - '28, South Park '28 - '43)
(Former Cleveland Tankers, Inc. vessel which last operated in 1969.)
(The Meteor is the last remaining "Whaleback" Great Lakes cargo vessel.)
Above two in use as museums in Superior, WI. Open seasonally, May to mid October.

Icebreaker Alexander Henry is open to the public at Kingston, ON. *(Roger LeLievre)*

Fleet #.	Fleet Name Vessel Name	Type of Vessel	Year Built	Type of Engine	Cargo Cap. or Gross*	Overal Length	Breadth	Depth or Draft*
MU-25	**SOCIETY FOR THE PRESERVATION OF THE CITY OF MILWAUKEE, 51 NINTH ST.,** **MANISTEE, MI — (231) 398-0328**							
	City of Milwaukee	TF	1931	R	26 rail cars	360' 00"	56' 03"	21' 06"
	(Former Ann Arbor Railroad System vessel.) Open to the public at Manistee, MI, 15 April – 15 November)							
MU-26	**STEAMER COLUMBIA FOUNDATION, P.O. BOX 43232, DETROIT, MI — (313)-331-9920**							
	Columbia {2}	PA	1902	R	968*	216' 00"	60' 00"	13' 06"
	(Last operated 2 Sept., 1991 — 5 year survey expired Jan. 1998 — Currently laid up in Ecorse, MI.)							
MU-27	**STEAMER STE. CLAIRE FOUNDATION, P.O. BOX 43232, DETROIT, MI — (313)-331-9920**							
	Ste. Claire	PA	1910	R	870*	197' 00"	65' 00"	14' 00"
	(Last operated 2 Sept., 1991 — 5 year survey expired May, 1993 — Currently laid up in Ecorse, MI.)							
MU-28	**THE CANADIAN NAVAL MEMORIAL TRUST, P.O. BOX 99000 STATION "FORCES",** **HALIFAX, NS — (902)-429-2132**							
	Sackville *[K-181]*	KO	1941	T	1,170*	208' 00"	33' 00"	17' 06"
	(Former Royal Canadian Navy "Flower" class corvette [K-181] which was stricken in 1982.) *In use as a museum in Halifax, NS.*							
MU-29	**UNITED STATES LST ASSOCIATION, TOLEDO, OH**							
	LST 325 *[LST-325]*	LST	1943	D	2,100	328' 00"	50' 00"	25' 00"
	(USS LST-325 '43 - '64, Syros [L-144] '64 - 2000)							
MU-30	**USS SILVERSIDES & MARITIME MUSEUM, P.O. BOX 1692, MUSKEGON, MI — (231)-755-1230**							
	LST-393	LST	1942	D	2,100	328' 00"	50' 00"	25' 00"
	(USS LST-393 '42 - '48, Highway 16 '48 - '99)							
	(Former Wisconsin & Michigan Steamship Co. vessel which last operated 31 July, 1973.) *(During World War II the Highway 16 earned 3 Battle Stars and participated in the Normandy* *Invasion of 6 June, 1944 as the USS LST-393.)*							
	McLane *[WMEC-146]*	WM	1927	D	289*	125' 00"	24' 00"	12' 06"
	(USCGC McLane [WSC / WMEC-146] '27 - '70, Manatra II '70 - '93)							
	(Former U. S. Coast Guard "Buck & A Quarter" class medium endurance cutter [WSC/WMEC-146] *which was stricken 31 December 1968.)*							
	Silversides *[SS-236]*	SS	1941	D/V	1,526*	311' 08"	27' 03"	33' 09"
	(Former U. S. Navy "Albacore (Gato)" class submarine [SS-236] which was stricken 30 June, 1969.) *(The USS Silversides is credited with sinking 90,080 tons during World War II.)* *Above three in use as museums in Muskegon, MI. Open seasonally, April to October.*							
MU-31	**WISCONSIN MARITIME MUSEUM, 75 MARITIME DR., MANITOWOC, WI — (920)-684-0218**							
	Cobia *[AGSS-245]*	SS	1944	D/V	1,500*	311' 09"	27' 03"	33' 09"
	(Former U. S. Navy "Emergency Program (Gato)" class submarine [SS/AGSS-245] which was *stricken 1 July, 1970.) (The Cobia earned 4 Battle Stars and sank 16,835 tons during World War II.)*							

MARINE MUSEUMS ASHORE

Hours and other information subject to change. Please call for times.

ANTIQUE BOAT MUSEUM, 750 MARY ST., CLAYTON, NY — (315) 686-4104
An impressive collection of historic freshwater boats and engines. Annual boat show is the first weekend of August. *Open May 15-October 15.*

COLLINGWOOD MUSEUM, MEMORIAL PARK, COLLINGWOOD, ON — (705) 445-4811
More than 100 years of shipbuilding, illustrated with models, photos and videos. *Open all year.*

DOOR COUNTY MARITIME MUSEUM, 120 N. MADISON AVE., STURGEON BAY, WI — (920) 743-5958
Located in the former offices of the Roen Steamship Co.; exhibits portray the role shipbuilding has played in the Door Peninsula. Refurbished pilothouse on display. *Open all year.*

DOSSIN GREAT LAKES MUSEUM, 100 THE STRAND, BELLE ISLE, DETROIT, MI — (313) 852-4051
Models, photographs, interpretive displays, the smoking room from the 1912 passenger steamer **City of Detroit III,** an anchor from the **Edmund Fitzgerald** and the working pilothouse from the steamer **William Clay Ford** are on display. *Open all year.*

FAIRPORT HARBOR MUSEUM, 129 SECOND ST., FAIRPORT, OH — (440) 354-4825
Located in the Fairport Lighthouse, displays include the pilothouse from the lake carrier **Frontenac** and the mainmast of the first **U.S.S. Michigan.** *Open late May-Labor Day.*

GREAT LAKES HISTORICAL SOCIETY, 480 MAIN ST., VERMILION, OH — (800) 893-1485
Museum tells the story of the Great Lakes through ship models, paintings, exhibits and artifacts, including engines and other machinery. Pilothouse of retired laker **Canopus** and a replica of the Vermilion lighthouse are on display. *Museum open all year. An affiliated operation is the* **U.S.S. Cod** *(see MU-6 above).*

GREAT LAKES MARINE & U.S. COAST GUARD MEMORIAL MUSEUM, 1071-73 WALNUT BLVD.,
ASHTABULA, OH — (216) 964-6847
Housed in the 1898-built former lighthouse keepers' residence, the museum includes models, paintings, artifacts, photos, the world's only working scale model of a Hulett ore unloading machine and the pilothouse from the steamer **Thomas Walters**. *Open Memorial Day-October 31.*

GREAT LAKES SHIPWRECK MUSEUM, WHITEFISH POINT, MI — (906) 635-1742 or (800)-635-1742
Located next to the Whitefish Point lighthouse, the museum includes lighthouse and shipwreck artifacts, a shipwreck video theater, the restored lighthouse keeper's quarters, and an **Edmund Fitzgerald** display that includes the ship's bell. *Open May 15-October 15.*

LE SAULT DE SAINTE MARIE HISTORIC SITES, INC., 501 EAST WATER ST.,
SAULT STE. MARIE, MI — (906)-632-3658
The 1917-built steamer Valley Camp, which once sailed for the Republic Steel Co., is the centerpiece of this extensive museum. Dedicated in 1968, the Valley Camp's three vast cargo holds house artifacts, ship models, aquariums, photos and other memorabilia, as well as a tribute to the **Edmund Fitzgerald** that includes the ill-fated vessel's lifeboats. Extensive gift shop offers a large selection of nautical books and other items. *Tours available. Open May 15-October 15.*

MARQUETTE MARINE MUSEUM, EAST RIDGE & LAKESHORE DR., MARQUETTE, MI — (906) 226-2006
Contained in an 1890s waterworks building, the museum re-creates the offices of the first commercial fishing and passenger freight companies. Displays also include charts, photos, models and maritime artifacts. *Open May 31-September 30.*

MICHIGAN MARITIME MUSEUM, 260 DYCKMAN AVE., SOUTH HAVEN, MI — (616) 637-8078
Exhibits are dedicated to the U.S. Lifesaving Service and U.S. Coast Guard. Displays tell the story of various kinds of boats and their uses on the Great Lakes. *Open all year.*

OWEN SOUND MARINE – RAIL MUSEUM, 1165 FIRST AVE., OWEN SOUND, ON — (519) 371-3333
Museum depicts the history of each industry (but leans more toward the marine end) through displays, models and photos. *Seasonal.*

THE PIER, 245 QUEENS QUAY W., TORONTO, ON — (888) 675-7437
Exhibits detail the development of the shipping industry from sail to steam on the Great Lakes and St. Lawrence Seaway, with a special focus on Toronto. The 79-foot steam tug **Ned Hanlan**, built in 1932, is also on display. *Open all year.*

PORT COLBORNE MARINE & HISTORICAL MUSEUM, 80 KING ST., PORT COLBORNE, ON — (905) 834-7604
Wheelhouse from the steam tug **Yvonne Dupre Jr.,** anchor from the propeller ship **Raleigh** and a lifeboat from the steamer **Hochelaga** are among the museum's displays. *Open May-December.*

U.S. ARMY CORPS OF ENGINEERS MUSEUM, SOO LOCKS VISITOR CENTER, E. PORTAGE AVE.,
SAULT STE. MARIE, MI — (906) 632-3311
Exhibits include a working model of the Soo Locks, historic photos and a 25-minute film. Also, three observation decks adjacent to the MacArthur Lock provide an up-close view of ships locking through. *No admission; open May-November. Check at the Visitor Center information desk for a list of vessels expected at the locks.*

WELLAND CANAL VISITOR CENTRE, AT LOCK 3, THOROLD, ON — (905) 984-8880
Museum traces the development of the Welland Canal. *Museum and adjacent gift shop open year 'round. Observation deck open during the navigation season. Check at the information desk for vessels expected at Lock 3.*

Canadian Olympic icebound in the Livingstone Channel south of Detroit December, 2000.
(Neil Schultheiss)

Extra Tonnage

Ports, Lakes & Locks

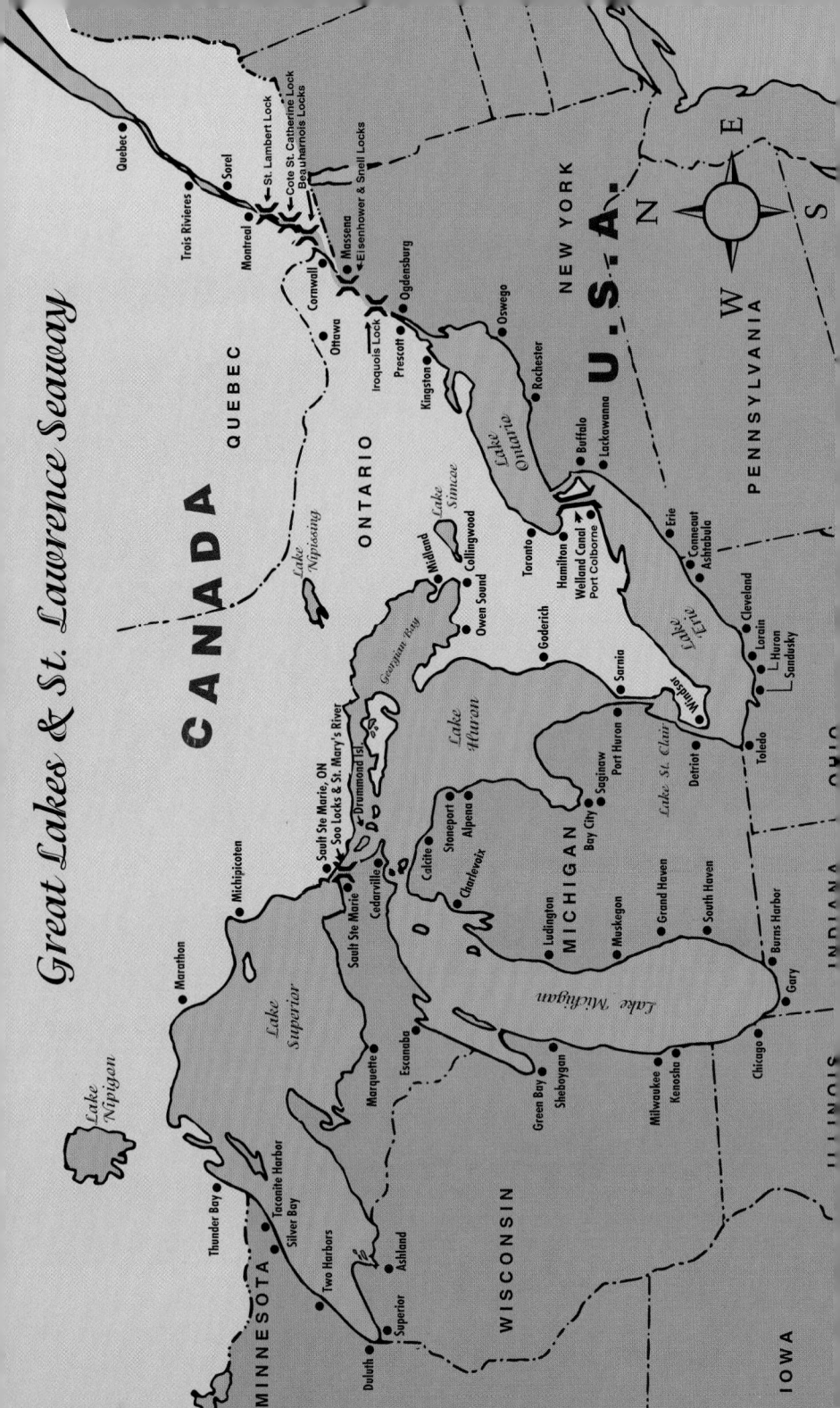

GREAT LAKES LOADING PORTS

Iron Ore	Limestone	Coal	Grain	Cement
Duluth	Port Inland	Superior	Thunder Bay	Charlevoix
Superior	Cedarville	Thunder Bay	Duluth	Alpena
Two Harbors	Drummond	Chicago	Milwaukee	
Taconite	Island	Toledo	Chicago	**Gypsum**
Harbor	Calcite	Sandusky	Sarnia	Port Gypsum
Marquette	Stoneport	Ashtabula	Toledo	Alabaster
Escanaba	Marblehead	Conneaut		

Petroleum

Sarnia

East Chicago

UNLOADING PORTS

The primary iron ore and limestone receiving ports are Cleveland, Lorain, Chicago, Gary, Burns Harbor, Indiana Harbor, Detroit, Toledo, Ashtabula and Conneaut. Coal is carried to a host of ports in the U.S. and Canada, much of it used to generate electrical power. Most grain loaded on the lakes is destined for export via the St. Lawrence Seaway. Cement is delivered to terminals stretching from Lake Superior to Lake Ontario. Tankers bring petroleum products to cities as diverse in size as Cleveland and Detroit or Escanaba and Muskegon. Self-unloaders carry road salt and sand to cities throughout the region.

MEANING OF BOAT WHISTLES

1 SHORT: I am directing my course to starboard (right) for a port to port passing.

2 SHORT: I am directing my course to port (left) for a starboard to starboard passing.

5 OR MORE SHORT BLASTS SOUNDED RAPIDLY: Danger.

1 PROLONGED: Vessel leaving dock.

3 SHORT: Vessel moving astern.

1 PROLONGED, SOUNDED ONCE PER MINUTE: Vessel moving in fog.

1 SHORT, 1 PROLONGED, 1 SHORT: Vessel at anchor in fog.

3 PROLONGED and **2 SHORT:** Salute.

1 PROLONGED and **2 SHORT:** Master's salute.

Some of these signals are listed in the pilot rules; others have been adopted through common use.

BOOKING A TRIP

Can the public buy a trip on a laker? The answer, unfortunately, is no. Great Lakes cargo vessels are not certified to carry passengers for hire. Some vessels do have guest quarters, but these are reserved for industry-related customers, technicians and others who have business on board. Occasionally, a charitable group may sell raffle tickets for a laker trip (see **www.knowyourships.com** for details), but that's about the only chance the public has for getting a ride.

Shiploader fills Wilfred Sykes' holds with 19,200 tons of Empire Standard taconite pellets at Escanaba, MI. (Roger LeLievre)

Mesabi Miner discharging a cargo of coal at Marquette, MI. (Rod Burdick)

THE GREAT LAKES

Lake Superior

According to most references, the Seaway system begins at the U.S. ports of Duluth-Superior, at the western-most end of Lake Superior. Taconite ore pellets from the Minnesota iron ranges, grain and low-sulfur coal from Montana and Wyoming start their long trip to the lower lakes from the twin ports region, as well as from nearby Two Harbors, MN, Taconite Harbor, MN, and Silver Bay, MN. Iron ore is also shipped from the Marquette Range, while grain is exported from the Canadian lakehead at Thunder Bay, ON. Lake Superior itself is the single largest body of freshwater in the world, measuring 383 miles (616.4 km) in length, 160 miles (257.5 km) at its widest point and 1,333 feet (406.3 m) at its deepest.

Lake Michigan

The western-most of the Great Lakes is 321 miles (516.6 km) long, 118 miles (189 km) wide and 932 feet (281.3 m) at its deepest. Vessels calling at Escanaba, MI, load taconite consigned to Chicago-area steel mills, while grain and manufactured goods ship worldwide from the ports of Milwaukee, Green Bay and Chicago. Port Inland, MI, at the lake's northern end, ships limestone to destinations around the Great Lakes.

Lake Huron

Lake Huron, at 247 miles (397.5 km) long, 183 miles (294.5 km) wide and 750 feet (228.6 m) deep, is fed from Lake Superior by the St. Marys River. Collingwood, ON, on Georgian Bay, has a rich shipbuilding history, while Goderich, ON, enjoys an active grain and salt trade. On the United States side, Calcite, MI, specializes in the shipment of limestone while Alpena is a major cement port.

Lake Erie

The shallowest of the Great Lakes is 210 feet (64 m) deep, 241 miles (387.8 km) long and 57 miles (91.7 km) wide. Ore and coal shipped to Toledo, Cleveland, Ashtabula, Conneaut, Erie and Buffalo feed the industries of the region, while the same ports are major trans-shipment points for overseas cargos. The Welland Canal, at its easternmost end, connects lakes Erie and Ontario.

Lake Ontario

The most easterly of the Great Lakes is also the smallest, measuring 193 miles (310.6 km) in length and 53 miles (85.3 km) in width. The ports of Toronto and Hamilton enjoy brisk grain and ore trades, while Cape Vincent, NY, marks the start of the St. Lawrence River that runs eventually into the Atlantic Ocean.

ANGRY LAKES

The **Great Storm** of 11-13 November 1913 is generally acknowledged as the worst to ever strike the Great Lakes in terms of life and property lost, with 10 vessels sunk, twice that number driven ashore and 235 lives lost. Also notorious is the 30 November **1905 Blow**, which hit particularly hard on Lake Superior, the **Black Friday** storm of 20 October 1916, which hit hardest on Lake Erie, and the 11 November 1940 **Armistice Day** storm, centered mainly on Lake Michigan.

ST. LAWRENCE SEAWAY

The St. Lawrence Seaway, which celebrated its 40th anniversary in 1999, is a deep waterway extending some 2,038 miles (3,701.4 km) from the Atlantic Ocean to the head of the Great Lakes at Duluth, including Montreal harbor and the Welland Canal. More specifically, it is a system of locks and canals (U.S. and Canadian), built between 1954 and 1958 at a cost of $474 million and opened in 1959, that allow vessels to pass from Montreal to the Welland Canal at the western end of Lake Ontario. The vessel size limit within this system is 740-feet (225.6 meters) long, 78-feet (23.8 meters) wide and 26-feet (7.9 meters) draft.

LOCK DIMENSIONS

Length	766' (233.5 meters)
Width	80' (24 meters)
Depth	30' (24.4 meters)

Vessels transiting the St. Lawrence Seaway locks pay tolls based on registered tonnage and cargo on-board.

Closest to the ocean is the **St. Lambert Lock**, which lifts ships some 15 feet (4.6 meters) from Montreal harbor to the level of the Laprairie Basin, through which the channel sweeps in a great arc 8.5 miles (13.7 km) long, to the second lock. The **Cote St. Catherine Lock**, like the other six St. Lawrence Seaway locks, is built to the standard dimensions shown in the table at left.

The Cote St. Catherine requires 24-million gallons (90.9-million liters) to fill and can be filled or emptied in less than 10 minutes. It lifts ships from the level of the Laprairie Basin, 30 feet (9.1 meters) to the level of Lake St. Louis, bypassing the Lachine Rapids. Beyond it, the channel runs 7.5 miles (12.1 km) before reaching Lake St. Louis.

The **Lower Beauharnois Lock**, bypassing the Beauharnois Power House, lifts ships 41 feet (12.5 meters) and sends them through a short canal to the **Upper Beauharnois Lock**, where they are lifted 41 feet (12.5 meters) to reach the Beauharnois Canal. After a 13-mile (20.9 km) trip in the canal, and a 30-mile (48.3 km) passage through Lake St. Francis, vessels reach the U.S. border and the **Snell Lock**, which has a lift of 45 feet (13.7 meters) and empties into the 10-mile (16.1 km) long Wiley-Dondero Canal.

After passing through the Wiley-Dondero Canal, ships are raised another 38 feet (11.6 meters) by the **Dwight D. Eisenhower Lock**, after which they enter Lake St. Lawrence, the pool upon which nearby HEPCO and PASNY power-generating stations draw for their turbines located a mile to the north. A visitor center at the Eisenhower Lock is popular with boatwatchers.

At the Western end of Lake St. Lawrence, the **Iroquois Lock** allows ships to bypass the Iroquois Control Dam. The lift here is only about one foot (.3 meters). Once in the waters west of Iroquois, the channel meanders through the beautiful Thousand Islands to Lake Ontario, the Welland Canal, Lake Erie and beyond.

In 1998, ships moved more than 39 million metric tons of grain, steel and other commodities through the Montreal-Lake Ontario stretch of the Seaway. It is estimated that 1.5-billion metric tons of cargo have been carried by vessels from more than 50 countries on the busy waterway since 1959. In 1998, administration of the waterway (including the Welland Canal) was assumed by the St. Lawrence Seaway Management Corporation.

WELLAND CANAL

The 27-mile long (43.7 km) **Welland Canal**, built to bypass nearby Niagara Falls, overcomes a difference in water level of 326.5 feet (99.5 meters) between lakes Erie and Ontario.

The first Welland Canal opened in 1829; the present (fourth) canal opened officially on 6 August 1932 with the passage of the steamer **Lemoyne**. Each of the seven Welland Canal locks has an average lift of 46.5 feet (14.2 meters). All locks (except Lock 8) are 859-feet (261.8 meters) long, 80-feet (24.4 meters) wide and 30-feet (9.1 meters) deep.

The maximum sized vessel that may transit the canal is 740-feet (225.5 meters) long, 78-feet (23.8 meters) wide and 26-feet (7.9 meters) in draft. Connecting channels are kept dredged to a minimum of 27-feet (8.2 meters).

Locks 1, **2** and **3** are at St. Catharines, on the Lake Ontario end of the waterway. At Lock 3, the Welland Canal Viewing Center and Museum houses an information desk (which posts a list of vessels expected at the lock), a gift shop and restaurant. At Thorold, locks **4**, **5** and **6**, twinned to help speed passage of vessels, are controlled with an elaborate interlocking system for safety. These locks (positioned end to end, they resemble a short flight of stairs) have an aggregate lift of 139.5 feet (42.5 meters) and are similar to the Gatun Locks on the Panama Canal. Just south of locks 4, 5 and 6 is **Lock 7**. **Lock 8**, seven miles (11.2 km) upstream at Port Colborne, completes the process, making the final adjustment to Lake Erie's level. A park and information center adjoin Lock 8.

In 1973, a new channel was constructed to replace the section of the canal that bisected the city of Welland. The bypass eliminated delays to ship navigation, road and rail traffic.

The average passage time for the Welland Canal is about 12 hours, with the majority spent transiting locks 4-7. Vessels passing through the Welland Canal and St. Lawrence Seaway must also carry a qualified pilot.

There are also 11 railway and highway bridges crossing the

Rt. Hon. Paul J. Martin, at 740' x 78', is the largest the Seaway will allow. (Jimmy Sprunt)

Welland Canal. The most significant are the landmark vertical-lift bridges that provide a clearance of 126 feet (36.6 meters) for vessels passing underneath. Tunnels at Thorold and South Welland allow vehicle traffic to pass beneath the waterway.

All vessel traffic though the Welland Canal is regulated by a control center. Upbound vessels must call **Seaway Welland** off Port Weller, ON, on VHF Ch. 14 (156.700 Mhz), while downbound vessels are required to make contact off Port Colborne, ON. Cameras keep vessels under constant observation, and individual locks (and most bridges over the canal) are controlled from the center.

THE SOO LOCKS

American Locks

MacArthur Lock

Named after World War II Gen. Douglas MacArthur, the MacArthur Lock is 800-feet long (243.8 meters) between inner gates, 80-feet wide (24.4 meters) and 31-feet deep (9.4 meters) over the sills. The lock was built by the U.S. in the war years 1942-43 and opened to traffic 11 July 1943. The maximum-sized vessel that can transit the MacArthur Lock is 730-feet long (222.5 meters) by 76-feet wide (23 meters). In emergencies, this limit may be exceeded for vessels up to 767-feet in length (233.8 meters).

Poe Lock

The Poe Lock is 1,200-feet long (365.8 meters), 110-feet wide (33.5 meters) and has a depth over the sills of 32-feet (9.8 meters). Named after Col. Orlando M. Poe, it was built by the U.S. in the years 1961-68. The lock's vessel limit is 1,100 feet long (335.3 meters) by 105 feet wide (32 meters). There are currently more than 30 vessels sailing the lakes restricted by size to the Poe Lock.

Davis Lock

Named after Col. Charles E.L.B. Davis, the Davis Lock measures 1,350- feet long (411.5 meters) between inner gates, 80 feet-wide (24.4 meters) and 23-feet deep (7 meters) over the sills. It was built in the years 1908-14 and now sees limited use due to its shallow depth.

Sabin Lock

Measuring the same as the Davis Lock, the Sabin Lock was built from 1913-19. Named after L.C. Sabin, the lock is currently inactive.

St. Marys River

Connecting Lake Superior with Lake Huron, the 80-mile (128.7 km) long **St. Marys River** is a beautiful waterway that includes breathtaking scenery, picturesque islands and more than its share of hazardous twists and turns.

Remote **Isle Parisienne** marks its beginning; the equally-lonely **DeTour Reef Light** marks its end. Between are two marvels of engineering, the **West Neebish Cut**, a channel literally dynamited out of solid rock, and the **Soo Locks**, which stand where Native Americans in dugout canoes once challenged the St. Marys Rapids. Vessels in the St. Marys River system are under control of the U.S. Coast Guard at Sault Ste. Marie, MI, and are required to check in with **Soo Traffic** on VHF Ch.12 (156.600 Mhz) at various locations in the river. In the vicinity of the locks, they fall under jurisdiction of the Lockmaster, who must be contacted on VHF Ch. 14 (156.700 Mhz) for lock assignments.

The first lock was built on the Canadian side of the river by the Northwest Fur Co. in 1797-98. That lock was 38-feet (11.6 meters) long and barely 9-feet (2.7 meters) wide.

The first ship canal on the American side, known as the State Canal, was built from 1853-55 by engineer Charles T. Harvey. There were two tandem locks on masonry, each 350-feet (106.7 meters) long by 70-feet (21.3 meters) wide, with a lift of about 9-feet (2.7 meters).

The canal was destroyed in 1888 by workers making way for newer, bigger locks.

1,000-footer Edwin H. Gott leaves the Poe Lock, while Oglebay Norton waits her turn to enter. The locks control tower is at left. (Neil Schultheiss)

A New Lock at the Soo?

Discussion continues about building a new lock in the space now occupied by the Davis and Sabin locks. It would relieve the pressure on the Poe, the only lock now able to handle vessels more than 730-feet (222.5 meters) long and/or 76-feet (23 meters) wide.

Cost of such a lock was estimated at $225 million in 1999. If built, it would be paid for by the U.S. federal government and the states surrounding the Great Lakes.

The Canadian Canal

The present Canadian Lock has its origins in a canal constructed during the years 1887-95 through the red sandstone rock of St. Marys Island on the north side of the St. Marys Rapids. The most westerly canal on the Seaway route, the waterway measures 7,294-feet (2,223.4 meters), or about 1.4 miles (2.2 km) long, from end to end of upper and lower piers. A 900-foot (274.3 meters) long lock served vessels until the collapse of a lock wall in 1987 closed the waterway.

In 1998, after $10.3 million in repairs, a much smaller lock opened, built inside the old lock chamber. Operated by Parks Canada, it is used mainly by pleasure craft, tugs and tour boats.

All traffic through the Soo Locks passes toll-free.
Locks in the Seaway system operate on gravity — no pumps are used.

FOLLOWING THE FLEET

Prerecorded messages help track vessel arrivals and departures.

Algoma Central Marine	**(905) 708-3873**	ACM vessel movements
Boatwatcher's Hotline	**(218) 722-6489**	Superior, Duluth, Two Harbors, Taconite Harbor and Silver Bay traffic
CSX Coal Docks/Torco Dock	**(419) 697-2304**	Toledo, OH, vessel information
DMIR Ore Dock	**(218) 628-4590**	Duluth, MN, vessel information
DMIR Ore Dock	**(218) 834-8190**	Two Harbors, MN, vessel information
Eisenhower Lock	**(315) 769-2422**	Eisenhower Lock vessel movements
Inland Lakes Management	**(517) 354-4400**	ILM vessel movements
LTV Lorain Pellet Terminal	**(440) 244-2054**	Vessel arrivals at the LTV dock
Michigan Limestone docks	**(517) 734-2117**	Calcite, MI vessel information
	(906) 484-2201	Ext. 503 - Cedarville, MI vessel info.
Oglebay Norton Co.	**(800) 861-8760**	O-N Vessel movements
Pilotage tape	**(905) 934-1836**	Saltwater vessel information
Presque Isle Corp.	**(517) 595-6611**	Stoneport, MI, vessel information
Soo Traffic	**(906) 635-3224**	Previous day's traffic – St. Marys River
Superior Midwest Energy Terminal	**(715) 395-3559**	Superior, WI, vessel information
Thunder Bay Port Authority	**(807) 345-1256**	Thunder Bay, ON, vessel information
USS Great Lakes Fleet	**(218) 628-4389**	USS vessel movements
Upper Lakes Group	**(905) 688-5878**	ULG vessel movements
Welland Canal	**(905) 688-6462**	Welland Canal traffic update

With a VHF scanner, boatwatchers can tune to ship-to-ship and ship-to-shore traffic, using the following guide.

Commercial vessels only	**Ch. 13** (156.650 Mhz)	Bridge-to-Bridge Communications
Calling / Distress ONLY	**Ch. 16** (156.800 Mhz)	**Calling / Distress ONLY**
Commercial vessels only	**Ch. 06** (156.300 Mhz)	Working Channel
Commercial vessels only	**Ch. 08** (156.400 Mhz)	Working Channel
Supply boat at Sault Ste. Marie, MI	**Ch. 08** (156.400 Mhz)	Supply boat **Ojibway**
Detour Reef to Lake St. Clair Light	**Ch. 11** (156.550 Mhz)	Sarnia Traffic - Sector 1
Long Point Light to Lake St. Clair Light	**Ch. 12** (156.600 Mhz)	Sarnia Traffic - Sector 2
Montreal to about mid-Lake St. Francis	**Ch. 14** (156.700 Mhz)	Seaway Beauharnois - Sector 1
Mid-Lake St. Francis to Bradford Island	**Ch. 12** (156.600 Mhz)	Seaway Eisenhower - Sector 2
Bradford Island to Crossover Island	**Ch. 11** (156.550 Mhz)	Seaway Iroquois - Sector 3
Crossover Island to Cape Vincent	**Ch. 13** (156.650 Mhz)	Seaway Clayton - Sector 4 St. Lawrence River portion
Cape Vincent to mid-Lake Ontario	**Ch. 13** (156.650 Mhz)	Seaway Sodus - Sector 4 Lake Ontario portion
Mid-Lake Ontario to Welland Canal	**Ch. 11** (156.550 Mhz)	Seaway Newcastle - Sector 5
Welland Canal	**Ch. 14** (156.700 Mhz)	Seaway Welland - Sector 6
Welland Canal to Long Point Light	**Ch. 11** (156.550 Mhz)	Seaway Long Point - Sector 7
St. Mary's River Traffic Service	**Ch. 12** (156.600 Mhz)	Soo Traffic, Sault Ste. Marie, MI
Lockmaster, Soo Locks	**Ch. 14** (156.700 Mhz)	Soo Lockmaster (call WUE-21)
Coast Guard traffic	**Ch. 21** (157.050 Mhz)	United States Coast Guard
Coast Guard traffic	**Ch. 22** (157.100 Mhz)	United States Coast Guard
U.S. Mailboat, Detroit, MI	**Ch. 10** (156.500 Mhz)	Mailboat **J. W. Westcott II**

FOR MORE INFORMATION ...

www.boatnerd.com

A treasure trove of web sites are

On-Line

available on the Internet, connecting to just about everything imaginable concerning ships and shipping. To start, visit **www.boatnerd.com**, the Great Lakes and Seaway shipping home page. In addition to news and rumors, vessel passages, winter lay-up ports and photos of Great Lakes vessels, Boatnerd links to hundreds of shipping-related addresses on the Web, among them links to shipwreck sites, museums, lighthouses, the Soo Locks and Welland Canal and Great Lakes and Seaway shipping companies.

To track vessel news, information and rumors in more traditional ways, join one or more of the marine societies around the lakes (send a stamped, self-addressed

In Print

envelope to **Marine Publishing Co.** for a free list including addresses and subscription rates). In particular, the Great Lakes Maritime Institute, the Marine Historical Society of Detroit, the Toronto Marine Historical Society and the Great Lakes Historical Society offer long-standing and informative publications.

John B. Aird, escorted by the cutter Griffon, makes port at Goderich, ON. (Duane Jessup)